# Democracy in Crisis?

## Politics, Governance and Policy

## Yannis Papadopoulos

palgrave
macmillan

First published 2013 by
PALGRAVE MACMILLAN

Palgrave Macmillan in the UK is an imprint of Macmillan Publishers Limited,
registered in England, company number 785998, of Houndmills, Basingstoke,
Hampshire RG21 6XS.

Palgrave Macmillan in the US is a division of St Martin's Press LLC,
175 Fifth Avenue, New York, NY 10010.

Palgrave Macmillan is the global academic imprint of the above companies
and has companies and representatives throughout the world.

Palgrave® and Macmillan® are registered trademarks in the United States, the
United Kingdom, Europe and other countries

ISBN: 978-0-230-53697-5 hardback
ISBN: 978-0-230-53698-2 paperback

This book is printed on paper suitable for recycling and made from fully
managed and sustained forest sources. Logging, pulping and manufacturing
processes are expected to conform to the environmental regulations of the
country of origin.

A catalogue record for this book is available from the British Library.

A catalog record for this book is available from the Library of Congress.

# ANALYSIS

Series Editors: B. Guy Peters, Jon Pierre and Gerry Stoker

Political science today is a dynamic discipline. Its substance, theory and methods have all changed radically in recent decades. It is much expanded in range and scope and in the variety of new perspectives – and new variants of old ones – that it encompasses. The sheer volume of work being published, and the increasing degree of its specialization, however, make it difficult for political scientists to maintain a clear grasp of the state of debate beyond their own particular subdisciplines.

The *Political Analysis* series is intended to provide a channel for different parts of the discipline to talk to one another and to new generations of students. Our aim is to publish books that provide introductions to, and exemplars of, the best work in various areas of the discipline. Written in an accessible style, they provide a 'launching-pad' for students and others seeking a clear grasp of the key methodological, theoretical and empirical issues, and the main areas of debate, in the complex and fragmented world of political science.

A particular priority is to facilitate intellectual exchange between academic communities in different parts of the world. Although frequently addressing the same intellectual issues, research agendas and literatures in North America, Europe and elsewhere have often tended to develop in relative isolation from one another. This series is designed to provide a framework for dialogue and debate which, rather than advocacy of one regional approach or another, is the key to progress.

The series reflects our view that the core values of political science should be coherent and logically constructed theory, matched by carefully constructed and exhaustive empirical investigation. The key challenge is to ensure quality and integrity in what is produced rather than to constrain diversity in methods and approaches. The series is intended as a showcase for the best of political science in all its variety, and demonstrates how nurturing that variety can further improve the discipline.

**Political Analysis Series**
**Series Standing Order**
**ISBN 9780333786949 Hardback**
**ISBN 9780333945063 Paperback**
**ISBN 9780230585386 Electronic Book Text**
(outside North American only)

You can receive future titles in this series as they are published by placing a standing order. Please contact your bookseller or, in the case of difficulty, write to us at the address below with your name and address, the title of the series and one of the ISBNs quoted above.

Customer Services Department, Macmillan Distribution Ltd
Houndmills, Basingstoke, Hampshire RG21 6XS, England, UK

# POLITICAL ANALYSIS

Series Editors: B. Guy Peters, Jon Pierre and Gerry Stoker

# Contents

# List of Figures

# Acknowledgements

I am indebted to a huge number of people for the ideas developed in this book. Although they are too many to mention individually, I am deeply grateful to all. Steven Kennedy of Palgrave Macmillan, who has been constantly supportive (although at some point I probably ceased to deserve his patience), deserves special thanks. Likewise, I am particularly grateful to Gerry Stoker, who took the lead in commenting on behalf of the series editors, and to an anonymous reviewer, for their insightful comments on earlier versions. I am also grateful to Isabelle Guisan for her reading of parts of the manuscript, to Soraya Ksontini and Karen Lang for editorial assistance, to Alec McAulay for copyeditorial work, and to Ildi Clarke for compiling the index. Indexing and English-language editing have been generously supported by research funds from the Faculté des sciences sociales et politiques of my home institution, the University of Lausanne. I am thankful to the Ecole normale supérieure and to Sciences Po for enabling me to make two research stays as a visiting professor in Paris, far from the vicissitudes of daily academic life. I am also thankful to the framework of the Swiss National Center of Competence in Research 'Challenges to Democracy in the 21st Century' for giving me the opportunity to discuss some of the arguments presented here at various events.

This book is dedicated to Sandrine and to my daughters Alba, Floria and Amalia, each having her own way of pulling me away from my writing activities, a welcome distraction, most of the time.

Lausanne, February 2013

# Introduction

Although often in quite imperfect form, democracy has spread throughout the world in successive waves (Diamond and Plattner, 1993; Merkel, 1999), and the number of democracies has tripled in the last 30 years (Morlino, 2008). The watchdog organization Freedom House counted 87 full democracies in the world in 2010, representing almost half of the independent polities and of the global population (Flinders, 2012: 8–9). Furthermore, anti-system parties challenging democratic institutions, such as those of the extreme Right in the inter-war period, or those of the far Left before the breakdown of communism, have nearly disappeared in most established democracies. It is thus no surprise that Russell J. Dalton (2008: 251) concludes his book *Citizen Politics* with the assertion that 'by some measures, the present may be considered the golden age of democracy'. But perhaps such an assessment is too optimistic. This is what the present book argues.

## Something happened to democracy

In 1975, a group of prominent social scientists drafted a report commissioned by the Trilateral Commission entitled *The Crisis of Democracy* (Crozier *et al.*, 1975). They maintained that democracies were threatened by an overload of demands and irresponsible claims, leading to uncontrolled expansion of government activities, and that political authority was increasingly undermined by critical media and intellectuals; these 'dysfunctions' were seen as conducive to the rise of 'anomic democracy'. Unsurprisingly, the authors of the report prescribed the rehabilitation of a sense of responsibility to safeguard governability. In their diagnosis, 'crisis' meant, to a large extent, too much democracy, or at least a democracy denatured by its excesses. Some assessments made by Crozier *et al.* (1975) – for instance those on the fragmentation of interests in contemporary highly differentiated societies, or on the decline of partisan appeal – were correct and retain their validity. However, the crisis of democracy that is discussed in the present book is based on a diametrically opposed diagnosis. My argument is that the influence of democratic politics on political decisions

1

has been weakened – not that it is too strong. While the capacity of democratically legitimized authorities to generate compliance does have limits, this does not prevent governability from being preserved or restored; however, this has often happened at the price of declining democratic accountability.

Sometimes, of course, there might be good reasons to limit the role of democratic politics. For example, it is often suggested that the protection of minority rights is not easily reconcilable with the majoritarian character of democratic decision-making. While this book acknowledges such trade-offs, they do not affect its core argument about the weakening role of democratic processes on public matters, an argument primarily of an empirical nature, whatever normative conclusions one might wish to draw from it.

I am not the first to argue that the 'victory' of democracy at the global level has been accompanied by a degradation of its substance in long-established democratic states. For example, a publication from the Council of Europe – the mission of which is 'to promote democracy and protect human rights and the rule of law' – suggested that while democracies are increasing in number, and offer, in some cases, more opportunities for participation, the room for democratic choice is at the same time restricted by the insulation of 'guardian institutions' (Schmitter and Trechsel, 2004). Or, as French political scientist Guy Hermet put it in an essay on the 'winter' of democracy: 'There is a confusion between extending and deepening democracy.... In a word, it is the triumph of democracy on the surface, so to say, that draws the attention of the public. By contrast, the lack of a deep substance of democracy remains largely and voluntarily unobserved' (2007: 9–10). As causes for the hollowing-out of democracy, Schmitter and Trechsel have in mind the proliferation of regulatory bodies that escape democratic control, while Hermet points to the proliferation of complex governance arrangements that evade accountability. Both are important, but I shall show that a range of other factors, such as the rapidly expanding internationalization of policy-making, successive waves of administrative reform, or the movement of 'judicialization' that empowers courts as policy actors, need also to be taken into account. These factors do not all produce the same consequences, but sometimes their joint action may have cumulative effects on democratic substance. Analysing their complex relationships contributes to a more fine-grained understanding both of the transformations of democratic political systems and of the forces driving them. This is what this book attempts to do.

An important argument made in this book is that degradation of democratic substance is not always obvious or immediately visible. The hollowing-out of democratic politics is not just the result of a 'democratic deficit' of supranational integration as it takes place in the European Union, nor more generally of the malevolent role of economic globalization and financial capitalism, which have become common places of public debate. I argue that a more fundamental challenge to the substance of democracy comes from a gap between the spheres of 'front-stage' and 'back-stage' politics, each of them operating according to a distinct logic. There is not much in common between the highly mediatized spectacle of party competition and the intricacies of complex policy-making processes that largely escape public attention. Such a gap has considerably broadened in spite of recurrent calls for more 'transparency' in the conduct of public affairs.

This means quite simply that the classic – standard, or 'textbook' – model of democracy based on the role of political parties and representative institutions no longer adequately describes our political systems. This model is historically situated. There is hardly any doubt that it has been a broadly appropriate description of a range of democracies in the periods that followed the advent of mass politics in the second part of the nineteenth century and the restoration of democratic politics after its breakdown in the 1930s. But this was actually a short period that did not extend beyond the immediate post-war decades. It did not take very long for mass parties – key actors in this description, both for the formulation of political options and for their translation into public measures – to start losing their mobilization and later a substantial part of their decision-making capacity as well.

In his book *Why Politics Matters*, Gerry Stoker points out 'a contradiction between the naïve conception of democracy that is often in our heads and the reality of the way that the governmental process works' (Stoker, 2006: 80). Nevertheless, the traditional conception of representative democracy continues to be widely used as a normative standard. This presents a problem inasmuch as real-world democracy is judged on the basis of a stylized ideal. In the classic representative model, the legitimacy of democratic regimes relies on the bottom-up delegation of power from citizens to their (partisan) representatives. It is because rulers are considered to be representative that they are authorized to make collectively binding decisions in a top-down manner. According to a congruence principle, those who have to comply with political decisions must have previously authorized the decision-makers to act in their name, so rendering the decision-making system legitimate (this is called procedural or 'throughput' legitimacy). In addition, the shadow of future competitive elections is a safeguard that induces representatives to behave in a responsive way. The normative attractiveness of such a circular model of representative democracy relies, then, on the existence of a direct line upward from 'we the people' to government, and downward from government to society (Hupe and Edwards, 2012).

However, several changes in the functioning of our democracies have undermined the effectiveness of this circular model of democratic 'inputs' that feed the political system and the 'outputs' it produces. They may be summarized as follows:

- The basis of authorization has become narrower and more fragile, with citizens becoming more independent of partisan loyalties and more critical, or even distrustful, of political elites.
- No matter whether those who are authorized to govern have deliberately delegated some of their power, or whether it has escaped from their hands, a substantial amount of power is now in the hands of actors who evade democratic accountability.
- Thus, the distance between policy-makers and policy-takers is larger, and the lack of congruence between them more conspicuous, in the view of attentive observers, at least.
- In partisan politics, electoral competition keeps on going as if politicians were the key decision-makers.
- As a result, a disjunction or divorce occurs between the increasingly distinct logics of the spheres of politics and of policy-making.

To give an example of that disjunction, '[S]ince 1960 there has been a significant expansion of the electoral marketplace on almost every dimension. More people have access to the polls, vote more often, at more levels of government.... On average, contemporary publics now have more opportunities to make electoral input on more offices at more levels of government' (Dalton and Gray, 2003: 34–5). However, at the same time, we are observing 'the rise of the unelected' (Vibert, 2007), that is, an increasing policy-making role for bodies that are not democratically accountable, such as transnational institutions, central banks, independent agencies, or courts. In addition, electoral pledges lose much of their relevance in situations where policy-making is increasingly negotiated because political systems face a range of functional pressures that limit their scope for steering. Take, for example, the combination of international pressure (likely to lead to policy convergence and uniformization) with the higher domestic differentiation of interests, values, and preferences – a paradox best portrayed by the neologism of 'fragmegration' (Rosenau, 2004). If citizens become aware of the disjunction between the logic of politics and the logic of policy-making, this may well reinforce the already-existing trends of rising citizens' distrust and declining voter turnout. It may thus lead to spiral effects through a new wave of disappointment with the fictitious character of the circular model of representative democracy sketched above, which continues to be presented as a legitimate benchmark.

Is this necessarily bad news for democracy? After all, if the influence of representative institutions is weakening, advocacy groups are gaining influence and pushing for more grassroots participation in politics and in policy-making: some would argue that this is a source of popular empowerment. According to this line of reasoning, parties and formal official decision-making bodies are often unrepresentative and ossified, and democracy can only benefit from a more vigorous and active civil society. I do not fully agree with such a diagnosis, as I will explain in the concluding chapter of the book, which builds upon the analyses developed in the preceding empirical chapters. Let me point to the centrality in representative democracy of competitive elections, which are both formal mechanisms of authorization to rule and of accountability of the rulers. Without idealizing representative democracy, such formal mechanisms are less developed, or even simply absent, elsewhere. For instance, several advocacy groups are self-proclaimed representatives of populations that have not mandated them to defend their interests, and to whom they are not accountable. Participatory additions to the partisan system may be welcome, most notably if they stimulate interest in politics and if they counterbalance the elitist bias of partisan organizations. However, participatory forms of policy-making are not, by essence, more pluralist or more egalitarian, and they may even offer less formal guarantees for equality among the participants than the 'one person, one vote' formula of representative democracy. Hence, they should not be idealized.

For instance, considering that policy-making increasingly takes place across state borders, the involvement of organized civil society is often deemed to offset the absence of parliamentary institutions beyond the European level. Not only is this a rather hasty and undifferentiated assessment, but it also overlooks the existence of numerous sites of technocratic governance that are permeated neither by representative nor by participatory forms of democracy (Papadopoulos, 2012). There are, of course, also numerous participatory devices involving lay-citizens more directly, in principle, without the filtering effect of organizations. However, in spite of their proliferation, such devices are generally confined to the local level. This is not to say that political decision-making taking place at this level lacks significance, but one should not act as if the other levels did not exist. 'Megaprojects' with high-risk consequences are seldom critically scrutinized in public deliberations: silence protects them (Keane, 2012). Besides, even at the local level, it is often hard to estimate to what extent the outcomes of participatory devices have decisive effects on collectively binding decisions (Papadopoulos and Warin, 2007).

To grasp such complex evolutions, one needs to take a bird's eye view of political systems. The next section emphasizes the specificity of this book in that respect, a perspective which distinguishes it from most of the recent literature on democratic institutions, politics, and policy.

## Trying to move beyond 'parochial' views of changes

This book offers a comprehensive view of the major observable trends in democratic governance, of the origins and context of these trends, and of their effects. It identifies the major transformations of our democracies that affect the 'input', 'throughput', and 'output' dimensions of political activities – respectively politics as competition for the allocation of goods and values, policy-making processes, and the production of collectively binding decisions. It examines the mechanisms at the root of the observed transformations, the linkages between the trends observed, and possible reinforcement effects – positive feedback loops – at work between them. It also points out the paradoxical aspects of some transformations, and seeks to elucidate their puzzling elements. It does so by connecting and putting into perspective distinct strands of research that seldom communicate.

In recent decades, research on political phenomena has expanded tremendously, substantially contributing to a better knowledge of our world. However, the other side of the coin of such an expansion is often specialization on narrow topics, through limiting conceptual lenses. As a result, the discipline of political science is today too fragmented along school, and, above all, subdisciplinary lines (for example, political sociology, policy analysis, European studies, international relations) to be able to offer an encompassing view of the changes affecting contemporary democracies.

The literature on elections and party competition, or on collective action and associations, focuses on changes in individual and group behaviour. As expressed by an influential analyst of group membership and of cooperative links between individuals (their 'social capital'), the erosion of social networks and withdrawal into the private sphere in our societies are epitomized in the metaphor of 'bowling alone' (Putnam, 2002). If the decline in the importance of group identities affects partisan ties, there are several other factors acting in the same direction: the growth of cynicism, distrust in politicians, and anti-establishment feelings, but also the diffusion of 'post-materialist' participatory beliefs that are suspicious of partisan straitjackets, or even the reorganization of political parties themselves in response to media pressure. With very few exceptions, this body of research is not concerned with the workings of institutions or with issues related to policy-making.

Researchers working on the institutional architecture, for their part, come to quite diverse, if not contradictory, conclusions about the fate of democracies, depending on whether their focus is on state reform, on participatory experiments, or on the role of 'guardian institutions' such as courts or independent agencies. While the vast majority of studies of participatory experiments are at least moderately optimistic about their contribution to citizens' empowerment, a number of studies of internationalized policy-making and of the delegation of regulatory tasks to depoliticized bodies deplore their deficient democratic accountability. Furthermore, studies usually emphasize a single trend and thus fail to notice the frequently contradictory character of changes in modes of policy-making. Few works are as perceptive as Kelemen's recent (2011) study *The Transformation of Law and Regulation in the European Union*, which suggests that the frequently observed rise of informal 'soft law' instruments (namely, the 'Open Method of Coordination') within the European Union is a red herring that distracts the attention from a more significant parallel trend towards legalization.

Policy studies emphasize variation in management modes, policy styles, or policy content arising from a number of changing contextual factors: globalization, European integration, socioeconomic and ideological change, and so on. Such research, however, usually concentrates narrowly on the study of policy outputs, and may suffer from a managerial and problem-solving bias that makes it reduce the issues of decision-making to a sort of 'administration of things' (to use an old concept from Marxist literature). Even when policy research is exempted from such a bias, the changing relationship of the citizenry to politics is not given due consideration, even as a mere background aspect. Besides, what is more surprising is that not much consideration is given either to the existence or not of a feedback effect of policy shifts and governance changes on the way the political game is played.

In other words, because of its concentration on politics as a means for the conquest of power, or alternatively, on the policy process and decision-making, the literature usually fails to capture the full range of phenomena that illustrate major transformations of democracies, and thus offers only a partial view of them. For instance, an edited volume entitled *Challenges to Democracy* (Dowding *et al.*, 2001) allotted little space to policy changes, and the same can be said of the more recent (and excellent) *Future of Representative Democracy* (Alonso et al., 2011). Another volume, *Democracy Transformed?* (Cain *et al.*, 2003), was more balanced with respect to changes on the 'input' and 'output' sides, but trends towards more technocratic forms of policy-making were not given sufficient consideration. For example, the editors' introductory chapter emphasizes pressures for new forms of democracy, but underplays trends such as the more powerful role of expert bodies, and fails to address the impact of changes in governance modes such as the development of public–private partnerships or of multilevel negotiation involving different jurisdictions. Naturally, the editors conclude with an optimistic assessment of the expansion of democratic opportunities, which requires qualification, especially as more weight should be put on the consequences of internationalization of policy-making. By contrast, the edited volume *Transformations of the State?* (Leibfried and Zürn, 2005) mainly scrutinized transformations attributed to internationalization, with only one chapter dealing with domestic legitimacy problems.

True, bringing together scholarly works that seldom speak to each other and drawing on empirical evidence pertaining to multiple facets of politics, governance, and policy-making is a mammoth task. However, this task is facilitated by the fact that the present book is not based directly on primary material, but relies on the secondary literature. Of course, this is not the only limit to the ambition of this book. Its observations may not apply beyond the universe of (mostly European) established democracies, and it concentrates more on general trends than on a systematic scrutiny of differences across countries. Since the scope of the book is broad, the substantive chapters probably do not offer the detailed view that specialists would prefer, but only an overview of what I consider to be the main issues and challenges for democracy in each field. And since the book does not rely on my own empirical research (which, in recent years, has addressed issues of accountability and participation in multilevel governance and in 'Europeanization' processes), I must acknowledge the huge debt I have accumulated to the numerous specialists of the topics that I address. Allusions to their work, and quotations, abound, and the reference list at the end of the book is fairly long. I hope that readers will not find this too irritating and will appreciate my concern for transparency about my (perhaps eclectic) sources of inspiration.

The final section of this introduction summarizes the argument of the book as it is developed in the subsequent chapters.

## Outline of the book: the argument in brief

*Chapter 1*, which follows this introductory chapter, begins with a reminder: political parties are the key actors in representative democracy. Some consider that the major contemporary parties today collude and construct 'cartels', and that in a context of the decline of ideological loyalties, several parties are seeking to retain their voters through constituency service facilitated by their penetration of the state and manipulation of public resources. However, the internationalization of policy-making and fiscal constraints reduce the number of tools and the magnitude of the resources that incumbent parties possess to serve their constituencies, and economic globalization produces losers who blame the incumbent parties for their misfortune. All this happens in a period during which, again for a variety of reasons (for instance, the increase in educational levels which makes citizens better informed and more critical), citizens' identification with parties decreases, electorates become more fluid, and voting becomes more instrumental, when it is not simply replaced by abstention. Since parties are less able to deliver side-payments, voters have no incentives to excuse the withdrawal of political elites into their closed world.

Political elites responded to citizens' disaffection by trying to restore competition. Party systems tend to become bipolar as parties seek to offer a choice between competing governmental teams. Bipolarization does not necessarily mean ideological polarization. The crucial issue is generally which governmental team is judged by voters as best able to carry out tasks of government on which there is an overarching consensus, such as avoiding inflation. In such a context, credible leadership is helpful, so we observe a *de facto* (informal) 'presidentialization' of political parties and politics. If the competitors are more or less similar and the outcome of the elections uncertain, then leadership becomes an asset. Party presidentialization also has an 'output' face: leaders deemed particularly appealing to the electorate are given more leeway to formulate their party's policy platform. Moreover, governments become less accountable to parties and parliaments, and power within them is increasingly concentrated in the hands of the prime minister and the core executive. Hence, presidentialization undermines the conditions that made for the success of the traditional party government model and is conducive to a (quasi-) plebiscitary model of democracy.

*Chapter 2* addresses another change that strongly impacts politics, the growing role of the mass media. If attention to political events is selective, and if only few people are loyal party followers, competition for media attention becomes stronger between parties. Editorialists become influential opinion-makers, and politicians strive to garner positive judgments from these figures: 'party democracy' has evolved into 'audience democracy' (Manin, 1997). The media itself has changed. It is largely autonomous from political parties, and its commercial side has become more prominent. Operating according to its own commercial imperatives, the media often tends to sensationalize political events, seek scapegoats, privilege scandal and the dramatization of conflict, and is more attracted by policy failure than by success. This changes the self-presentation of parties, which are under pressure to deliver ready-made information to the media to avoid their dependence on it. The media's role also affects the power balance within parties: the influence of spin doctors increases at the expense of militants. The media also favours personalization, reinforcing the trends towards presidentialization. Some media outlets also use simple arguments and reinforce distrust of politicians, thus facilitating the task of anti-establishment actors. Furthermore, the media is in search of news value, so it selects only what counts as 'events', and may not offer adequate descriptions of increasingly complex policy-making activities. There is a widening gap between mediatized 'front-stage' – mostly partisan – politics, and policy-making, a significant part of the latter taking place 'back-stage', and often involving non-elected actors.

This has consequences on the impact of 'new' (electronic) media on politics and governance. Its rise is deemed to alleviate the negative effects of the colonization of politics by increasingly commercialized media. According to a 'cyber-optimistic' scenario, the internet produces virtuous effects by making the communication landscape more plural and by favouring more horizontal patterns of deliberation and more extended forms of mobilization. The internet is deemed to empower actors other than politicians with high media profiles or the spin doctors who advise them. However, these virtuous effects are disputable, and, given the uncoupling between front-stage and back-stage politics, even if new information technologies help challengers of the established political order there is no guarantee that the challengers will become influential in policy-making channels.

The first chapters of this book basically focus on politics within the nation-state, with the exception of the discussion on the role of the internet, which operates across borders. Yet, as pointed out in *Chapter 3*, the process of internationalization of political decision-making has important consequences for national democratic systems. With the globalization of regulation, most nations become 'rule-takers rather than rule-makers' (Braithwaite and Drahos, 2000: 3). Also, in several cases of transnational decision-making, there are no rules guiding the inclusion of actors in policy-making in a satisfying way, and there is no institutionalized political competition between organized interests or advocacy groups to safeguard pluralism. The increasing involvement of NGOs in transnational governance has generated changes in the structure of international regimes and organizations. However, the impact of NGOs on international affairs and the responsiveness of international bodies to their claims should not be overestimated. Moreover, as already argued in this chapter, the inclusion of civil society organizations is no substitute for traditional mechanisms of representation, given that usually they are not formally authorized to act by the populations whose interests they claim to represent, and are only weakly accountable to them. Furthermore, trends toward the privatization of governance, which give a central role to democratically unaccountable entities, are more pronounced at the transnational level.

As for the European Union, it is a complex and sophisticated polity whose institutional architecture increasingly resembles national federal systems. Although its 'democratic deficit' is less acute than in other sites of governance beyond the nation-state, it remains multifaceted. In addition, the internationalization of decision-making and 'Europeanization' (that is, the EU's impact on domestic policy-making) both increase the domestic influence of the core executive that is observed with 'presidentialization'. They lead to a strengthening of unelected bureaucracies and to the marginalization of parliamentary institutions, the influence of which on the policy process is in decline.

Is this, however, too static an account? Parliaments undergo learning processes and react to 'deparliamentarization', but they mainly gain policy influence through informal channels, so that 'reparliamen-tarization' does not necessarily mean better accountability to the citizenry.

It is also asserted that the influence of supranational bodies in policy-making leads to multilevel governance structures. This means that the formulation or the implementation of public policies takes place in networks that involve public agents (politicians and administrators) belonging to different decisional levels, together with various non-public participants (economic agents, interest representatives and stakeholders, and experts). Thinking in terms of networks leads to a more pluralist image of policy-making than thinking in terms of executive dominance. However, multilevel structures are often arenas of informal negotiations between decisional units. These are largely prepared by technocrats, are not the object of media scrutiny, and thus lack visibility, which is a precondition for public control and the allocation of responsibilities.

Depending on the decisional sites beyond the nation-state, the most influential actors are members of executives, experts, or even members of transnational interest groups. With the many facets of internationalization, the lack of congruence between policy-makers and policy-takers is on the increase, and the role of democratically accountable political action is diminished. Decisions resulting from European integration are thought to escape national democratic control and are then criticized because they are produced in remote decisional circles or because they negatively affect the condition of 'modernization losers'. Such issues are put on the agenda primarily by nationalist parties that succeed in presenting themselves as alternatives to a mostly pro-European political class. Therefore, Europeanization reinforces distrust and populism. However, what citizens do not seem to see (yet?) is that the democratic deficit is much larger at the transnational level beyond the EU. It may then be hypothesized that there is potential here for more contestation.

The shift from 'government' to 'governance', or, in other words, the advent of cooperative forms of policy-making, is not limited to multilevel interactions. As explained in *Chapter 4*, it is related to the state's relatively restricted ability to steer our complex and fragmented societies, which obliges states to negotiate (and undertake joint action) with non-state actors in matters of policy-making. It is, notably, a consequence of public authorities' limited resources (of finance, organization, knowledge, or authority) that they depend for the exercise of their power on resources held by other, non-public, actors. This translates into *de facto* power fragmentation even in systems of government in which the locus of power is thought to lie in the hands of the prime minister and a small group of people around him or her. The development of various forms of policy 'co-production' in governance networks may be seen as a counter-trend to the dynamics of 'presidentialization'. Paradoxically, concentration of power in the core executive can go hand in hand with a weakening of the government, which diminishes its policy-making capacity. The core executive thus has more power, but the scope of its power may become narrower.

Are cooperative forms of policy-making, which take the form of networks that also involve non-state actors, a promising step towards more inclusive and horizontal forms of decision-making? One problem is that the task of managing and 'governing' governance networks may be delegated to the bureaucracy. In addition, collaborative governance stresses the inclusion of particular interests, replacing the egalitarian principle of 'one person, one vote' with the principle of stakeholderism. The actors who matter are those who can credibly claim that they have intense preferences and interests to defend. Besides, it is an open question to what extent the integration of civil society claims into policy-making is authentic. We know that the representation claims of NGOs are disputable, that NGOs may themselves suffer from elitism or lack of transparency, and that the cooption of some NGOs into policy networks may reinforce inequalities between organizations, for example, between those more 'cooperative' and the rest, or between those able to provide the resources necessary for policy-making (such as their expertise) and the rest.

Collaborative governance also leaves its mark on regulatory instruments. 'Hard' law is losing its grip as an instrument of political regulation. The shift to 'soft' law has the same origin as the shift to collaborative governance: the inability of the state to impose regulation in a top-down manner. But soft law tends to also be fuzzy law. Negotiated agreements, for instance, are almost inevitably vaguely formulated. The margin for the interpretation of law is broadened, and this reinforces the growing influence of the judiciary (see below). Hence, the traditional representative circuit of party-parliamentary democracy loses its influence again. But probably even more alarming with respect to the quality of democracy is another risk: elected politicians are seldom influential in policy networks, and in addition, parliamentary bodies are losing their indirect influence, which lies in their formal capacity to overrule decisions formulated in networks, making the latter operate under the 'shadow of hierarchy'.

Along with reforms in policy styles involving organized interests, one should not overlook the fact that there are reforms that are driven by a concern to involve ordinary citizens; these are presented and discussed in *Chapter 5*. The two reform streams do not completely overlap. Collaborative governance primarily results from the need to increase the expertise of public authorities and the legitimacy of their policies. Several participatory experiments, by contrast, appear to embody a genuine desire to allow lay-persons to express their claims on policy-making or to educate citizens to become involved in public matters and to formulate an informed opinion about them. Although more instrumental and top-down concerns about enhancing policy legitimacy through participation are not absent either, one common principle of participatory experiments is that neither elected officials nor large, organized collective actors should be the key players. All sorts of experiments in participatory forms of policy-making are proliferating nowadays, not only in OECD countries, but also in developing countries. Some of these devices have found international resonance, such as the participatory budgeting process first established in the Brazilian city of Porto Alegre. Not only has the scope of innovations been extended to numerous policy areas, but new information technologies also allow the involved parties to proceed with online and partly interactive consultations on the internet.

Participatory experiments are so numerous and diverse that it is difficult to draw general conclusions about their implications. They are not designed as alternatives to traditional mechanisms of electoral representation. However, this poses the problem of their coupling with overall institutional (representative) architecture. Anecdotal evidence can support the argument that these devices are influential on collectively binding decisions, but can also argue against it. As a whole, only a few devices lead to the formulation of policy options endorsed by public authorities. Hence, it would be bold to argue that their development can compensate for the loss of influence of democratically elected officials on policy-making. The growth of participatory forms of policy-making does not take place in a vacuum, but in a context of wider transformations of policy-making, marked by the diffusion of new modes of governance. This book shows that most of these modes are not genuinely participatory or even not participatory at all.

Chapter 5 also discusses the impact on political regulation of changes inspired by 'New Public Management' (NPM) doctrines and their derivatives. Although primarily guided by concerns about efficiency, these changes are also part of an 'accountability' agenda, and thus imply a closer attention to the needs of policy addressees. NPM reforms originated in economic thinking and fit well into the neoliberal paradigm that idealizes the operation of private firms. However, since there is a quest for greater accountability to service users, too, it is not so easy to distinguish 'client orientation' from concerns at the origin of the development of the participatory procedures described in the first part of Chapter 5. In principle, the clienteles of administrations are supposed to gain influence through more direct channels of expression open to the specific segments of the population that are personally affected by service delivery. This may present advantages with regard to the degree of state responsiveness to public needs, as these segments may know better the kind of public action that meets their needs. However, as we know, a high degree of organization may be necessary to become a credible spokesperson for the interests of 'clients', so not all those affected have the same opportunity to make their voice heard.

To what extent has administrative reform modified the degree of political control over the bureaucracy? Unlike collaborative governance, in which bureaucracy seems to keep the upper hand in the design and management of policy-making networks, reforms seem to have triggered a reassertion of the power of politicians, although they initially implied that the administration would be awarded more autonomy. Those politicians who truly accepted the enhancement of administrators' operational autonomy realized that they ran the risk of committing *hara-kiri* with regard to their own roles and prerogatives. Thus, they initiated a new wave of repoliticization of the civil service. In that respect, the 'partyness' of the government seems to have increased during a period of dissolution of the partyness of society, as suggested in Chapter 1. Members of the executive appear, therefore, to be the ultimate winners of this cyclical process. Furthermore, since reforms also led to administrative fragmentation, they generated demands for more 'joined-up government', which usually means more intervention from the top. In addition, reforms enhancing administrative discretion make it more difficult to hold members of executives accountable in cases of policy failure, because the reforms facilitate blame-shifting to highly exposed top managers. It may well be that we are facing an executive drift in that case, too, as with the internationalization of politics discussed in Chapter 3.

More generally, the consequences of administrative reform for democracies are multifaceted and even contradictory. The 'downward' accountability of the bureaucracy is now – in principle, at least –

enhanced vis-à-vis narrow populations who, as in collaborative governance, can make credible claims about how they are affected by state policies. However, in reality, 'consumer' empowerment does not seem to be the primary concern. Even when feedback by service users takes place, its interpretation often lies in the hands of politicians and managers who can use it as an instrument for their own strategic purposes. In addition, accountability for conduct in government at large through electoral mechanisms becomes less effective, given the primacy conferred to accountability relationships at the street level and due to the elongation of the accountability chain between citizens, parliaments, governments, and administrations.

*Chapter 6* discusses limits to majority rule that result from the growing power of non- and counter-majoritarian institutions, such as independent agencies and courts. Courts are expected to ensure minority protection and to safeguard individual rights. The rationale of regulation by independent bodies is not so much to protect rights, but to safeguard the public interest from the alleged self-interest of politicians, or from the risk of capture of decision-making by particular interests.

'Agencification', that is, the proliferation of independent agencies, especially in the field of regulation of market competition, is yet another reform trend in the administration of contemporary political systems that aims – at least in principle – to free members of the bureaucracy and experts from political pressure. NPM influence is discernible in features of such agencies. However, unlike NPM, agencification should not be viewed as a correlate, but rather as a side-effect of the spread of neoliberal policies. Following the international diffusion of policies of deregulation, a need for re-regulation appeared. And although it extends far beyond the OECD world, the growth of 'regulatory capitalism' appears closely related to European integration. The EU has become a major promoter of regulation. In many sectors, EU legislation requires member states to create independent agencies, and the EU seeks to propagate 'best practices' by encouraging the formation of multilevel networks involving regulatory bodies at European and national levels. The 'regulatory state' is also a consequence of 'risk' society. The domains of pharmaceuticals, food, and the environment require the production of regulations and their implementation by bodies in charge of tasks as diverse as avoiding accidents or ensuring sustainability.

Agencification means that formal rule-making remains within the realm of classic parliamentary and governmental bodies, but single-purpose independent agencies, rather than the traditional state bureaucracy, issue important individual binding decisions that clearly impact the market or an economic sector. The search for credibility implies that regulatory bodies should remain immune from partisan politics and be staffed by experts. Unlike the establishment of participatory procedures or even of collaborative forms of governance, agencification is technocratic in spirit. For example, while proximity to stakeholders is positively valued in collaborative governance, proximity to the regulatees is often viewed as entailing the risk of capture for agencies. Mirroring fears about the unreflective practice of democratic politics, delegation to independent bodies exemplifies a 'logic of discipline' (Roberts, 2010). Although independent regulatory agencies have been portrayed as 'guardian' institutions endowed with the task of protecting the public interest, the question 'Who Guards the Guardians?' (Shapiro, 1988) is indeed crucial. On the other hand, politicians can also content themselves with cosmetic delegation of their power, while retaining in reality control over the operation of agencies (Hood, 2011: 21). Formal and *de facto* agency independence are not necessarily correlated. We shall also see that, as with NPM, agencification has led, in several cases, to the reassertion of the power of politicians over the bureaucracy. For instance, the autonomization of some administrative agencies was offset by appointments of board members following a political logic. Thus, the questions posed about the outcome of NPM reforms can also be posed about agencification: What is ultimately the capacity of elected officials to control and hold accountable those to whom they delegate their power, and who among these officials are more successful in carrying out this task?

Another facet of the inclination to put checks on the power of political majorities is the process of 'judicialization', which is also discussed in Chapter 6. Judicialization can be defined as the increased influence of courts on policy-making. Courts influence the law instead of merely applying it, and this challenges the formal separation of powers. For instance, since World War II, most legal systems have developed in ways that increase the power of judges to control political decisions. This yields indirect effects: legislators have to anticipate possible court vetoes, and they are thus constrained to self-limitation. Therefore, judicialization also contributes to the declining role of the partisan representative circuit. It can be considered part of a broader process of juridification of society, in which social issues are increasingly framed in legal terms. An important manifestation thereof in the political realm is the 'constitutionalization' of national legal orders: fundamental individual rights and freedoms become constitutionally entrenched and judicially enforceable. Particularly in deeply fragmented societies, political majorities wishing to retain their legitimacy must prove to be other-regarding with respect to the protection of minority rights. Yet individuals, too, feel now that they deserve to be protected against violations by state authorities.

Judicialization is also driven by internationalization. It seems that an international human rights regime enjoys an increasingly global consensus, and at the regional level, there has been a 'domestication' of the European Convention on Human Rights by national legal orders. To this, one should add in EU member-states the constitutionalization of core principles of European integration that took place largely under the leadership of the European Court of Justice, which enjoys an atypical degree of discretion as a court. Within the EU, 'multilevel' networking between courts is relevant to the diffusion of legal integration, similarly to the multilevel networking between agencies that is an important feature of the agencification process. Incidentally, there are links between agencification and judicialization, as the requirement of agencies to 'give reasons' as a counterweight to their enjoying increased discretion has expanded the scope of judicial oversight over administrative practice.

Nevertheless, contrary to agencification or to soft law, which may appear as constitutional or legislative anomalies, improvements in the quality of decision-making – such as less arbitrariness and more fairness – expected from judicialization can be justified by referring to the classic requirements of the rule of law, which should be respected by those in power. Judicialization is primarily a core manifestation of the gradual prevalence of a liberal or constitutionalist conception of democracy over a populist one (Mény and Surel, 2002). The role of the judiciary is legitimized because it injects impartiality into the policy process, which can compensate for power asymmetry between rulers and their subjects. However, legal doctrine and political theory are profoundly divided in their normative assessments of such a role. It is often argued that one should not have an idealized picture of the judiciary, and that its lack of democratic accountability is a problem, especially in a context of increased judicialization. Because the courts are the least representative branch of government, critics of judicialization denounce 'juristocracy' or the 'government of judges'. Moreover, even if disadvantaged segments of society or marginalized concerns can benefit from litigation, expertise and financial resources are necessary to appeal to the courts with reasonable chances of success, thus reproducing social inequalities. But what about the practical legitimacy of a trend like judicialization? Some (for instance, Mény and Surel, 2002) consider that the erosion of the populist component in established democracies lies at the origin of the kind of anti-establishment protest discussed in Chapter 1. Yet it can also be argued that, in a context of distrust of politicians, courts enjoy larger legitimacy, at least if they are not themselves politicized (just as administrative bodies situated at arm's length from government may satisfy those concerned about the lack of impartiality of partisan decision-making bodies). Anyway, in spite of its pervasiveness, judicialization does not seem to feature largely in media coverage or political debates. Although some might welcome it while others would disapprove of it, it is one of the long-term evolutions that are not generally subject to public scrutiny.

In sum, this book argues that most significant evolutions are taking place back-stage. The problem is that several lead to a widespread degradation of democratic quality, which can be epitomized in four key challenges to democratic politics and governance:

- the marginalization of parliamentary institutions;
- the 'technocratization' of political decisions;
- the advent of 'advocacy' democracy;
- the divorce between the spheres of 'politics' and 'policy-making'.

These challenges are presented in the concluding chapter of the book, which also points out that they may lead to spiral effects, although they are not devoid of paradoxes and contradictions. The tone of this final *Chapter 7* is inevitably rather sceptical about the prospects for democracy, but it also provides some suggestions for a 'de-hollowing-out' of representative institutions with regard to their control functions, and for a more robust impact of participatory procedures over political decisions.

It is of crucial importance for political science to provide people, especially those who are dispossessed from their legitimate power of self-determination, with the instruments that they need to evaluate critically evolutions that concern them and, if they judge them to be negative, the tools to change them. Perhaps this book can contribute, even marginally, to what is admittedly an ambitious but, in my view, essential task.

# Chapter 1

# Party Democracy Challenged

As mentioned in the introduction, representative democracy is above all party democracy, in the sense that political parties are the main actors in representative institutions. In some countries, such as Italy and Belgium, the role of political parties has been, or still remains, so prominent that the countries have been labelled 'partitocracies'. Party domination of political life has been enabled by the deep penetration of party organizations into society, a phenomenon that specialists call the partyness of society. Traditionally, parties not only recruit political leaders but also play a crucial role in expressing, aggregating and filtering social demands in the process of 'input-formulation' in the political system. They are also key players in making collectively binding decisions and in the authoritative allocation of public resources: this process of 'output-formulation' is typically the realm of 'party government'.

Parties are subject to several challenges, leading to substantial transformations in their profiles and functions: these transformations constitute the subject of this chapter. It will show why and how the major contemporary parties have evolved into 'cartel' machines (Katz and Mair, 1995), and explain why parties need to reinstate competition and how competition leads to the advent of a plebiscitary-style democracy – a style that does not apply to the whole range of political activities, but only a section of them.

Confronted by the erosion of ideological loyalties in society, the cartel party typically seeks to attract and retain voters through the allocation of 'club' goods that it can offer to its followers, thanks to its deep penetration of the state. However, we shall see that a number of factors have limited the ability of incumbent parties to serve their clientele generously. This is happening at a time when, for a variety of reasons, party loyalties continue to decline. As parties are less able to deliver side-payments, sceptical voters have no incentives to overlook the withdrawal of political elites into their closed world. Those excluded from the benefits of the cartel system desert partisan politics or are increasingly mobilized by anti-elitist protest parties. Those with

20

a high level of political sophistication either become politically volatile or opt for alternative channels of political mobilization through single-issue or cause groups. The conventional forms of political participation, such as voting, are increasingly replaced by participation in policy-oriented cause groups. Dalton *et al.* describe this as an evolution toward 'advocacy democracy' (2003: 267ff).

Political elites have responded to voters' disaffection by trying to restore competition. Party systems have tended to become bipolar as parties seek to offer meaningful choices between competing governmental teams. However, note that partisan bipolarization does not mean ideological polarization. The crucial issue is which governmental team is judged by citizens as best able to carry out governing tasks on which there is an overarching consensus, such as avoiding inflation. In this context, credible leadership is helpful, so that we observe a *de facto* 'presidentialization' of political parties (Poguntke and Webb, 2005, 2005a; Webb and Poguntke, 2005; Webb *et al.* 2011). Both established and anti-establishment parties tend to rely increasingly on personalization, because this strategy seems to attract votes. This diffusion phenomenon is the result of 'contagion' from first-movers in the direction of presidentialization. Party presidentialization has an output face: leaders deemed particularly appealing to the electorate acquire more leeway to formulate their party's policy platform. Moreover, governments become less accountable to parties and parliaments, and power within them is increasingly concentrated in the hands of the prime minister and the core executive. Hence, presidentialization is conducive to a (quasi-) plebiscitary model of democracy. However, this is only part of the story. While politics is increasingly dominated by a competitive logic, in the policy-making sphere there are strong constraints, which are likely to lead to compromise or to the depoliticization of decisions. This major disjunction tends to lead to a spiral in which popular dissatisfaction and distrust of politics are reinforced.

## The cartel strategy and its limits

The story of the cartel strategy starts with the so-called 'end of ideologies', the title of an influential book (Bell, 1960) that characterizes the cultural atmosphere of the decades immediately after World War II. Sustained by economic growth and generous social policies, a wide ideological consensus allowed big parties to become catch-all machines (Kirchheimer, 1966); they were able to satisfy multiple clienteles who were no longer divided by deeply antagonistic interests. However, this situation also had a negative consequence for parties: given the weakening of their links with specific social segments, more of their clientele became ideologically volatile and, as a result, more likely to be won over by rival parties.

The decline in partisan attachments can be explained by broad social trends. Modernization brought about a loosening of ties between the individual and the community, be it a class, ethnic or religious milieu. Because partisan loyalties were largely derived from such forms of social belonging, their erosion had a negative effect on party identification (Dalton and Wattenberg, 2002: 11). In a sense, modernization has made democratic societies less heterogeneous, with individuals having less distinct and less dense social identities (notwithstanding the more recent trend towards multiculturalism due to immigration). Yet, paradoxically, society has become more heterogeneous in another respect: individuals cultivate and even idealize their particularisms. This individuation process is epitomized in Robert Putnam's formula 'bowling alone', which 'refers to the trend for the individual to acquire – due to changes in working conditions, living situations, family structures, personal mobility and cultural contexts – a set of interests (or passions) that is increasingly specific to the individual' (Schmitter, 2008: 206). Putnam (2000) suggested that, in the United States, the decline of interpersonal networks has translated into the decline of participation in voluntary associations, which has been mirrored in detachment from politics.

However, evidence also exists to show that social capital – measured by the degree of involvement in community life – may actually be increasing (Pharr and Putnam, 2000). The World Values Survey found that, even in the United States, membership in cause groups increased from 6 per cent in 1980 to 33 per cent in 1999, and the same upward trend in civic association membership was observed in Great Britain and in Germany (Dalton, 2008: 46). Hence, the erosion of partisan ties is not necessarily tantamount to a privatization of the individual. It may be accompanied by the rise of other forms of political participation, such as mobilization in favour of interest or single-issue groups that gain in attractiveness, especially among individuals with higher cognitive skills, who more easily develop feelings that their action can make a difference.

The advent of advocacy alongside party democracy is thus related to a social process of 'cognitive mobilization' that negatively impacts the partyness of society. With the spread of education, the political sophistication of voters increases, and better-educated citizens develop critical attitudes to partisan messages. As a result, the growth of non-partisanship disproportionately affects those citizens who have sufficient cognitive resources to detach themselves from party discourse (Dalton and Wattenberg, 2002: 33). In addition, the omnipresence of televized media reduces the need to rely on partisan information. With cognitive mobilization, the gap in terms of cultural capital between part of the citizenry and political elites has dramatically decreased, so that citizens with high cognitive skills are less deferential towards authority figures. However, disaffection from parties is not solely related to high cognitive skills that facilitate independence and predispose individuals to reflexive attitudes. People with low levels of education also tend to desert the established parties, but for a different reason: they feel that these parties are insensitive to their concerns. 'Dissatisfied' and 'stealth' democrats coexist (Webb, forthcoming).

These are typical supply-side explanations for the weakening of parties' links to society: the supply of human capital to party organizations has become scarce. However, demand-side explanations can also be given for the same phenomenon (Scarrow, 2002: 83). The transformation of parties into catch-all enterprises reduces partisan demand for mass involvement in their organizational life. The weakening of links between parties and society does not mean that parties are less efficient electoral machines. Rather, a shift in function has taken place: previously the agents of social encapsulation, party organizations are now directed primarily towards performance in 'volatile electoral markets' (*ibid.*: 99). The ensuing ideological flexibility of parties makes the setting of partisan competition more fluid. In such a context, parties less frequently act as channels of social integration, focusing instead on campaigns that allow them to attract, often quite provisionally, less party-dependent voters. This is a self-reinforcing process: parties become electoral machines because they have lost their social function, but focusing mainly on their electoral role prevents them from creating more stable links with their environment. More than 50 years ago, the economist Anthony Downs (1957) assumed that parties and voters perform like rational actors in a market and was repeatedly criticized for overlooking the constraints of parties' ideological commitments as well as structural determinants, such as class and religious ties, which significantly reduce the freedom and aptitude of voters to choose among competing political options. According to this line of criticism, such constraints prevent flexibility both on the supply side – party programmes – and on the demand side – voters' preferences. Today, it is apparent that the Downsian economic metaphor of politics has become more valid.

In order to retain their clientele in the context of the decline of structurally and ideologically based politics, big parties have also sought – in addition to focusing on their electoral function – to capture governmental machinery. They have gradually become deeply entrenched in the state, transforming themselves largely into cartel parties, as depicted in a thought-provoking piece by Katz and Mair (1995). Parties, now remote from voters, must capture the state to acquire essential resources that society no longer provides. It would not be an exaggeration to speak of the withdrawal of political elites into 'the closed world of the governing institutions' (Mair, 2005: 29), and this implies two distinct things. On the one hand, 'parties become part of the state apparatus itself' (Katz and Mair, 1995: 14); they become 'semi-state agencies' (*ibid.*: 16) able to absorb and then distribute state resources to their clienteles, such as jobs in the administration of the state or in publicly owned companies, public contracting to 'friends', housing facilities, and the like. On the other hand, according to the cartel thesis, parties collude with each other to ensure that they remain in power and share state resources.

Thanks to cartel politics, parties are able to partially offset the weakening of their links with society. They serve their clienteles through targeted advantages, such as, on the left, more services and, on the right, lower taxes (Katz and Mair, 2009: 757). Organizational survival and the perpetuation of political elites are the main goals of the cartel system. A century ago Roberto Michels (1962 1st edition 1911) identified similar tendencies within parties, but today politics as a profession – more precisely as a full-time job – is much more prevalent than it was in the past. Politicians' income is more dependent on their re-election, so that the stakes of political survival become higher, and parties have a joint interest in providing for their own security (Katz and Mair, 2009: 758). For that purpose, they need to be recognized as indispensable elements of the state and want to be treated as 'public utilities' or 'public goods' (van Biezen, 2004). Interestingly, this is happening in a period when a significant portion of the population definitely does not perceive them as such!

By the end of the 1980s, almost all parties of note had experience of holding government office at national level (Katz and Mair, 2009: 755), and today parties often benefit from state funding: 'A form of payment that was exceptional even as late as 1975 had become very much the norm by the start of the twenty-first century', according to Scarrow (2006: 621). Parties are in need of subsidies, not only because electoral campaigns become decisive when voters are less attached to parties, but also because these campaigns incur high costs, owing to the fact that they increasingly require professional expertise in political marketing. As Koole puts it: 'Party work and party campaigning is professionalized and almost exclusively capital intensive; labour-intensive organization and campaigning have become unimportant' (1996: 308). Public subsidies are not devoid of virtues: they reduce parties' dependence on private money from self-interested donors, thus enhancing the quality of democracy. But these virtues are probably overstated. Although subsidies are believed to equalize the conditions of electoral competition, Scarrow found no significant positive effect of subsidies on these conditions (2006: 631, 633). Furthermore, because they are distributed in a self-serving manner by partisan governments in a context of widespread distrust of parties, subsidies can also be seen as a protectionist measure in favour of 'lame ducks', support for whom is justified by social functions that most people would agree are not best performed by parties.

Cartel politics appears to be an adjustment by major parties to the fact that they are becoming increasingly remote from society and that, nowadays, they have only tenuous links with social segments conveying distinct political subcultures (such as working-class or religious values), which are losing their cohesion and force. Thus, the emergence and development of party cartels is, above all, a response to the loosening of partisan bonds to society. Parties hope to offset weakening ties with the electorate through the benefits they can distribute to their clientele, thanks to their penetration of the state; hence, contemporary politics is characterized by a revival of patronage, usually considered a feature of pre-modern or developing societies. Today, however, patronage is no longer tantamount to personalistic politics dominated by local notables, a pattern common in traditional societies; patronage currently takes the form of a collective enterprise, where the party – in close operation with the state machinery – becomes a broker, ensuring access to public resources: 'Patronage can therefore compensate for otherwise decaying organisational networks, and rather than being eliminated by modernisation, it might well prove to be its product' (Mair and Kopecky, 2006: 3).

Having said this, the cartel party thesis suffers from excessive generalization, because the diffusion of collective patronage is subject to cross-country variation. Its amplitude is larger in countries where parties control the public allocation of significant resources (or in some cases, even resort to illegal funding), and direct public funding is probably not the most decisive in that respect. The cartel thesis also probably

overstates the phenomenon of collusion between parties. Cartel politics is more likely in countries with a tradition of inter-party cooperation and negotiation and of inter-partisan agreements (sometimes only
tacit); the so-called *Proporzdemokratien* and *consociational* polities,
such as Austria and Belgium, are examples of obvious candidates. In
these countries, the allocation of 'spoils' among major parties is determined by consensus, usually in proportion to parties' electoral strength
and thanks to 'patronage-based penetration of the civil service,
publicly owned companies, and even private sector companies closely
linked to state agencies' (Kitschelt, 2000: 163).

In addition, as acknowledged by the proponents of the cartel party
thesis themselves, 'the cartel inevitably generates its own opposition'
(Katz and Mair, 1995: 24). As with cartel behaviour in economic
markets, policies that favour particular constituencies may yield collectively suboptimal outcomes: either costs are externalized to less influential segments, or these segments receive a reduced allocation of
resources. This creates a reservoir of dissatisfied voters. In the party
system, there are outsiders who are not part of the cartel – either because
they do not want to be or because cartel parties treat them like pariahs.
They are not involved in consensual agreements and are excluded from
the allocation of resources. These outsiders capitalize on popular
discontent, so that anti-establishment parties and movements prosper
thanks to their proclaimed willingness 'to break up what they often
refer to as the "cosy" arrangements that exist between the established
political alternatives... . The cartel parties are often unwittingly providing precisely the ammunition with which the new protesters of the right
can more effectively wage their wars' (Katz and Mair, 1995: 24).
Furthermore, the increasing importance of mass media in politics (see
Chapter 2) nurtures anti-establishment feelings and discourse: accusations of collusion or, worse, corruption are widely publicized today by
largely influential media looking for sensational events, and this further
undermines the legitimacy of parties suspected of cartel practice.
Opposition to established parties is also boosted by the internationalization of policy-making, which is scrutinized in Chapter 3. The most
successful opposition to established parties comes from nationalist
circles: the populist, anti-establishment rhetoric is combined with
rhetoric of national sovereignty that resonates strongly in the context of
cultural, economic and political globalization. Parties that are at the
same time populist and nationalist blame – according to them, self-
interested or incompetent – political elites for surrendering national
sovereignty.

Anti-establishment rhetoric combined with 'sovereignist' concerns is a favourite recipe for success for protest parties because internationalization is generating a new, wide, socioeconomic division between its winners and its losers (Kriesi *et al.*, 2006), in a period when traditional disparities have diminished in relatively affluent societies. Globalization winners – or, more accurately, those who perceive themselves as such – favour supranational integration because they assume they can benefit from it, whereas losers favour national demarcation, expecting it to shield them from the threats of globalization. Those who perceive themselves as losers form a heterogeneous block of mainly blue-collar workers and unemployed people together with small-firm owners and shopkeepers active in local markets (the traditional 'petty bourgeoisie'), as well as farmers. In European Union countries, mainstream parties are generally in favour of supranational political integration (including a substantial part of the Left, which is otherwise critical of globalization); therefore, opposition at the partisan level is confined to anti-establishment parties. An apparent paradox is that national-populist parties have been particularly successful in wealthy countries or regions such as Switzerland, Norway, Denmark, Austria, Flanders and northern Italy, which cannot be considered losers in the internationalization process. It is noteworthy, however, that most of these political systems are of the consensual type, with governments often composed of coalitions of the major parties, so making good targets for accusations of cartel behaviour. Furthermore, even in these regions, people with low levels of education and few market skills fear that free trade and immigration will deprive them of the advantages that they were able to gain in years of steady economic growth. For example, they advocate 'welfare chauvinist' measures in social policy, reserving benefits for the native population.

Nevertheless, the social basis of this kind of populism is broader, because it also includes people who have experienced different forms of social vulnerability not necessarily linked to internationalization and relatively affluent people who fear a loss of status. Voters in populist parties often share traditionalist or authoritarian values which are hostile toward the multiculturalist and politically correct discourse of the intellectual elite. They feel themselves to be losers not only as a result of economic but also of cultural globalization. They are alarmed by insecurity and crime (usually viewed as related to immigration) and advocate a meritocratic ideology according to which only those who deserve benefits should receive them, asserting that some beneficiaries of the welfare system profit from it unduly (for example, immigrants or recipients of unemployment benefits who do not actively seek jobs). In a sense, this segment of the population, composed of 'small–medium' people (Cartier *et al.*, 2008), feels deceived by both those on the top and those below them. However, none of this has much to do with narrow economic determinants of political behaviour. According to Mudde (2007: 119), given that national-populism is strongly concerned with the politics of identity, it definitely cannot be reduced to economic concerns. The fact that it is nurtured by anti-elitist feelings generated by cartel forms of partisan behaviour also points in the same direction.

Not only does the cartel system generate its opponents, but established parties face the additional constraint that they now have fewer resources to distribute and less discretion in distributing them. This is the consequence of limited governmental capacity to deliver the public goods that are likely to satisfy the multiple demands of the mass public. As suggested by Kitschelt (2000: 161, emphasis in the original):

> The new political-economic challenges force politicians to cope with *substantive trade-offs* among several policy objectives all of which voters would like to see realized and with *inter-temporal trade-offs* compelling politicians in executive office to choose when to represent voter preferences best... . Politicians face difficult substantive policy trade-offs because majorities of west European voters simultaneously wish to lower unemployment, improve income equality, maintain a sound fiscal system with low public deficits, and possibly achieve all this with low taxes.

Internationalization is also relevant here: supranational political integration reduces the tools available to national governments (as in the case of monetary policy delegated in the Eurozone to the independent European Central Bank), and economic globalization narrows the policy options of incumbent parties (as in the case of capital taxation, which can lead to capital 'exit' if perceived as excessive by firms). As regards the allocation of clientelistic benefits, European integration can be an obstacle to it. EU directives and competition rules, for example, make patronage more difficult, and EU regional policy often bypasses the national level, thus diminishing 'parties' ability to use regional policy to reward their constituents' (Raunio, 2002: 416). As we shall see in Chapter 3, this is not the only consequence of internationalization that matters for domestic politics, and internationalization is not the only factor that negatively influences the ability of governments to allocate benefits to their constituencies. The failure of Keynesian interventionist policies, which social-democratic parties have also acknowledged, the financial crisis of welfare states, and, more recently, deliberate power shifts in favour of non-partisan regulatory bodies (see Chapter 6) have negatively affected the capacity of incumbent parties to redistribute resources.

Parties are indeed closer to the state, as maintained by the proponents of the cartel thesis, yet the state's room for manoeuvre is limited. As Akkerman (2005: 3) puts it: 'Voters can no longer hire politicians', and, when fewer side-payments are possible, the 'withdrawal' of politicians into the state sphere is less tolerable. Moreover, close media scrutiny makes collusion more difficult, and it contributes to making elections more competitive and more polarized, contrary to the cartel logic. Cartel politics produces so-called positive feedback: it nourishes anti-establishment feelings and populism and contributes to the fact that a growing proportion of the citizenry is losing partisan identification and deserting conventional politics. It amplifies the decline of the representative function of parties, with originally largely predictable cleavage-based voting – based on group affiliation or ideological motivation – increasingly replaced by voting for more instrumental reasons. This change is making already fickle electorates even more volatile and more eager to express their dissatisfaction when parties do not deliver on their pledges. As the author of an extensive survey on the subject writes, citizens 'have grown distrustful of politicians, sceptical about democratic institutions, and disillusioned about how the democratic process functions' (Dalton, 2004: 1). Such changes are visible in several respects (Dalton *et al.*, 2002).

## The challenge to parties of an unfriendly environment

Dalton's comparative survey of 19 advanced democracies shows that, in 17 of them, party identification has steadily declined: a striking pattern, according to the author, given the large variety of countries under consideration (2004: 32–3). Differences in electoral systems, number of parties, or social cleavages did not influence this declining trend, which affected both categories of party identifiers and strong partisans (Dalton and Wattenberg, 2002: 25). The decline in party identification is mirrored in three interrelated trends that cartel politics has not been able to curb: lower party membership, higher electoral volatility and lower voting turnout.

Parties are continuously losing their capacity to recruit members. 'Taking a broad sample of countries and parties from the 1960s to the mid-1990s yields a picture of post-war membership decline, whichever membership measure is chosen', writes Scarrow (2002: 88), a trend also regularly confirmed in self-reports in surveys. Since the turn of the century, most European countries have undergone a further decline in party membership. As a result, in all of the long-established democracies membership rates have fallen by 25 per cent or more since the 1980s. To give some examples illustrating this trend, Britain, Norway and France have lost over half of their party members in the last three decades, and Sweden, Ireland, Switzerland and Finland have lost close to half. The consequence of membership decline is that party members are increasingly an unrepresentative group of citizens, not to mention the fact that most members are politically inactive (Van Biezen *et al.*, 2012). Van Biezen *et al.* argue that, in terms of their social profile (older, better-off financially and more highly educated than the average citizen) and employment (often public), party members might have more in common with the party in office than with the party on the ground (2012: 39).

Unsurprisingly, in a context characterized by the erosion of partisan loyalties, electoral volatility – measured by the proportion of shifts of votes from one election to another – is increasing. By the 1990s, the average volatility 'score' (12.6) in OECD democracies was larger by half than in the 1950s, and voters increasingly report in surveys that they have shifted their vote (Dalton *et al.*, 2002: 40–44). Lower turnout in elections is yet another symptom of the reduced attractiveness of party politics. Turnout in 17 of 19 OECD countries was lower in the 1990s than in the 1950s (Wattenberg, 2002a: 71–2). Another study shows that, in all EU-15 member states, with the exception of Denmark, turnout decreased more or less significantly from the 1980s to the 2000s (Schmidt, 2006: 169). Low turnout is especially prevalent among younger generations, who are not socialized to the norm that voting is a moral obligation and have weaker group identities and links; in the United States, for instance, turnout among 18–24-year-olds fell by about 15 per cent between 1972 and 2000 (Chadwick, 2006: 145).

The decline in voting turnout can be related to a more general process of individuation; yet, it is noteworthy that it occurs during periods when the interest in politics has increased (Dalton *et al.*, 2002: 56), which indicates that citizens do not necessarily withdraw into their private spheres. Several works in the United States have emphasized that citizens hardly seem keen on influencing policy choice and are willing to delegate this task to professional politicians (Putnam, 2000; Hibbing and Theiss-Morse, 2005; Macedo, 2005). However, this may be a case of North American exceptionalism, and, if we look beyond the electoral arena, we see that Americans, and especially the younger segments of the population, are active in various forms of direct-action techniques, such as campaigning, contacting, political consumerism or contentious activities, including on the internet (Dalton, 2008: 55, 71). Therefore, remoteness from parties should not be regarded as a symptom of generalized political apathy and lack of interest in politics, but rather as a sign that people are critical of 'omnibus' machines such as parties that claim to deal competently with all social problems. Laments on the depoliticization of the mass public were heard as early as the 1950s as a consequence of broad consensus built on socioeconomic foundations of growth and prosperity in the post-war period. Although it is a recurrent theme, it should be strongly qualified.

Rather, people are behaving in politics more like consumers than believers (Blumler and Kavanagh, 1999: 210). Reviewing the 1983 general election in the United Kingdom, Rose and McAllister (1986) posited, slightly provocatively, that 'voters begin to choose', referring to the shift from 'closed-class to open election'. This meant not only that voters were becoming more volatile between traditional parties, but also that some voted for newcomers, such as parties articulating regional or environmental concerns, and anti-establishment parties, and that other people decided to abstain. Party systems have long had a reputation for being 'frozen', meaning that successive social cleavages between the second half of the nineteenth and first half of the twentieth centuries gave rise to religious, conservative, liberal, socialist and agrarian parties, but that the party landscape has not changed since then. Such a picture of stability belongs to the past, and changes in party systems translate into more fragmentation, with new parties emerging, usually at the margins. Furthermore, fragmentation is also visible in the fact that elections are becoming more candidate-centred – as we shall see, the rise in the importance of mass media contributes largely to that – and that, where it is possible, voters increasingly vote for candidates from different parties on the same election day ('ticket-splitting').

The remoteness from established parties and the willingness to 'begin to choose' are also influenced by the diffusion over the last few decades of so-called post-materialist values into the mass public

(Inglehart, 1999). This long-term trend has not been affected by episodes of economic crises, which only temporarily led to a resurgence of the primacy of 'materialist' concerns about economic wealth. Nowadays, although most people value both material and post-material goals, the proportion of those privileging post-material goals is on the rise. Post-materialists are more libertarian and less deferential about authority, they criticize democratic systems for providing insufficient opportunities and channels for political participation, and they favour less bureaucratic and hierarchic forms of organization than political parties (with the exception of New Left parties, whose emergence is largely a by-product of post-materialism). These more critical citizens often belong to the new middle class of public service employees involved in welfare-state activities, such as health professionals, social workers and teachers. They are, in a sense, 'monitorial' citizens who constitute the human capital of a 'monitory' democracy (Keane, 2009), in which the action of political officials is under the close scrutiny of different sorts of groups and organizations.

Among these often highly educated citizens, voting abstention does not mean low interest in politics. Post-materialists are strongly interested in politics, but they opt for protest activities because they find them more effective and convivial channels of influence than the partisan circuit. They are 'citizens-on-standby' (Hajer, 2009: 180) who are more likely to mobilize for single causes, and they form the social basis of new social movements, such as pacifist, environmentalist, feminist or humanitarian organizations. These 'new independents' are 'apartisan' but definitely not apolitical: they have the skills to follow actively the complexities of politics, but they have less need of parties and have fewer affective ties with them. This is eloquently described in the metaphor coined by Dalton (2008: 189): 'It is as if the most sophisticated fans of the sport of politics are becoming disengaged with the partisan players they see on the field.'

The partisan arena thus loses its aggregative function to the benefit of alternative arenas of protest politics and 'advocacy' democracy in which grassroots organizations and cause groups are the key players. In such groups, individuals are 'more likely to be in full agreement with a narrower range of concerns, and [to] feel they can make a difference' (Katz and Mair, 1995: 15). As van Biezen and Katz note, 'citizens participate directly in the process of policy formation through channels of direct democracy, or through substitutes such as interest groups and social movements, rather than the conventional representative channels of the political party' (2005: 5). Citizens are not irrational in their belief that elections and party pledges do not matter much when it comes to having their preferences translated into policy. In times of ideological convergence between the major parties, partisan politics loses its significance as an expression of preferences.

It should be added, however, that lack of commitment to partisan life and abstention from elections are signs not only of disillusionment with conventional politics but also of structural inequalities in the capacity to participate in politics (Perrineau, 2007: 16). Political stratification mirrors social stratification: people with low levels of education in the underprivileged stratum of society more frequently feel that politics is alien to them, and this feeling does not apply only to partisan politics but also to alternative political arenas that attract 'post-materialists' from the new middle class. Sociological surveys refer to this as a feeling of political alienation. Democracies are, therefore, still plagued by an oligarchic legacy that is part of their 'broken promises' (Bobbio, 1987), and their 'chorus sings with a strong upper-class accent', as American political scientist Elmer E. Schattschneider eloquently put it in a famous assertion five decades ago (1960: 34–5). Relying on cross-national data from the European Social Survey, Borgonovi (2008) came to the astonishing conclusion that every additional year of education raises the likelihood of voting in national elections by a remarkable three percentage points. French political sociologist Daniel Gaxie (1978) referred in his work to the existence in democracies of a 'hidden poll tax' (*cens caché*), because poorly educated people tend to feel that they lack the necessary cognitive resources to be 'authorized' to express political judgment and to influence the course of things. Politics appears too remote and too complicated for them, and, as a result, these people do not participate. Such an attitude can be portrayed as a sort of self-censorship with respect to political participation, and is not irrational for individuals who face very high costs of information when asked to make a choice. It usually derives from a feeling of powerlessness mixed with a sense of fatalism, or with cynicism, a feeling that 'they do what they want' regardless (for more details, see Hay, 2007). It is, therefore, no surprise that 'alienated' citizens are core targets for anti-establishment parties that promise to voice their resentment.

A growing proportion of citizens are critical of the operation of the political system, which they view as closed and insensitive to the preoccupations of the man in the street. They are disillusioned when politics seems reduced to 'politicking' – in other words, when it obeys its own self-referential logic that remains opaque for outsiders – and as such becomes an object of suspicion for the profane. Interestingly, however, abstention due to a feeling of lack of efficacy in influencing politics has not increased. This can be explained by the fact that, as a whole, the population in our democracies is better educated than in the past and that populist parties are now succeeding in bringing members of the lower social strata back into the electoral game. Disappointed citizens certainly continue to opt for a silent 'exit' from party politics (abstention), but they are also candidates for mobilization by anti-establishment parties ('voice'). As suggested previously, anti-elitism is not the only key to the success of these actors: the general phenomenon of globalization is leading to the distrust of national elites, too. Political authorities are viewed as major promoters of supranational integration, which is perceived as a threat on several dimensions: economic (pressure on the labour market), cultural (loss of identity) and political (demise of national sovereignty). Nevertheless, one should not underestimate the existence of a more diffuse 'politics of anti-politics', with variations across countries in amplitude; for example, anti-establishment sentiment has been boosted in countries like Italy and France by scandals and corruption cases affecting prominent politicians.

Disaffection from partisan politics is thus symptomatic of a general decline of trust in politicians. Dalton reported that the proportion of cynical Americans increased from 60 per cent in 1973 to 76 per cent in 1993, and that Americans' scepticism about the ethical and moral practices of federal governmental officials also increased (2004: 27–8). At approximately the same time, the number of Canadians who believed that politicians cared about their views decreased from 52 per cent to 32 per cent. But erosion of public support for politicians is more widespread and takes place 'regardless of recent trends in the economy, in large and small nations, in presidential and parliamentary systems, in countries with few parties and many, in federal systems and unitary states' (Dalton, 2004: 30–31). According to data from the European Social Survey 2003 on eight European countries (France, Germany, Great Britain, Italy, Netherlands, Poland, Spain and Sweden), in all of them nearly all of those interviewed expressed only mixed trust in political elites, and in six (with the exception of the smallest countries in the sample, the Netherlands and Sweden) the minority that expressed little trust was much larger than the minority expressing strong trust (Perrineau, 2007: 19). More recent data (2005 and 2007) from the European Social Survey downloadable brochure confirms this picture: examination of 17 European states reveals that the average rate of personal trust in politicians measured on a scale ranging from zero to ten is higher than five only in one country (Denmark). According to *Eurobarometer* data, in 2004, only 17 per cent of EU citizens expressed trust in their national parties, much less than the trust expressed for other institutions such as charitable organizations (Kies, 2010: 85). And according to more recent (2010) data from the same source that includes information on 32 states, there is not a single country in which the proportion of those tending to trust parties exceeds the proportion of those tending not to trust them.

Interestingly, lack of trust in politicians and parties is not tantamount to lack of identification or sympathy with the democratic regime as such. It may be coupled with, or even generated by, a strong commitment to democracy. For instance, whereas trust in government in the 15 member-states of the European Union decreased from an average 44 per cent in 1993 to 31 per cent in the fall of 2003, satisfaction with national democracy increased in the same period (Schmidt, 2006: 172). There is, in fact, a 'deepening commitment to democratic principles' (Dalton, 2004: 192), and it is significant that nowadays most anti-establishment parties are not anti-system parties, unlike the fascist or Nazi parties of the interwar period or the later communist parties of the Cold War period. Even if our democracies experience the success of anti-establishment parties, mass anti-system parties – hostile to the democratic regime as such – no longer exist. Right-wing, populist parties, for instance, are very critical of the authorities but remain supportive of democracy and usually do not challenge parliamentary institutions. The same applies to their voters, although some traditionalist segments may also support authoritarian values. As for New Left post-materialists, they are genuinely dissatisfied or disenchanted democrats; if they are critical, it is because they consider democracies not to be sufficiently democratic or, in Bobbio's words, not to keep their promises (1987). Dalton (2004: 68–9) reported that post-materialists are particularly supportive of democratic regime forms and do not manifest any significant distrust in democratic institutions.

More generally, although trust in government has decreased in established democracies, and a large proportion of the public displays little confidence in institutions of representative democracy, such as national legislatures, support for democracy as the best form of government remains nearly universal (Dalton, 2008: 244–250). With widespread support for democracy, nevertheless, democratic 'expectations have risen faster than performance' (Dalton, 2004: 199). These expectations have generated a perception of performance gaps that are a major cause of dissatisfaction with the virtues and skills of political elites. Political competition increases public expectations, only for these expectations to be dashed as the incumbent parties either seek to renege upon some of their commitments because of their political costs or fail to achieve their proclaimed goals (Flinders, 2009). As a result, abstention from elections is growing among young and educated people, who belong to the new middle class and, unlike structural abstainers, do not feel politically alienated. This more critical and less fatalist abstention is a novel sign of disillusionment with established parties and mainstream politicians. Sometimes intermittent, and depending on the salience of elections, it is, then, also contingent on the ideological 'supply' of competing parties: in other words, the credibility of their policy proposals.

Reporting on survey data that shows that, of 15 named institutions, political parties enjoy the lowest level of trust, Dalton and Wattenberg asked: 'can political parties successfully be the central institutions of parliamentary democracy with such low public support?' (2002a: 264). In practice, parties are no longer central, and it is no accident that critical citizens opt for alternative forms of action. It should not be forgotten, however, that advocacy democracy lacks the egalitarian dimension of the principle of 'one person, one vote', as the kind of activities it implies often require skills even less equally distributed than the feeling that one is able to decide in a competent manner between parties running in elections. Urbinati and Warren, for instance, affirm that, in the non-electoral domain, there is no equality of voice, and 'the advantages of education, income, and other unequally distributed resources are more likely to translate into patterns of over- and under-representation' (2008: 405). According to survey data, level of education plays a much less prominent role in people's decision to vote in parliamentary elections than in the decision to sign a petition, to participate in a citizen action group or to attend a demonstration (Dalton *et al.*, 2003: 262–3). Moreover, 'exit' from the partisan field leaves it vulnerable to capture by relatively small minorities of highly motivated citizens ('intensive' minorities: Kriesi, 2005: 17), especially since societies are strongly fragmented, which makes solidarity among their segments less likely.

Political parties are not the only actors to see their representative function being whittled away: interest groups such as trade unions are also losing their integrative function, as the constituencies they claim to represent become more heterogeneous. Furthermore, claims of representativeness are now based on a much broader variety of grounds

(Saward, 2005), expressing a high fragmentation of interests and what Max Weber called 'value polytheism', that is the fact that, in our complex societies, there is no undisputed hierarchy among conflicting values.

Given that individuals are increasingly heterogeneous, volatile, remote from parties and suspicious of their pledges, the parties concentrate on their electoral role. Although established parties no longer have major programmatic differences, each must emphasize its own distinctiveness in order to attract increasingly sceptical voters; therefore, paradoxically, elections are highly competitive, even between quite similar parties which, once in government, are often compelled to negotiate and compromise with each other in policy-making. This is a symptom of the divorce of electoral politics from the decision-making process, which we shall revisit.

To return now to the discussion of the cartel phenomenon: in electoral campaigns, cartel parties do not appear as such, but rather as competitors, and the party cartel provisionally breaks up. But how can a cartel party distinguish itself credibly from another cartel party? When party platforms are similar, when voters do not care much about them or do not take them seriously, emphasizing the positive attributes of a competent party leader may be a helpful strategy to distinguish him or her from the competitors.

## Another partisan response to challenges: the presidentialization of politics

Political elites attempt to respond to citizens' disaffection from partisan politics by adjusting to 'the declining market for the parties' product' (Wattenberg, 2002: 76). Establishing a cartel to share and distribute public resources was the first rational reaction to weakening links with society. Contrary to the prevailing stereotypical image of parties as today's 'dinosaurs', they should rather be viewed as 'highly adaptive, investing heavily in time and resources in the new campaign technologies, professionalizing and centralizing their organizations (particularly around their top leaderships), and paying far more attention to image and specific campaign issues as opposed to traditional ideological standpoints' (Farrell and Webb, 2002: 103).

Parties have sought to restrict competition in order to jointly distribute resources, but they are also under pressure to restore competition to make partisan politics attractive again. Lacking a stable and loyal electoral reservoir and no longer able to count on the partyness of society, they must invent new strategies to generate support. This implies a change in all functional aspects of parties: in their relation to the electorate, as organizations and as governing institutions (Dalton and Wattenberg, 2002: 1). With the decline of traditional social cleavages and following a path inaugurated by the 'catch-all' party of the post-war era, they are trying to convince parts of the electorate outside their traditional, but eroding, constituencies. As noted by Mair, 'the vote has become more free-floating and available, but so also have become the parties themselves', producing 'socially inclusive appeals in search for support from socially amorphous electorates' and 'chasing more or less the same bodies of voters with more or less the same persuasive campaigning techniques' (2008: 220, 222). As disaffection with parties grows, voting decisions are made later, and electoral campaigns thus gain in importance (Dalton *et al.*, 2002: 48). Campaign management necessitates professionalism and familiarity with the media (see Chapter 2), requiring coordination from the top, while grassroots activism becomes less necessary.

Given that parties have an interest in making elections salient, and are seeking to offer choices between competing governmental teams, party systems tend to become bipolar. Bipolar competition characterized a minority of West European party systems in the 1950s and 1960s, but a majority of nearly two-thirds of them in the 1990s and 2000s (Mair, 2008: 221). 'Through the creation of competing pre-electoral coalitions which tend to divide voters into two contingent political camps' (*ibid.*: 226), bipolarism prevails now even in consensual small countries of the continent. In Austria, for example, it has made the grand coalition between conservatives and social-democrats frequently unmanageable, and in Switzerland, there is a broad ideological gap between two of the major governmental parties, the increasingly popular national-populist SVP and the Social Democratic Party. Paradoxically, however, bipolar does not necessarily mean ideologically polarized: 'The parties might still compete with one another for votes, sometimes even intensively, but they came to find themselves sharing the same broad commitments in government and being bound to the same ever-narrowing parameters of policy-making' (Mair, 2008: 216). The narrowing of policy options – certainly a consequence of globalization and of delegation of sovereignty to the supranational level, but also of the fashionable belief that some areas of policy-making should be depoliticized (Chapter 6) – leads to ideological convergence 'into a mainstream consensus' (Mair, 2008: 212). This, in

turn, shifts the debate to the 'performance' issue of governmental efficiency: which team is more apt to best achieve political goals that –
unlike in 'position' issues – are broadly consensual? Which parties can
convince of 'their capacity as good governors, administrators, and
managers of the polity' (Mair, 2009: 9)?

Party politics nowadays well fits the definition of democracy
provided by the eminent theorist Joseph Schumpeter several decades
ago (1994 1st edition 1942). Schumpeter defined democracy primarily
as a competition among political elites very much centred on the issue
of which team would win the elections. Moreover, as parties find it
hard to credibly distinguish themselves from each other, appealing
leadership becomes an asset for the team. Due to the lack of major
differences between mainstream parties, distinctiveness becomes
closely related to a party leader's charisma, in the same way that oil
companies, selling the same product, try to broaden their appeal
through distinct marketing strategies. We observe, therefore, a *de facto*
(informal) 'presidentialization' of parties and of electoral competition
(Poguntke and Webb, 2005, 2005a; Webb and Poguntke, 2005; Webb
*et al.* 2011). This is yet another form of partisan adjustment to the
changing nature of politics: 'The "presidential" leader may well be able
to bypass the long and painstaking process of building a power-base in
the party by the sheer force of his electoral appeal: the party may cede
powers to such a leader on the basis that it will benefit electorally'
(Poguntke and Webb, 2005a: 8). Interestingly, in that respect, there is a
general democratization of elite recruitment, but this trend affects
above all the less influential partisan circles. While there seems to be a
trend within parties towards a more open selection process of candidates for the legislature, such a movement is slower in regard to the
selection of national party leaders (Kittilson and Scarrow, 2003:
68–73). It may indeed be suspected that the democratization of the
choice of leaders offers no sufficient guarantee of their charismatic
qualities necessary for 'presidentialized' parties.

The appeal of presidentialization is enhanced by the relative
decomposition of traditional social cleavages, which undermines
party loyalties and the structural basis of voting choice. Parties have
less latitude in policy-making as a result of structural constraints such
as globalization, and less interest in formulating clear policy
programmes, as their constituencies are increasingly heterogeneous.
Both established and anti-establishment parties tend then to rely
increasingly on personalization, which seems rewarding in terms of
electoral success and to compensate for weak partisan 'vote-structuring

capacity' based on class, religious or ethnic affiliation (Allern and Pedersen, 2007: 73). 'The presidentialization of party politics is a competitive phenomenon and the success of highly presidentialized parties such as Silvio Berlusconi's Forza Italia puts all major competitors under pressure to adapt' (Poguntke and Webb, 2005a: 17). There is, then, a diffusion phenomenon that can be explained in terms of the 'contagion' of presidentialized parties; if the competitors are very similar and the outcome uncertain, then strongly visible leadership will be considered helpful by all of them. It is indeed the perception of the contribution of leadership that matters: 'Even if leaders actually have a modest direct effect on voting behaviour, the fact that the strategists tend to be convinced of their importance nevertheless results in campaigns which are increasingly centred on party leaders. This, in turn, furnishes leaders with additional legitimacy (and hence power), as they are increasingly able to claim a personalized mandate to lead their party' (Webb and Poguntke, 2005: 346).

With party presidentialization, personalism no longer appears as a characteristic only of pre-modern politics but also of its 'post-modern' – weakly ideological – version. The revival of personalism in the contemporary era presents similarities with the revival of patronage linked to the cartel party, as both are party responses to the decline in citizen–partisan identification. Although the supply of charisma is, of course, contingent on politicians' personalities, the demand for charisma has become a structural phenomenon, driven by the erosion of group identities, by the convergence among parties on policy options and, as suggested in the next chapter, by an increase in the importance of the mass media. The mass party related to strong group loyalties was apparently a historical parenthesis.

Contemporary personalism differs, however, from its traditional version: personalization is no longer related to an individual's capacity to deliver patronage benefits to local constituencies, and – much like contemporary patronage – it manifests itself at the central and highest levels of party organizations. Personalization has a strong 'electoral face': it is driven by strategic calculations and especially by the desire of parties to attract the floating 'swing' voters, those who are decisive for an electoral victory and who, in the context of general ideological decline, are the most volatile and least attached to a particular party ideology.

Those leaders deemed particularly appealing to the electorate outside the party also acquire more internal leeway to formulate the party's policy platform; they gain flexibility and autonomy (Farrell and Webb, 2002: 122). Party organizations serve less as mediating instances, and the link between leaders and voters becomes more direct. This aspect is not entirely new; it was emphasized as early as the 1960s by Otto Kirchheimer, portraying the characteristics of the 'catch-all' party, and by Leon Epstein, with his thesis on 'contagion from the right' – according to which, left-wing parties traditionally structured around mass organizations such as trade unions progressively lost their tight links to them (Scarrow *et al.*, 2002: 129). For example, most parties seem relatively unconcerned about their (usually shrinking) memberships and are more interested in conducting professional campaigning and using sophisticated marketing techniques to reach the wider public. It is even argued that parties have given up their ambition to be mass organizations (Van Biezen *et al.*, 2012: 40–42).

In the post-war period, party leaders had to gain autonomy in order to strategically adjust party messages to the demands of diverse segments of the electorate that shared a lack of strong ideological identities. Parties nowadays are even less closely linked to specific social groups with strong preferences, and mediatization, coupled with the more decisive role of electoral campaigns, requires professionalism that further increases the leadership's internal power. Moreover, parties have become more accountable to voters, while the accountability of party leaderships to less numerous and less indispensable party militants has weakened. In order to re-establish contact with the 'ground', parties increasingly adopt primaries to select party leaders and candidates for office, and this can be seen as recognition by the parties themselves that their memberships are no longer representative (Van Biezen *et al.*, 2012: 39). Clearly, primaries highlight the blurring of the distinction between party members and non-members (Katz and Mair, 2009: 755).

Parties adjust to changes in their environment, but this adjustment then implies a shift in the power balance within them. The distance between leadership and organization becomes considerable, and this is especially likely to happen when parties are in government. Parliaments as institutions and parties as organizations become less effective in holding executives accountable, and their effectiveness is also undermined by factors such as internationalization (see Chapter 3); the partisan mark on representative democracy is less apparent. Not only is domestic governmental accountability weakened with internationalization, but power within governments is concentrated in the hands of the prime minister and the circle of collaborators who give him advice. The traditional monopoly of expertise retained by the civil service is diluted by the admixture of consultants, think tanks or research institutes. In the United Kingdom, for instance, the number of advisers employed at Downing Street rose from 71 in 1970 under Edward Heath, to 107 under John Major and to more than 200 under Tony Blair (Bevir and Rhodes, 2006: 673).

We are here at the confluence of the input and output sides of the political system: the party and the executive face of the phenomenon of presidentialization, respectively. In a recent book on the United Kingdom and Canada, Donald J. Savoie (2008) emphasized the advent of 'court' government. This kind of government is 'dominated by the prime minister with an informal cabal containing her or his favorite political staff and perhaps a few trusted ministers and public servants' (Aucoin, 2012: 185). In the United Kingdom, political scientists and insiders 'argue that Blair has manipulated his personal resources and expanded his institutional power to achieve a degree of predominance unmatched in British history' (Bevir and Rhodes, 2006: 672); for example, informal contacts between the prime minister and ministers of his government have tended to replace cabinet meetings, whose frequency and content are said to have diminished significantly (Bevir and Rhodes, 2006: 674). The idea that this kind of system is a sort of elective dictatorship may now be truer than ever, especially as some members of the court, such as communication specialists or political advisors, are not democratically accountable. It is argued that, in court government, effective power is concentrated in the hands of the prime minister and his court on matters important to them, whereas the decision-making process is more collaborative and inclusive for other matters (see also Chapter 4).

Presidentialization undermines the conditions that lay at the origin of the success of the traditional model of party government. Strengthening the autonomy of political leaders leads to the development of a model of democracy with plebiscitary traits. The latter resembles the model advocated by the famous German sociologist – and at times political activist – Max Weber, who pleaded at the beginning of the Weimar Republic for a plebiscitary leadership democracy (see Weber, 1994: 220ff.). In fact, controversies on leadership autonomy within parties are not new: as early as 1911, Roberto Michels had formulated his 'iron law of oligarchy', according to which even allegedly democratic mass parties fighting for democracy – Michels narrated his own experience from socialist parties – were inevitably subject to rule by elites. We also know now that, in the 1960s, leadership autonomy vis-à-vis party members appeared to be a correlate of the catch-all party (Kirchheimer, 1966). Such parties needed to be ideologically flexible to adjust to the changing moods of volatile electorates; hence, party leadership required more ample room for manoeuvre. In addition, leadership professionalism was a defining feature of the 'electoral-professional party', as described by Panebianco over twenty years ago (1988). It seems, however, that leadership autonomy has increased in recent decades: 'There appears to have been a fairly uniform trend towards the strengthening of the powers and resources of the centre over the last two decades or so' (Goetz, 2003: 83). Apart from the United Kingdom and Italy, countries as diverse as Spain, Germany and Hungary are cited as cases in point, and 'even in multiparty systems where coalitional and consensus models of politics are the norm, it is fascinating to observe that premiers have apparently often become more "presidential"' (Webb and Poguntke, 2005: 341). Unlike the situation in traditional party government, in presidentialized government political leaders do not govern through, but past, their party (Poguntke and Webb, 2005: 9).

## The uncoupling between politics and policy-making: spiral effects and paradoxes

I have argued in this chapter that, as a result of a process of adjustment to changing and challenging social environments, the major parties are now closer to state than to society and present themselves above all as potential governmental teams under the aegis of a 'presidentialisable' or 'prime-ministerisable' leader. Figure 1.1 presents a stylized image of the cartelization and presidentialization processes in party politics described in this chapter.

However, it should be asked how effective is the governing capacity of such governmental teams? Different political systems face similar limits to governing, such as those arising from globalization or from the depoliticization of policy-making, as we shall see below (Chapters 3 and 6). In addition, since most party systems are multiparty, once they are in power, parties must negotiate with their partners and are forced to water down their electoral pledges.

There appears to be a structural problem: on the one hand, the very nature of electoral competition favours 'over-promising' by leaders who target their messages to an increasingly remote electorate and base their credibility on their alleged efficiency as problem-solvers. On

Figure 1.1.   *The cartelization and presidentialization processes in party politics*

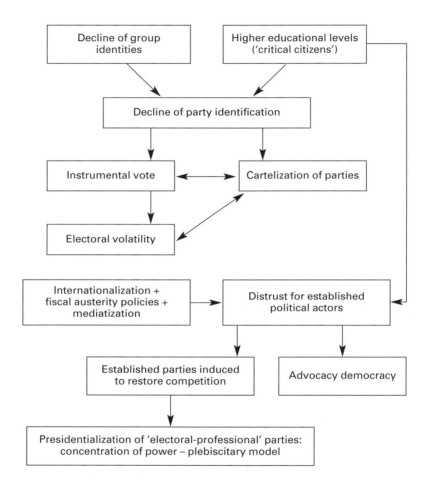

the other hand, the nature of the exercise of power often calls for compromise between institutions, between collective organizations, or even within amorphous networks of actors of different nature (see Chapter 4). While politics is increasingly dominated by a competitive logic, policy-making becomes technocratic or cooperative. Reflection takes place to work out policies that are adequate for problem-solving, and bargaining is done to work out broadly accepted solutions. It is no accident that, in this respect, a shift from top-down governmental steering to cooperative forms of governance was first posited by researchers such as Rhodes (1997) who studied the UK prototype of Westminster-style democracy in which, as mentioned, power is considered concentrated in the hands of the prime minister and a narrow circle of people around him.

Bipolarism prevails, then, in the sphere of politics, whereas in the policy-making sphere the incentives for depoliticization and negotiation are strong; this is a major disjunction to which I referred in the introduction. As a result, there is a risk that voters will be unhappy with the fact that their electoral preferences cannot really be translated into a governmental programme, because the conditions for partisan control over public policies – what has been portrayed as party government – are missing. According to Mair (2005a), this disjunction reinforces the trend towards a decline in election turnout, and, more generally, is likely to widen the gap between rulers and ordinary citizens. The uncoupling of the sphere of politics from the sphere of policy-making can lead to dissatisfaction with policy performance and to a demand for new charismatic alternatives (Grande, 2000), especially under the influence of the mass media, which seeks to dramatize and personalize politics for its own commercial reasons. But more disappointment may arise if those initially charismatic leaders cannot fulfil their unrealistic promises, thus leading to a vicious circle of political distrust, to which the media also contributes.

In the next chapter, the impact of the rise in the influence of mass media on politics will be scrutinized in more detail, and in Chapter 3 we shall see that internationalization – as also noticed by the advocates of the presidentialization thesis – contributes to power concentration. In Chapters 3 and 4 we suggest, however, that internationalization and other developments may lead to less visible forms of policy-making through networks that, to a large extent, escape media scrutiny, and whose cooperative logic strongly deviates from the increasingly bipolar logic of party competition. For instance, studying British politics under Tony Blair, Bevir and Rhodes (2006: 671) refer to a 'paradox between presidential claims and the governance narrative', with the latter emphasizing fragmentation and multipolarity. They suggest that 'personalization is a prominent feature of media management and electioneering', while 'the prime minister's influence is most constrained in the policy implementation' (Bevir and Rhodes, 2006: 681–2). For example, politicians probably become less dependent on the bureaucracy but, at the same time, they lose control over concrete policy formulation and implementation because networks steered by bureaucrats acquire considerable latitude, and perhaps not only on issues that do not matter to elected officials. There may well be a paradoxical evolution: as a result of several other trends described later in this book, power is more concentrated with presidentialization, but also more diffused.

## Chapter 2

# Mediatization and Audience Democracy

This chapter addresses the consequences of another change that strongly impacts politics: the growing role of the media. Mediatization of politics – a manifestation of the more general trend towards a 'media society' in which the media penetrates most social spheres – means that the media becomes a political actor in its own right and that it has become the predominant player that informs the public about politics. The media is increasingly necessary for political communication at a time when communicating is of paramount importance for political actors. Consequently, politicians try to make their behaviour compatible with media requirements, so that the media logic – the rules and norms under which the media operates – penetrates the political system (Esser and Pfetsch, 2004: 387; Schulz, 2004: 89). A trade-off occurs: to gain media influence, political actors accept that they will lose their autonomy and that their behaviour to a significant extent will be dictated by the rules of the game that the media sets. Not only are parties now more heavily dependent on the media than in the past, but the media is also more independent from them.

The dependence of parties on the media is enhanced by the political changes discussed in the previous chapter: links between parties and homogeneous sociocultural segments are weaker, fewer people are 'loyal' to parties, and, more generally, the influence of group identities on individuals is declining. Convergences are taking place in policy programmes, and this is likely to reduce public interest in politics, while attention to political events is, in any case, selective. All this introduces uncertainty about the part of the electorate on which political parties can count and makes highly mediatized electoral campaigns more decisive in a party's election victory. Moreover, as elections become more competitive, parties are obliged to attend to their media profile continuously. Hence, competition for media attention between parties is fierce. Mediatization changes partisan campaign strategies and forces parties to become permanent campaigning machines, as

47

suggested by the concept of the 'campaign party' (Beus, 2006: 14). In his book *Principles of Representative Government*, Bernard Manin (1997) described this trend as a shift from 'party democracy' to 'audience democracy'.

At stake are the parties' and politicians' reputations, which are key resources in politics. Since reputation is now largely supplied by the media (Street, 2001: 7), the need for it creates dependence on it. For example, editorialists become influential opinion-makers, and politicians are in need of positive judgments from them. Not only does media logic colonize politics (Meyer, 2002), but the media system is also, for its part, highly differentiated from politics. The media has changed, and its commercial side has become more prominent. The media's logic is primarily guided by newsworthiness, and, as such, it is different to the logic of political actors, or even inimical to it. Parties have to adapt to this logic by changing their self-presentation, and they are obliged to devote significant resources to that purpose. The necessity for this kind of investment may even sometimes induce corrupt behaviour, rendering established parties vulnerable to the attacks of populist challengers (see Chapter 1) or ... attacks by the media itself!

This chapter identifies other effects of mediatization. The media's actions affect the power balance within parties. The influence of communication professionals increases, at the expense of militants. The media also favours personalization, reinforcing the trend towards presidentialization. Since the media is in search of news value, it selects only what counts as 'events'; therefore, descriptions of complex policy-making activities may only be shortcuts. Plebiscitary and personalized politics is to a large extent uncoupled from decision-making activities, and this is reflected in the nature of media coverage. The mediatization of front-stage – mostly partisan – politics contrasts with the fact that a significant part of policy-making takes place back-stage, is less subject to media scrutiny, and may involve non-elected actors. This uncoupling should also be considered in assessing the impact of new media on politics and governance. The rise of internet-based comment and news is asserted to alleviate the negative effects of the penetration of politics by increasingly commercialized media. However, even if information technologies help challengers of the established political order to go public, there is no guarantee that the challengers will become influential in policy-making circuits.

Figure 2.1 summarizes the description of the mediatization process (and of its limits) that is provided in this chapter.

Figure 2.1.  *The mediatization of politics and its limits*

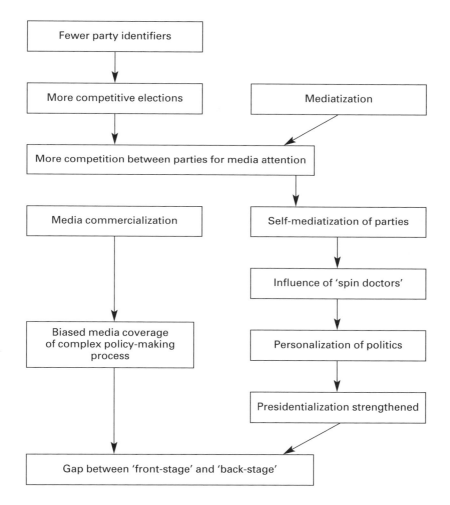

## The impact of media commercialization on politics: complex and multifaceted

In an influential article, Blumler and Kavanagh (1999) classified changes in the relationship between political and media actors into three distinct periods. They described the first two decades after World War II as the 'golden age of parties', because parties had the upper-hand over political communication. That golden age was characterized by a still-vivid party press, by a dense network of party satellite organizations, and by the fact that a large part of the citizenry still had sufficiently close ties to parties to be strongly influenced by their messages. By the 1960s, when partisan loyalties began to erode, nationwide television became the main medium for mass communication. This centralization of the provision of political information is characteristic of the second age, in which parties started losing their privileged position in political communication. This induced a change in their strategies:

> It is very plausible that the unprecedented reach of electronic media, and their ability to carry messages to the entire population simultaneously, across social and political divisions, changed political communication in important ways, encouraging political parties and other organizations to abandon earlier forms of communication in favor of centralized use of mass media as well as to target audiences outside their original social bases. (Hallin and Mancini, 2004: 33)

In several, although not all, democracies, public service organizations escaped governmental or partisan control and remained committed to respecting the public interest and to norms of fairness and impartiality. To this day, the BBC is often cited as a case in point, and the mission of press or audio-visual councils is to ensure that media organizations actually subscribe to such an ethos. Gradually, television reached new and more volatile segments of the electorate who remained immune to party messages, and the latter competed with those of the new medium. Partisan identification through long-term processes of socialization – in the family, for example – started being challenged by more contingent factors amplified by television news, such as governments' immediate performance, or criticism by opposition parties (Blumler and Kavanagh, 1999: 212). With the prevalence of television in the second age of political communication, campaigning started becoming permanent and professionalized.

The third age of communication is marked by an explosion in the number of television channels and, more generally, by media abundance, ubiquity, and fragmentation, although, unlike the first age, fragmentation is no longer mainly along party lines. It now has to do with the fact that, increasingly, commercial media must mirror the complexity of society: customization often requires specialization, the targeting of media content to specific audiences. Thus, commercialization necessitates the development of 'niche' products: it does not necessarily bring about homogenization, although that is a common assertion. In a nutshell, in the so-called first age of communication, differentiation between the political and the media system was low, with the former strongly controlling the latter; differentiation increased in the second age; in the third age, the logic of the media system has tended to infiltrate the political system.

The media system operates in what is described as a 'self-referential' manner, with its own aims and rules (Mazzoleni and Schulz, 1999: 249). However, the aims and rules are now, to a large extent, the expression of the dominance of a commercial logic. This is most notably evidenced in the concentration of ownership and in dependence on advertisers. These are features of which the audience is seldom aware, and lack of awareness of such connections precludes a critical reading of media messages. In the first and the second ages, the rules of the media game were – although in different ways – largely set by political elites; this no longer holds true in the third age, in which the rules are much more dependent on the economic imperative of profit. Today, political and media systems are differentiated spheres with distinct rationales. Yet, success in politics depends more strongly than in the past on media goodwill.

Although the mediatization of politics is a long-term process that started in the early days of radio propaganda, and although traditional routines of partisan communication were already being challenged in the second age of communication, the rate of change has significantly accelerated in the third age. In the current age, the professionalization of political communication has reached a peak, and political advertising has made a breakthrough as well. Parties are subject to new challenges through 'the relentless scrutiny and "unmasking" of the manipulative strategies and devices of politicians and their advisers by sceptical journalists' (Blumler and Kavanagh, 1999: 217), and their messages have to compete with dissonant messages from many other sources. It is in this age that political parties' dependence on the media has become more pronounced, not only because commercialized media logic is more alien to them than in the past, but also because the decline of party identification makes support for parties more contingent on their ability to convey credible messages through the media.

This is not to say that political actors are mere victims of media logic: they adopt it because doing so benefits them, and it penetrates the political game because it is critical to achieving political goals. In a sense, mediatization is also 'self-mediatization' by political actors (Meyer, 2002). In fact, there is an interdependent relationship between media and politics: 'There is the power *over* the media – what gets shown or reported – and there is power *of* the media – what gets changed by the media' (Street, 2001: 4, emphasis in the original). Nevertheless, parties are under pressure to deliver ready-made information ('event-marketing') to the media, so as to limit their dependence on them. Meyer suggests that 'you can only control the media by submitting to them' and that 'those who think they can escape the iron-clad rules of preliminary stage-management affecting the media are either ignored by it, or – in the best case – used as unformed raw material for the media's own productions' (Meyer, 2002: 52–53). Mediatization forces political actors to select and emphasize those issues most likely to find media resonance and to frame them in ways that the media will find attractive, particularly because there is much competition for space in media coverage between politics, on the one hand, and sports and lifestyle coverage, on the other. Interestingly, the symbiotic relationship between politics and media persists even though politicians are cynical about journalists and journalists are equally cynical about politicians (Brants *et al.*, 2010).

As for the commercialization of the media system, it does not fall from heaven: media developments are not unrelated to general socioeconomic trends. It may happen that commercial imperatives conflict with the political preferences of media ownership or management and do not necessarily eclipse them. However, the force of media commercialization is related to the fact that it is an aspect of the more general trend of the marketization of social relationships. As Hallin and Mancini (2004a: 302) suggest:

> The process of commercialization, though it may accelerate the differentiation of the media from political institutions, tends to subordinate them to the logic of the market and of the corporate struggle for market share, often diminishing the autonomy of journalists and other communication professionals. In this sense the media become less differentiated from economic institutions as they become more differentiated from political institutions.

Media differentiation from the political sphere occurs, then, in parallel with a lack of media differentiation from the economic sphere, visible in the crucial influence of market actors on media management and policy and in the prevalence of profit-linked considerations– mainly through advertising – in media activity. Therefore, in several countries, the media itself has changed. Now it is largely autonomous from political parties, while, at the same time, its commercial side has become more prominent: just like any other industry, the media sells commodities. And, like politicians, the media must function in a highly competitive market in which the potential receivers of a message can easily be distracted by another message from a competing source. There is much 'competition for readers and viewers with an ever-expanding range of media sources to choose from' (Street, 2001: 44).

Mediatization expresses itself primarily (but not only) in the role of television in politics, and the expansion of privately owned television channels leads to the diffusion of their own rules into the public broadcasting sector. The whole television landscape tends to become commercialized, with parties no longer having at their disposal many valuable alternative communication channels that are not impregnated by a commercial logic. Commercialization has also been referred to as 'Americanization'. This is not to say that other countries deliberately mimic the highly commercialized media system that prevails in the United States, but rather that various factors – such as the dynamics of economic and technological globalization – favour the replication of North American practices. The 'commercial deluge' embodied in the growth of multinational multimedia conglomerates such as Rupert Murdoch's no doubt leads to an 'international media culture' (Hallin and Mancini, 2004a: 251 and 274) and to the greater – although not complete – homogeneity of media products across nations.

It should not be forgotten, however, that the trend towards media commercialization is also a consequence of political decisions that led to the opening up of national media markets, deregulation, and privatization. Media regimes emanate from choices made by public authorities. This is true both for policy regarding press concentration and for policy regarding the regulation of private access to broadcasting. Although the dependency of politicians on the media has increased, the media as a set of commercial organizations also needs politicians who are in power. Referring to Rupert Murdoch, Street (2001: 172) writes that 'commercial success is not just a product of commercial resources; it depends on constant negotiations with governments who both need his corporations and have the capacity to set the terms under which they operate'. This is yet another consequence of the interdependence of media and politics, and, also, of both with the economy, because, although some conglomerates are active only in the media field, others embrace a broader range of activities and thus have a complex web of economic interests to defend, for which they require support from influential public officials.

The mediatization of politics is a complex process indeed. Many cross-national differences persist, including the architecture and practices of media systems, the organization of parties, the style of political campaigns, and the political communication culture of both politicians and journalists. Rather than homogenization, it may be more appropriate to speak of hybridization, a combination of features influenced by the American model but with country-specific traditions (Esser and Pfetsch, 2004: 406). In Europe – and especially in Scandinavian countries – media regimes are more favourable to a public service model that privileges hard news over commercialization and infotainment, and media regimes do matter for the political consequences of mediatization: 'The quality of national news media may have a big impact on how well informed citizens are about politics' (Newton, 1999: 581). Thus, the commercialization of the media system is not inescapable; rather, it seems to be contingent on path dependent mechanisms, that is, on long-term national traditions and trajectories that may limit convergence towards Americanized media practices. Blumler and Kavanagh (1999: 219) have suggested, for instance, that 'the impact of multichannel competition in a fully privately owned and commercially run media system may differ from its impact in media systems shaped at an early stage by the establishment of large public service organizations'.

Therefore, the convergence on an Americanized model of 'media-oriented political communication culture' (Pfetsch, 2004) is partial and does not affect equally all mature democracies. This has been observed in other fields as well: the 'varieties of capitalism' literature (Hall and Soskice, 2001) suggests that, notwithstanding pressure from economic globalization, regional models of capitalism only partially converge on the liberal Anglo-American model: they retain some of their major specificities, such as concerted action between business and trade unions, the political regulation of economic competition, or interfirm cooperation in vocational training. Hallin and Mancini (2004) distinguish between three types of media systems: the liberal model, which prevails in Britain, Ireland, and North America; the democratic corporatist model, which prevails across northern continental Europe; and the polarized pluralist model, which prevails in southern Europe. Briefly stated:

> the Liberal Model is characterized by a relative dominance of market mechanisms and of commercial media; the Democratic

Corporatist Model by a historical coexistence of commercial media and media tied to organized social and political groups, and by a relatively active but legally limited role of the state; and the Polarized Pluralist Model by integration of the media into party politics, weaker historical development of commercial media, and a strong role of the state. (Hallin and Mancini, 2004: 11)

In addition, Hallin and Mancini point out that references to models overstate the homogeneity of national situations, to say nothing about the obfuscation of cross-country differences (2004: 12). An obvious example is the unequal market share of 'yellow' or 'boulevard' press across countries. Even across countries considered to belong to the same liberal model, convergence is partial precisely because of path dependency. Comparing, for instance, national electoral campaigns in the United Kingdom and the United States in 1980 and again in the second part of the 1990s, Blumler and Gurevitch (2001) not only reveal that campaigns in the UK remained somewhat sheltered from commercialization and infotainment tendencies, but also that the USA moved further in this direction, thus broadening the initial gap.

Hallin and Mancini also acknowledged, however, that there are strong forces of convergence towards the liberal model: in the third age of communication, the prevailing media model comes closer to the original American one, with commercialization as a core component. For instance, in the previous communication ages, 'a strong emphasis on public affairs content was clearly one of the distinctive characteristics of European public service broadcasting. Its most important manifestation was the placement of substantial news broadcasts in the heart of prime time, often simultaneously on all available channels' (Hallin and Mancini, 2004: 34). Today, news departments are under pressure to adjust their routines to a more commercial imperative. In an infotainment regime, news value is diluted, and the proportion of 'soft' news, dealing with celebrities, entertainment, and sport increases at the expense of 'hard' news. As Blumler and Kavanagh (1999: 225) put it:

> key boundaries that previously shaped the political communication field seem to be dissolving – for example, between 'political' and 'nonpolitical' genres, between matters of 'public' and 'private' concern, between 'quality' and 'tabloid' approaches to politics, between journalists serving audiences as 'informers' and as 'entertainers', and between 'mass' and 'specialist', 'general' and 'attentive' audiences.

This changes the social functions of journalism, 'as the journalist's main objective is no longer to disseminate ideas and create social consensus around them, but to produce entertainment and information that can be sold to individual consumers' (Hallin and Mancini, 2004a: 278). Politicians, for their part, must do their best to be portrayed as 'people' or 'media stars'. They must show that they possess extraordinary attributes and, at the same time, that they are human beings like others: they draw then 'upon the language, icons and expertise of popular culture' (Street, 2001: 61). Even in countries like France, where the distinction between public and private life of politicians used to be a core value, we note a narrowing of the divide (Blumler and Gurevitch, 2001: 392).

Considering these trends, it may be argued that the supply of information has considerably increased with the deregulation of public television systems, but this information is now more superficial as deregulation has led to commercialization. Despite resistance mainly (but not only) from public television, linked to the fact that the presence of serious news coverage legitimizes all – including commercial – television channels (Brants, 1998: 321), the supply of politically relevant information suffers from the commercialization of the media landscape. Ordinary voters are usually not sufficiently motivated to search the media for political information. Much of their exposure to political news occurs precisely by accident, from inadvertent encounters while they are waiting for a sitcom to start, or driving their cars. People 'fall into' rather than 'jump into' political news (Newton, 1999: 596), and infotainment reduces the probability of such fortuitous encounters with politically relevant information. The available comparative data shows, for example, that the public is better politically informed in countries where the media regime is less marketized (Newton, 1999: 598). In addition, marketization of the media is suspected of generating simplified images and narratives – sound bites – that reflect less and less the complexity of contemporary policy-making.

Nevertheless, research on opinion formation has not proved systematically that the media have direct effects on mass values and attitudes. The weakness or strength of media effects on opinion formation depends on a number of circumstances, and there is no simple path for determining media influence. For example, those who do not know much about a political issue are more receptive to media messages, and the same applies to the part of the population whose ideological predispositions are congruent with the orientation of media messages. Nevertheless, according to the cognitive mobilization thesis (see

Chapter 1), voters are now better educated and have a greater interest in politics, which may predispose them not to be 'media victims'. Furthermore, for the media to be believed, it has to be trusted: but it appears that the level of trust the media enjoys is low (Newton, 2006: 216–17), although usually a little higher than trust in political parties. In the United Kingdom, where tabloids dominate the market, the proportion of those tending not to trust the press reaches 79 per cent (*Eurobarometer* 11/2010). However, it is also plausible that, because contemporary problems are often complex, and because more citizens lack party identification and thus ideological cues, the propensity to have public opinion shaped by media messages is higher.

The important point is that politicians do not feel compelled to pay attention to the media because the latter is powerful in and of itself. The power of the media is largely based on its reputation, that is, the media is powerful because participants in the political process ascribe a powerful role to it. It suffices that politicians believe the media affects public opinion, namely through its influence on opinion leaders who subsequently convey further the media message to the less attentive segments of the public (Dalton, 2004: 73). And even if politicians doubt media power, it might be risky for them to ignore it. Therefore, even if the media may not have a strong direct or independent effect on political demand (that is, on the values and preferences of the mass public), there can be no doubt that it affects political supply (party strategies). Since prominent editorialists are supposed to be influential opinion-makers, for instance, politicians strive to win a positive endorsement from them. The media is now widely considered able to manufacture public opinion by setting the agenda and framing the issues in their own way. 'Mediality' – the *sui generis* reality manufactured by the media – becomes the only reality most people recognize (Mazzoleni and Schulz, 1999: 250); therefore, it may be argued that, in quite a number of cases 'those who control the image control the reality' (Street, 2001: 5). The following constitutes an example of such mediality: because violent crime attracts viewers, television in the United States concentrates on it, despite the fact that the level of such crime has been significantly reduced. Young offenders in particular are newsworthy (Gilliam and Iyengar, 2007).

In a world in which the attention paid to political events is scant and selective, and in which fewer people are loyal to parties, competition for media access (which is selective) is stronger. Furthermore, politicians' responsiveness to voters' preferences is very much mediated by their responsiveness to media claims. Parties find it difficult to identify the preferences of a citizenry that is increasingly opaque to them, in spite of the development of sophisticated polling techniques. Not only has society become more fragmented and public opinion more volatile, but the fact that parties' links to society have become more tenuous also makes it harder for them to identify social preferences (Mair, 2009: 13). Therefore, politicians not only try to use the media to manufacture public opinion: because they believe that the media mirrors public opinion, they also rely on it to inform them about public opinion. Politicians are also dependent on the media because their deeds and misdeeds are now subject to increased media scrutiny. Of course, one might praise the contribution to public accountability of media control over what politicians do, but the possible distortions generated by the media's framing of politics should not be discounted. Interestingly, media scrutiny is held to be necessary for the accountability of officials, but the operation of private media, at least, escapes political accountability in capitalist-democratic polities. This does not necessarily mean that the media is not animated by any concerns of responsibility, but rather that the only sanctions it risks are through the market or through legal action. Although many often lament that this contributes to a democratic malaise, an oversimplified, 'apocalyptic' (Mazzoleni and Schulz, 1999: 248) view should not be adopted: the media is not omnipotent; as a result, the rise of scandal politics, for instance, only becomes possible because courts also increasingly intervene in political life (see Chapter 6).

Yet, it remains rational for commercialized media to search for news value and therefore to sensationalize political events and trivialize politics by treating political competition and debates as 'titanic struggles' similar to 'sporting encounters' (Street, 2001: 47). As a result of media commercialization, journalists are under increased pressure to adapt their discourse to what media ownership or management believes readers expect. Several media organizations tend, therefore, to employ simple arguments, to replace reporting on substantial debates with 'horserace' narratives, to overvalue the point of view of the 'ordinary citizen' (Hallin and Mancini, 2004a: 278), which is usually presented as common sense to which readers should identify, and to induce – or at least not to counteract – the cynicism or distrust of politicians (Stoker, 2006: 127–31). Longitudinal studies suggest that, in many countries, the content of news about the political process has become more negative and more critical of politicians (Dalton, 2004: 71). The shift from a deferential to a more irreverent treatment has been depicted as 'attack' or 'accusatory' journalism: some media organizations can become aggressive and search for scapegoats, privilege scandal, or dramatize conflict. Moreover, commercial media is more attracted by gossip, the unusual, and policy failure than by routine performance or success ('negativism').

Journalists acquire a new ethos wherein they consider themselves self-proclaimed representatives of public opinion, enjoying authority thanks to their professional credentials. This new ethos is backed by higher educational levels – like citizens in general, well-educated journalists are more critical and more independent of political parties – and by increased specialization within large media organizations, through which journalists gain expertise (Hallin and Mancini, 2004: 37–8). Parties and politicians deploy considerable efforts to manage the media, but the more journalists feel under pressure, the more they are tempted to offer products on the news market that cannot be suspected to be influenced by partisan strategies: 'What politicians have to say is subordinated to the stories that journalists decide to tell' (Coleman and Blumler, 2009: 52). Like most professionals, journalists value their distinctiveness, and a reputation for autonomy and critical thinking can be rewarding in terms of a journalist's career.

The journalistic ethos may often serve commercial imperatives, but it does not always do so. The disclosure of political scandals, for instance, is jointly nurtured by commercial imperatives and by the desire of journalists to build professional prestige based on their investigative capacity (Hallin and Mancini, 2004a: 279). In this case, commercialization and professionalization deploy converging effects by putting politicians under pressure. It may well be, however, that they enter into conflict, as in cases in which journalists wish to 'assert the integrity of journalistic criteria *against* purely commercial ones, and their own autonomy against the intervention of owners, marketers, and advertizing sales staff' (Hallin and Mancini, 2004a: 289, emphasis in the original). Investigative journalism may indeed collide with the interest of the media organization for which journalists work, and this may result in the restriction of resources devoted to it. Investigative journalism may uncover corruption, but the economic and political interests of media ownership may inhibit this kind of journalism, or investigative journalism may be considered to be less attractive for readers or advertisers than superficial infotainment. In that sense, the professionalization of journalists that marked the increasing emancipation of the media from partisan control may well have been followed more recently by a reverse movement of deprofessionalization: media organizations working under commercial imperatives need less experienced journalists and can increasingly rely on a low-skilled and cheap labour force composed of trainees, students, and the like.

Be that as it may, both the 'noble' investigative journalism uncovering scandals and 'trivial sensationalism' (Street, 2001: 150) in which the watchdog role of journalists is denatured by commercial imperatives – focusing, for example, on private lives – can destroy politicians' image. Politicians are thus under increased pressure to adapt their conduct to what they consider to be media expectations or style. Thinking about such expectations or style is often influenced by the content and form of tabloid newspapers – a sort of catch-all press (Hallin and Mancini, 2004: 38). Of course, it can be believed that 'quality' newspapers escape the trend towards sensationalism and negativism, perhaps only because both journalists and readers of the elite press tend to identify with the establishment. Owing to sheer competitive pressure, however, this media segment may not be insensitive to stories manufactured by tabloids, often based on the 'If it bleeds, it leads' belief. A media analysis based on a corpus of top-quality newspapers in the United States, the United Kingdom, and Switzerland concludes, for instance, that 63 per cent of newspaper statements question or deny the legitimacy of their political objects, and only 37 per cent evaluate them positively (Hurrelmann *et al.*, 2005: 125). Furthermore, the tabloid press has the broadest readership, and its readers are most likely to rely heavily on the commercial televised media. This does not ease the life of established political actors: a study of eight nations (Dalton, 2004: 73) suggests that high levels of television viewing appear related to less incumbent support, lower support for democratic values, and a higher support for the national community, all of which are typical features of the anti-establishment nationalist–populist voter.

Is it then an exaggeration to suggest that protest parties benefit from mainstream media's framing of issues (such as crime and security, or immigration), which are susceptible to sensationalism? There does, indeed, appear to be a convergence between issues 'primed' by the media and issues that are part of protest parties' 'ownership'. Since anti-establishment parties receive public support because they capture issues that are high on the media agenda, it can be argued, in a sense, that the media may not hesitate to offer for their own reasons cheap publicity to critical claims couched in attractive, simplistic language. And when the media challenge the collusive 'cartel' of established parties, they inevitably provide some sort of legitimization to anti-elitist protest. As suggested by Coleman and Blumler (2009: 60):

The present system disseminates an oversupply of oxygen for cynicism through the visibility of manipulative publicity efforts and the increased flow of negative messages. A related product is a highly pejorative, oversimplified and, in many cases, probably unfair stereotype of the standard politician as someone who cares only for power and personal advancement, is not bothered about problems that matter to ordinary people and is constitutionally incapable of talking straight. Audience disillusionment with political leaders and their utterances is a natural outcome of such a bombardment. Credit is not given to government even when it deserves it.

Yet, there is a 'chicken-and-egg' problem (Newton, 1999: 583): for example, high levels of television viewing are usually negatively correlated with the viewer's level of education, and the latter is also a strong determinant of the protest vote. Or, to take another problematic correlation, 'attack journalism' may undermine trust in politicians, but, again, those who read this kind of press or watch this kind of television show are the least educated – they lack trust in politics to begin with, and there is not necessarily a 'spiral of cynicism'. For example, a recently published study of the American presidential election of 2000 shows that those with low levels of political trust did not become more or less trusting following news exposure, regardless of the news source (Avery, 2009). The robustness of the empirical evidence in support of the 'video-malaise' thesis has thus been questioned. An alternative 'virtuous circle' thesis has even been formulated: although exposure to political news is a function of prior political knowledge, when it happens it increases knowledge of, trust in, and favourable predispositions towards civic activity (Norris, 2011: 172). In any case, straightforward media effects should not be overestimated, and the media impact follows complex causal paths.

Consider, for instance, the famous Monica Lewinsky case at the end of the 1990s, a sexual affair between Bill Clinton and an intern at the White House, in which it appeared that the then president lied about his conduct, which led to his being impeached. The Monica Lewinsky scandal was the object of unprecedented and enduring mediatization. The pessimistic conclusion is that 'national politics had been reduced to a sometimes amusing, sometimes melodramatic, but seldom relevant spectator sport' (Delli Carpini and Williams, 2001: 178). The 'outing' of the sex scandal did not affect public support for the US president, however, because support was already polarized along partisan lines, and Bill Clinton was regarded as having successfully achieved both peace and prosperity, as well as broadly accepted policies (Zaller, 2001). According to Delli Carpini and Williams, the public created their own narrative of the issue, which was not consonant with media framing nor with the framing of the president's supporters and critics. People believed that the president had an affair and lied about it, and this indeed damaged Clinton's reputation. But, at the same time, the public considered the affair a private matter and separated it from the question of whether Clinton was able to govern efficiently. Interestingly, the MoveOn website launched a petition that advocated 'moving on' to more serious issues than the Lewinsky affair. By the end of 1998, 450,000 people had signed the petition (Chadwick, 2006: 122).

This suggests that 'media events may play a greater role in setting the public agenda than in framing it' (Delli Carpini and Williams, 2001: 178). The media would be more successful in deciding which issues to put to public debate than in deciding the lines along which this debate is conducted. This would be another limitation of direct media power on media consumers, although politicians are probably not aware of such subtle nuances. They most likely overestimate media influence, and hence, due to this (mis)perception, the public, and increasingly the private, conduct of politicians is largely dictated by dependence on media approval. The impact of mediatization on party politics is multifaceted, even though it has not been possible to prove that media effects on individuals are stronger than in the past, or that they are ubiquitous across national democratic systems (Newton, 2006).

For instance, the fact that the place occupied by the media as the target of party strategies can affect the power balance within parties should not be overlooked: it may be argued that mediatization contributes to the trend towards party presidentialization. Comparative media content analysis posits that the media now refers more often to leaders than to parties (Dalton *et al.*, 2002: 51), but also that media coverage is not necessarily candidate-centred (Adam and Maier, 2010; Kriesi, 2012). This kind of evidence is inconclusive, but it suffices for parties to believe that the media are candidate-centred to make them emphasize political leadership. Political leaders thus gain visibility, and, among them, the more charismatic are more likely to move to the forefront. In Italy, Silvio Berlusconi understood how important media control is, but this is by no means the only example of media-driven 'controlled semi-populism' (Hermet, 2007: 178) on behalf of established parties: Tony Blair in the United Kingdom,

Gerhard Schröder in Germany, or, more recently, Nicolas Sarkozy in France are cases in point.

In 'professional-electoral parties' (Panebianco, 1988), the support of experts in media-handling who are able to make use of communication-management tools becomes necessary. Their influence increases at the expense of militants, given that campaigns are less labour-intensive and require sophisticated communication skills. Parties need more public relations and political advocacy professionals such as spin doctors and image-makers who package politics (Mancini, 1999). Depending on the parties, these are either external consultants, or have become part of the party apparatus. A telling example is that of the Strategic Communications Unit created by Tony Blair in 1997 and directed by Alastair Campbell, whose 'job was to monitor the news and provide a rapid response, expounding the government's position and, where necessary, rebutting any criticisms of government policy' (Bevir and Rhodes, 2006: 675). At the same time, parties increasingly rely on opinion polls to measure not only the acceptance of proposed policy measures or the strength of parties in society, but also the popularity of individual leaders. Polling is intimately related to mediatization: true, some polls are used confidentially by the parties, and their results, particularly if they are unfavourable, are not disseminated, but polls are also highly mediatized if they are deemed likely to influence public opinion favourably.

All this shows that parties do not remain passive actors in a context of mediatization; rather, they try to attract maximum media attention and to ensure appropriate media coverage. To achieve this, political actors must play according to media rules; therefore they depend on experts familiar with these rules. With the help of press officers and media advisers carrying out news management, parties and interest groups try to lobby the media and influence the agenda in line with their priorities. They 'work hard to fashion the news in their own interests and to draw attention away from issues that might prove politically embarrassing' (Mulgan, 2003: 73). Mulgan described this as a primarily governmental activity, but, given the importance of having a positive image in the media, it is reasonable to conjecture that many kinds of political actors try to gain some influence over media reporting. Let us conclude this section then with an eloquent summary of the breadth of partisan activities aimed at managing the media (Beus, 2006: 14). Parties:

> manage media by direct contacts with owners, editors and reporters; off-the-record talks; press conferences; embedding (journalists in

airplanes and buses); party events (organized with the sole purpose of media exposure); and selective appearance in different types of media and broadcasting. They manage information by controlled assignment of items and messages to different classes of privileged journalists; framing of issues in terms of party ownership; hiring 'spin doctors'; and bypassing vested networks and dreaded interviewers. They manage image by electoral research, focus groups, media monitoring, media training, Internet sites of prominent politicians (weblogs), advertisements (such as political spots on prime time), appearances in popular yet apolitical (even anti-political) television shows, and human-interest stories (the friendly face or feel good factor of parties and candidates). And they manage internal relations of the party in order to show unity and enthusiasm and to keep political opponents and journalists from exploiting division and pessimism within the party.

## Can the media see behind front-stage?

Professional campaigning and media management eclipse the role of party militants. Moreover, Litton and Maccartaigh (2007: 57) suggest that the influence of spin doctors on governments may even overshadow that of administrators: 'The role media advisors play now indicates that management of appearances has a high priority ... . [Civil servants] find themselves sidelined as ministers turn to media and other advisers for guidance.' And even if this does not happen, civil servants are 'under pressure to engage in media management, including government advertising, in ways that support the government' (Aucoin, 2012: 181).

This erosion of bureaucratic autonomy seems the reverse of the technocratic drift induced by developments such as internationalization (see Chapter 3). Admittedly, it is hard to get the big picture of current shifts; sometimes contradictory trends coexist. For instance, communication specialists may gain power in those policy fields that are under strong media scrutiny, or there may be a tacit division of roles between policy experts influential in decision-making and public relations experts whose task is to justify policy to a broader audience. Furthermore, bureaucratic influence can indeed be weakened by mediatization, but its erosion can be counterbalanced by other changes, such as transformations of policy-making styles in the direction of 'collaborative governance' that confer a leadership role on administrators (see Chapter 4). Hence, mediatization does not entirely permeate the political process.

The media needs to focus on discrete events, to relate them to people, and to tell simplified and dramatized stories. There is not always fertile soil for that, therefore media logic colonizes the part of political activity that is more prone to be mediatized: front-stage politics. This most visible part of politics can more easily become the object of dramaturgy. But this is not all the essence of politics, as numerous careful studies of policy-making have shown. Policy-making usually appears as a complex process entailing negotiation and compromise and the involvement of the bureaucracy, organized interests, and other non-elected actors (see Chapter 4). True, in their decision-making activities, politicians need 'something to show now' (Pollitt and Bouckaert, 2004: 8). They are thus under increased pressure to take into account the short-term media agenda, the timescale of which is much shorter than the traditional electoral agenda. Yet, policy-making also implies long-term considerations because it requires some continuity, and there are influential actors in the bureaucracy for whom media constraints are not the primary concern. Moreover, the degree of complexity of policy-making activities is probably increasing. Hence, the widening gap between mediatized front-stage – mostly partisan – politics and the more complex policy-making activities, a significant part of which mostly takes place back-stage and may involve non-elected actors. This is not to say that there is no media coverage of policy-making activities, and recent research shows that, at least in metropolitan areas, the media recognizes as crucial players in policy-making actors such as public-private bodies or civil society organizations that do not count among the usual suspects (Christmann *et al.*, 2012). Media coverage may even affect policy-making styles by inducing what has been portrayed as symbolic politics: spectacular actions instead of genuine problem solving. However, there is not necessarily significant overlap between the policy agenda and the media agenda.

We know now that, because the media is in search of news value, it selects only what counts for it as 'events'. The consequence of such a filtering process is that 'ideas, programs, intentions, interpretations, expectations, texts, and projects that fail to qualify as events, or that cannot plausibly be honed into or at least linked up with events, have little chance of being considered as the raw materials from which the media might construct their version of reality' (Meyer, 2002: 29). The media needs to provide simple accounts, and this is not compatible with the treatment of policy problems that are often complex and not always salient in the eyes of the public. As a result, 'the media spotlight can never illuminate more than a small slice of the plenitude of policy projects that are being planned or readied for implementation in the political-administrative system at any given time' (Meyer, 2002: 96). Even journalists specializing in investigative activities may focus on, and also applaud or blame, only the visible tip – the most 'theatralized' – of the iceberg (front-stage). As suggested by Hajer (2009: 176–7):

> While media attention gives a boost to the authority of the centre, actual problem-solving requires complex forms of network governance... . Hence, while the autonomous power of the centre to change events diminishes, its press coverage soars.... Network governance features those who know most about the substance, not those who like to be on stage. Should some enlightened spirit try to connect that roundtable to the mediatized politics, all that network governance can offer is a meeting room filled with administrators, some stakeholders, expert reports, and a folder with minutes and draft agreements. This can hardly be made into an interesting story, and is therefore neglected by journalists and remains invisible to the general public.

Significant aspects of policy-making escape media attention because they are not interesting in commercial terms or because journalists lack the background to apprehend them. This is all the more the case if policy issues are deliberately depoliticized, as happens when private bodies are in charge of regulatory tasks (see Chapter 3) or when these tasks are delegated to independent agencies (see Chapter 6). Hence, although 'it sometimes seems that "politics" *is* what appears on TV or in the press' (Street, 2001: 5, emphasis in the original), this is by no means a general rule. There is indeed a contradiction between the logic prevailing in policy-making activities and media logic. A prominent illustration thereof is the fact that negotiation and the search for compromise frequently are necessary ingredients of decision-making, but they cannot take place unless some degree of secrecy is guaranteed. Schrott and Spranger (2007: 6) point out that:

> A decisive prerequisite of successful negotiation is the exclusion of the public from the bargaining process. ... This atmosphere of privacy provides participants with the opportunity to demonstrate willingness to compromise without losing their credibility as loyal representatives of their respective interests. Threats and promises

are more credible in this context, since they can't be relativized in public or be denied when they don't become public in the first place. Positions and arguments can be flexibly deployed and withdrawn when actors don't have to worry about losing face in public. Negotiated agreements require careful re-phrasing once they are made public, with successes characterized as a collective achievement and individual contributions suppressed. Finally, a successful negotiation is only possible when each participant can walk away with something to display to his clientele and to the public at large as evidence that he 'won' the negotiation. Both are only possible when the intimacy of negotiations can be preserved.

Exposure to media scrutiny is likely, for instance, to move the behaviour of bargaining actors towards more radical positions and confrontational strategies in order to satisfy the demands of the rank-and-file, and thus to inhibit the forging of compromises on controversial issues. Of course, participants in negotiation processes are not mere media victims: they are aware of media pressure and do not remain passive in the face of it. Each of them can unilaterally decide to instrumentalize the media for reasons of self-promotion or by organizing leaks that he or she believes to strengthen his or her bargaining position. Negotiating actors can also jointly try to ignore media pressure or to manage media demands through a concerted information policy. But, in any case, if the media displays an interest in policy negotiations, actors have to consider it and reflect on how best to deal with media pressure (Spörer-Wagner and Marcinkowski, 2011).

Given the constraints of problem solving, it is also likely that participants in the policy process opt for 'informalization' strategies and use them as escape routes to avoid media scrutiny and the risk of negative reporting. The more frequently formal negotiations become the object of media curiosity, the more will bargaining actors be induced to negotiate informally. Hence, although it is difficult to object to transparency, it is questionable whether mediatization actually produces the claimed positive effect on public accountability. And policy-makers should not be blamed unilaterally for this, because their fears of distorted media coverage are not always unfounded. However, the problem is that if informalization strategies are disclosed, they will not only be the object of media attacks, but may feed accusations of lack of transparency, an attractive strategic argument for populist challengers, who may then exploit it to generate a new spiral of citizens' distrust of the established actors involved in the policy process. In other words, myopia on behalf of the media results in parts of the political system remaining immune to mediatization, but, if this fact is mediatized, it may generate a self-reinforcing process through which disclosed elite 'subterfuge' further erodes public trust.

## New media: a change of logic?

Mediatization refers to the role of traditional media, with television as a key figure. It is primarily 'televisualization', notwithstanding the fact that the tabloid press follows a similar logic as commercial television, and that the degree of television commercialization varies, depending on media regimes. There is still a strong reliance on television as the major medium through which political discourse is transmitted; it remains the main source of news on politics, despite the growth of digital media. Even in the Internet Age, television remains the trendsetter, and we have not reached yet the stage 'in which the rules of the television age will lose much of their relevance' (Meyer, 2002: 118). To give an example: according to empirical studies, a few years ago television still was more effective than the internet in reaching undecided voters (Klotz, 2004: 64) who, as we know, compose a significant part of the electorate and sometimes even a plurality (see also Chadwick, 2006: 175). Overall, the internet has had only modest success in displacing traditional media sources (Hindman, 2009: 92).

Is there, however, anything substantially new about the impact of the information and communication technology (ICT) and of the new media on democracy? There may indeed be a 'cyber-optimistic' scenario (Schultz, 2004: 94–5) based on arguments, all of which emphasize that the constraints of the television era are removed in an upcoming phase of 'e(lectronic)- or cyberdemocracy' (a buzzword which has even come to include merely technical improvements in terms of 'e-administration', that is, routine communication over the internet between administrations and service users):

- The mass audience of television dissolves into a large number of fragmented virtual communities.
- Information becomes more plethoric and diverse, and each receiver has much more freedom of choice.
- Internet users produce their own messages and communicate interactively (in online forums, chat rooms, and so on), instead of passively consuming television products: 'For the most part, the

information that circulates on the Internet is not produced by journalists and news media' (Mazzoleni and Schulz, 1999: 258). This can be described as a democratic trend that conflicts with the claims of journalists to possess a monopoly of professional expertise on news production (Coleman and Blumler, 2009: 67).

• Political actors can also use their own direct channels of information and bypass the media.

According to this scenario, the internet will reduce the dependency on mass media that is characteristic of the third age of communication. Meyer (2002: 118) observes that cyber-optimists:

> expect a great deal of the Internet, even that its technical potential might be engaged to revive a version of direct democracy characteristic of the ancient Athenian *polis*, except now on a virtual plane. Its technical infrastructure and the software required to use it seem capable of converting the old, hierarchical, one-to-many structure of communication into a new, many-to-many pattern. If so, it could usher in a non-hierarchical, essentially symmetrical form of communication accessible to everyone, which could move the public sphere closer to the discursive ideal of an assembly democracy open to all citizens.

In such an optimistic scenario, not only would the gate-keeping function of traditional media be bypassed, but parties and representative institutions would also lose their weight as filters. Moreover, within parties themselves, the internet can reinforce grassroots autonomy and control over leaderships (Chadwick, 2006: 148), reversing the trend towards leadership power that results from catch-all, cartel, and presidentialized politics (see Chapter 1) and from traditional forms of mediatization.

So far, however, the informational revolution has not led to a revolution in politics. Innovations and advantages do not equally benefit everyone. This is the notorious 'digital divide' between internet users and 'offliners', between info-rich and info-poor. It has two components: first, the availability of infrastructure, in which there is a huge gap between the developed world and developing countries; and second, basic skills and electronic literacy, which are unequally distributed among the population mainly according to age, income, and level of education. Optimists argue that the digital divide will become ever less acute. At the global level, the disappearance of the digital divide is far too optimistic a prediction, because the growth rates of internet penetration have stalled in the least-developed and the developing countries. In countries such as Bangladesh or Ethiopia, the proportion of frequent or occasional internet users does not exceed 1 per cent. The global digital divide is here to stay, and it might even become wider (Chadwick, 2006: 53–63). It is, of course, possible to say that time will tell what will happen, but this book is about the current state of things in democracies, not about the future. And recent empirical evidence – for example a survey of Americans in 2008 – has concluded that the internet did not significantly contribute to a decrease in participatory inequality in politics (Schlozman *et al.*, 2010).

Of course, we all know that the internet presently contributes to the mobilization and campaigns of fringe parties and other political groups, just as cell phone technology does (Bale, 2005: 178). It also accelerates the formation of cross-border activist protest as a reaction to economic globalization, against military action, or on environmental issues. Thanks to the internet, not only is the geographical dispersion of diffuse interests no longer an obstacle to (virtual) community-building, but inequalities in financial resources matter less: 'Having a big bank account may mean less if the Internet creates inexpensive channels of communication' (Rethemeyer, 2007: 202). Furthermore, some participatory experiments such as those described in Chapter 5 require ICT for their deliberations (see Smith, 2009: 144–7, for example, on '21st Century Town Meetings' organized by *America Speaks*). The internet also generates more horizontal forms of communication within organizations that escape control by leaderships. It enhances the transparency of established institutions and is a major challenge to dictatorships, which can no longer rely only on controlling traditional media to block the circulation of information. Recently, social networks on the internet contributed to mobilizations in favour of democratization in the Arab world.

The internet also allows for a more efficient scrutiny of politicians' and parties' records in office, increasing their accountability, at least among the most motivated citizens who are willing to support the costs of information-seeking. Further, the internet erodes the agenda-setting function of the traditional media, obliging it increasingly to take up issues first raised online by other sources. Overall, the internet is a vector of pluralism: 'One can see an expansion in terms of available communicative spaces for politics, as well as ideological breadth, compared to the mass media. Structurally, this pluralization not only extends but also disperses the relatively clustered public sphere of the mass media', writes Dahlgren (2007: 152). In a similar vein, Chadwick (2006: 23) notes: 'The power of large media organizations and political communication professionals to shape public opinion will be steadily diluted as self-publishing by a multitude of groups or individuals becomes the norm.' It is hardly questionable, then, that the development of the internet increases the variety of information available and facilitates interactive deliberation. For example, according to a survey carried out during the campaign for the American midterm elections of 2006, 31 per cent of American adults or 46 per cent of internet users reported that they went online during the campaign to exchange views or at least to gather information: these figures represent more than 60 million people. In the fall of 2006, the top ten advocacy groups on Facebook counted almost half a million members (Dalton, 2008: 53). A survey conducted in 2007 among citizens of the 27 EU member-states revealed that one in four young citizens has posted political comments on an online forum in the last year (Kies, 2010: 68–71).

These developments are not necessarily synonymous, however, with the better quality of political communication. Does the internet contribute to extend participation? It appears, for instance, that those who visit campaign websites are mostly partisans or, more generally, the usual suspects. For example, during the French presidential campaign of 2007, the users of the parties' websites were predominantly heavy users of the internet, and strongly interested in the campaign (Kies, 2010: 87). This fact has been acknowledged by the most successful sites, which solicit activists and donations and do not aim to reach undecided voters. Experiments have shown that asking internet users to find a political candidate's website is a difficult challenge, which is clearly a sign of deficient electronic literacy with respect to political matters (Hindman, 2009: 16 and 69).

True, in Putnam's (2000) terms, web communities may produce 'bridging' social capital, which may help transcend boundaries between groups. Interestingly, a study of online debates by Kies (2010: 164–6) shows that 'the forums that are perceived as having a strong political impact are more likely to be characterized by respectful and reciprocal exchanges and to encourage active and passive users to revise critically their own positions and beliefs'. However, web communities also produce 'bonding' capital. The latter 'develops within relatively closed groups and rests on trust and repeated interaction. … Once established, the links reinforce the preexisting affinity' (Rethemeyer, 2007: 208). Hence, a corollary of the pluralization of content brought about by the internet seems to be 'balkanization'– that is, fragmentation of the public sphere into 'cyber ghettos' (Dahlgren, 2007: 152). Sunstein (2001) nicely described this phenomenon in his book *Republic.com*. He spoke about 'enclave deliberation', which is limited to like-minded people employing arguments that all develop in the same direction and that are not exposed to alternative views. Such a situation is well illustrated by the logic of hyperlinks available on webpages, which can be considered as signs of the existence of virtual communities. According to a recent study in the United States, only 2.6 per cent of the traffic from one of the 50 most visited political websites to another crosses ideological lines. Conversely, roughly two-fifths of the queries were directed at specific political sites and organizations, and such searches are not likely to lead internet users to divergent political perspectives (Hindman, 2009: 66 and 77). A process that Sunstein called the 'law of group polarization' reinforces common beliefs rather than calling them into question. In other words, deliberation on the internet tends to generate islands of group-think and segmentation in partial communities. The consequences can be very negative: thanks to the lack of the disciplining effect of face-to-face interaction, and the lack of regulation, we find on the internet much intolerant, uncivil discourse, and all sorts of information with frankly racist content. The internet intensifies 'attack' styles of political communication that appear to be a corollary of mediatization (Chadwick, 2006: 174).

Perhaps more importantly, the assertion that the internet redresses imbalances of power is disputable, because mainstream actors use it, too. It is no surprise that a study conducted in 2003 among 163 parties in Europe revealed that almost half of them hosted an online forum for debates (Kies, 2010: 87–8). 'Blogging', for instance, has enormously stimulated do-it-yourself and often critical news production, but it has also stimulated the trend towards the personalization of electoral campaigns. Millions of people maintain a blog, but, in the United States, 'only a few dozen political bloggers get as many readers as a typical college newspaper' (Hindman, 2009: 103). The most popular blogs in the 'blogosphere' continue to be written by political insiders or journalists (Chadwick, 2006: 174 and 304–5). Reading blogs requires a certain level of skills and motivation, but the skills required to offer content that will be widely read are much less common: free time and professionalism are necessary to maintain a blog.

A good example of such professionalism is provided by Barack Obama's campaign for the US presidential election of 2008. Obama's management succeeded to orchestrate a campaign that strongly relied on the internet. For example, Obama published hundreds of 'tweets' – short messages on Twitter – over a long period, starting much earlier than his competitors. This, however, required considerable financial investment and significant fundraising activity. The ruthless conclusion of a recent empirical survey (Hindman, 2009: 123) is that:

> Almost all the bloggers in the sample are elites of one sort or another. More than two-thirds were educational elites, holding either an advanced degree or having attended one of the nation's most prestigious schools. A hugely disproportionate number of bloggers are lawyers or professors. Many are members of the elite media that the blogosphere so often criticizes. An even larger fraction are business elites, those who are either business owners or corporate decision makers. Also hugely overrepresented in the blogosphere are technical elites, those who are paid to work with technology.

Even if the plethora of information on the internet is pluralistic, demand does not necessarily present the same characteristics: online audience concentration on a small number of very successful sites equals or even surpasses that observed in the traditional media (Hindman, 2009: 17 and 51). Rethemeyer (2007: 201, emphasis in the original) asserts that 'The Internet *does* make mobilization cheaper, easier, and faster.' Yet, he considers this development 'a "shock" to all organizations that have an interest in an area of policy'. They will all seek to adjust to this new state of things, and, therefore, the structure of communication will not be profoundly altered. 'Politics as usual moves online' is the major tenet of the so-called 'normalization' thesis. As a matter of fact, 'by the early 2000s, most if not all major interest groups in the United States had established online presences and were using email, websites, bulletin boards and instant messaging to organize existing supporters, fund-raise, and reach out to old and new constituencies of support' (Chadwick, 2006: 118, see also 149). It may be suspected that wealthier organizations will also be able to invest more resources in a more professional fashion in websites, communication on the internet, and so on. For example, more and more professionals work as consultants for internet campaigns. Furthermore, although information available on the internet may reduce the gap between leaders and the grassroots members of organizations, conversely, the more associations and movements have a 'virtual' component – that is, a gathering of people who never meet each other – the less will these people be able to know what professional staff or leaders are undertaking in their name (Schmitter and Trechsel, 2004: 59). This gap can reinforce disenchantment, and the same applies if people realize that even if recent technological developments facilitate interactive dialogue, this does not necessarily mean that elite communication becomes less top-down and more responsive (Coleman and Blumler, 2009: 86).

In addition, because the internet undermines the gate-keeping role of traditional media (Chadwick, 2006: 148), powerful media react by investing in the web too, and commercial interests colonize it. As Meyer (2002: 121) suggests, 'we can observe a widespread tendency for the older media to colonize the new ones. The editors of newspapers and radio stations have successfully invested major resources to place their products on the internet, where they are used in more or less the same way as in the classic mass media.' Not only does entertainment continue to dominate the media environment, but its supply on the internet has expanded much more than the supply of information (Schulz, 2004: 97), in a totally uncontrolled manner. Politics is completely overshadowed on the internet by other aspects of life, such as sex. Only a tiny proportion of websites deal with political issues: 0.12 per cent according to a US study (Hindman, 2009: 61), a much lower share than in the print or television media. Under such conditions of supply, there is no reason to think that those who prefer infotainment to politically relevant information will behave differently on the internet. Even if more politically relevant information or data is available, the problem remains on the demand side: frequently, the good that is most scarce is not information, but attention. There is an overload of information on the internet, a great deal of attention is required to sort it out, and few people are able or willing to make that effort. This is not favourable to the development of mass audiences for political websites: not one political site is included in the list of the 500 most visited sites in the United States: news and media sites receive 30 times more visits than political sites do, and politically related queries are only a small portion of the searches sent to news sites by internet users (Hindman, 2009: 63–6, 74).

But perhaps the most important reason why we should not have too-high expectations of the positive impact of the internet on democracy is that although the internet may indeed change the style of political communication as well as pressure strategies to influence office-holders, most developments on the internet have no formal connection to political decision-making. The internet may affect how we discuss politics and how we try to have an impact on decisions that affect us, and it will also increasingly influence how organizations or individuals are consulted, but it does not fundamentally alter the structures of policy-making. We should not forget that 'there can be all kinds of political communication and debate in circulation, but there must be structural connections – formalized institutional procedures – between these communicative spaces and the processes of decisions-making' (Dahlgren, 2007: 152).

Today, the internet is increasingly used by public authorities as a tool for the online consultation of citizens and organizations, including outside the circle of the 'usual suspects'. Democracy, however, is not defined only by one's capacity to express one's preferences, but primarily by an equal capacity to participate in converting social inputs into political outputs and thus to contribute to decision-making. Online and more general public consultations are valued by citizens, but the question remains whether there is actually 'anybody listening' (Coleman and Blumler, 2009: 189). If consultations are viewed as essentially public relations exercises, they are likely to generate 'consultation fatigue'. And, if they are seen as futile, this may increase, rather than reduce, public distrust of politics. To prevent this, it would be advisable to follow guidelines such as those of the Australian government's Information Management Office e-consultation code, according to which 'agencies need to inform participants at the outset about how their input will be received and used in policy-making. Once a decision has been taken, agencies should indicate how citizen input through online engagement has been used' (cited in Coleman and Blumler, 2009: 192). Although public authorities can try to manipulate this kind of information, they cannot easily succeed because their behaviour is often closely monitored by stakeholder groups.

As we shall see in much more detail in the next two chapters, the conversion process from inputs to outputs often takes place in so-called policy networks. The decisive issue, then, is whether the internet affects power relationships within these networks. There is no systematic research on that question, but anecdotal evidence provided by Rethemeyer (2007) and based on two case studies in adult education and mental health policy in an anonymous state in the USA does not encourage optimism.

Rethemeyer (2007: 201) defines policy networks as:

> sets of public agencies, legislative offices, and private sector organizations (including interest groups, corporations, and non-profits)

that have an interest in public policy within a particular domain (e.g. health, education) because (1) public decisions affect the ability of members to continue their operations and meet the goals of internal and external stakeholders and (2) members are interdependent. Such organizations constitute a network because they communicate frequently about issues they care about and must exchange resources (e.g. money, support) in order to survive. Decisions are made collectively through consultation and based, in part, on swapping resources, favors, and support across multiple decisions (i.e., 'logrolling').

Rethemeyer's concern is whether the internet helps network insiders or outsiders – in other words, to which among three possible outcomes it leads: democratization, stalemate, or intensified corporatization. He writes that 'with virtually no exceptions, the organizations reported that their Internet communication partners were drawn strictly from the same circle of interlocutors that existed before they began using the Internet.' (Rethemeyer, 2007: 204). Based on his findings, he suggests that 'the Internet may be better suited to furthering organized and organizational interests rather than the citizens in unorganized or informal sectors that many Internet optimists wish to empower. ... The Internet appears to foster and intensify closed, corporatized policy networks' (199). He continues: 'The Internet, it seems, is being used primarily by those who are highly influential, highly endowed with resources, and well positioned as brokers or public authorities to enrich their communications with one another.... . These findings again support the intensified corporatization hypothesis' (205). Given that 'there is much evidence that the Internet is increasingly a tool of the powerful, entrenched, and organized rather than the unorganized or reform minded' (212), he concludes that 'the dark side of this reality is that the Internet may be exacerbating the inherent status quo bias of policy networks' (209).

Of course, this is not the definitive answer to the question. Fieldwork on these cases was conducted in 1998 and 2001, and things may change rapidly, although Rethemeyer checked to see if a possible narrowing of the 'digital divide' influenced his findings. Although generalization is hardly possible from isolated case studies, in the light of this study's conclusions it requires indeed a good dose of optimism to anticipate the democratization effects of the internet on policy networks. Ultimately, although Rethemeyer's work should be seen as a pilot study, a word of caution on prediction is necessary: the internet sphere is subject to contradictory trends and to rapid change, so that any 'snapshot' is likely to lose its accuracy quickly.

## The limits of audience democracy

The rise of the new media was expected to alleviate the negative effects of the colonization of politics by increasingly commercialized media. This cyber-optimistic scenario must be qualified, and, for a book on transformations of governance, what matters above all is the connection of the opinion-making process, which may indeed be influenced by electronic media, to the decision-making process. Now, even if new information technologies are an important tool for political communication and mobilization and wired activism is helpful to challengers of the established political order in their role of opinion-makers, there is no guarantee that these challengers will become influential in their policy-making role. This is a facet of a more general problem.

As a matter of fact, although mediatization seems pervasive in audience democracy and has led to major adjustments in the strategies of all sorts of political actors, its effect is only partial. There is often a gap between mediatized front-stage politics and policy-making, a significant part of which takes place back-stage. Some communications scientists and policy analysts are aware of such a gap.

In his book on the colonization of politics by the media, Meyer (2002: 54) refers to a 'dualism of politics' and to the fact that 'because of the colonization of politics by the media system, the most decisive aspects of the politics, those that directly affect the public, are moving behind the drawn shades of the media-dominated public sphere'. He asserts that 'instrumental political action (the "production" side of politics) at the level of programs and substantive policy-making is, under prevailing conditions, largely disconnected from the ways politics presents itself in public' (Meyer, 2002: 63). Meyer is right in his diagnosis, although the fact that decisive aspects of political decision-making are not subjected to media scrutiny is not just a reaction to the colonization of politics by the media but is also a consequence of media lack of attention. Klijn (2008: 24), a specialist of policy-making at local level, points out that:

> a strange split occurs, in which a significant part of empirical decision-making takes place within complex processes in which involved interests, including involved groups of citizens, attempt to

intervene themselves, or at least to become involved. This is where politics is conducted intensively, but not always recognizably, and where processes require long-term dedication and a lot of network management in order to bring them to a favourable conclusion. On the other hand, the politics visible to the media and the citizen takes place more and more in an almost surrealistic media landscape, which requires powerful imagery, quick decision-making and clear steering. ... The rules of the drama-democracy, the stress on theatre, quick communication and individuals, seem to clash hard with those of complex decision-making processes in governance networks.

If Klijn's diagnosis is correct for the local level, the split he refers to is more accentuated when one moves up to the national and transnational level of political activities (see Chapter 3). This split weakens the impact both of traditional and new media on governance practices and signals limits to the pervasiveness of mediatization.

# Chapter 3

# Internationalization, Europeanization, and Multilevel Governance

The previous chapters dealt with important changes that affect a large number of established democracies. Changes such as the transformations of parties or the impact of media on politics manifest themselves at the domestic level; however, one must consider additional changes – those that develop beyond the nation-state, but affect the domestic political arena.

Economic globalization is thought to restrict the sovereignty of national governments; for example, it enhances the bargaining and blackmailing power of transnational firms, and, more generally, of mobile capital. Cultural homogenization – also referred to as 'Americanization' (see Chapter 2) – is thought to generate identity reactions and lead to a 'clash of civilizations'; this perverse dialectic has been portrayed – perhaps caricatured – by Benjamin Barber (1996) as a fight between 'McWorld' and 'Jihad'. Since the impacts of economic or cultural globalization are the subjects of a vast body of work, this chapter focuses rather on the political dimension of internationalization, as defined by Hurrell and Menon (2003: 401):

> According to this view, a vast array of rules, laws, and norms that are promulgated internationally affect almost every aspect of how states organize their societies domestically.... Proponents of this view.... highlight the tremendous growth in the number of international organizations; they point to the vast increase in both the number of international treaties, and agreements and the scope and intrusiveness of such agreements; and they suggest that important changes are occurring in the character of the international legal system, such as the appearance of 'islands of supranational governance'...; the blurring of municipal, international, and transnational law; and the increased importance of informal, yet norm-based, governance mechanisms, which are often built around complex transnational and transgovernmental networks.

Regulation at the international level appears to be a functional imperative because more and more issues, including migration, global trade, and the environment, are extraterritorial, in the sense that 'they are not contained by any existing territorial polity' (Urbinati and Warren, 2008: 390). As a response to that development, one can consider the increasing number of intergovernmental organizations (Barnett and Finnemore, 2004: 1). But one should add to this the progress of supranational integration in Europe, or the explosion of transnational regulation (Djelic and Quack, 2003). Zürn and Leibfried (2005: 21) provide some eloquent examples of this trend, which takes a multitude of forms:

> The international merchant law (*lex mercatoria*), but also the *ICANN* – the private Californian organization with authority over the world wide web (*lex informatica*) – and the large international sport federations (*lex sportiva*) have also, partly with the support of state courts, developed transnational legal forms that function outside the realm of the nation-state, as the handling of doping in national and international sports events makes apparent.

Not only are national competences delegated beyond the nation-state, but also a significant part of national legislation – though varying across policy fields – follows some form of external input or is constrained by external regulations. Alec Stone Sweet (2004: 122) suggests that, 'As the world has shrunk – that is, as physical space imposes fewer constraints on trade, travel, and other forms of global communication – the classic techniques of rationalized state rule (public, authoritative, territorially based regulation of social exchange) have been undermined'. It can be argued that state action made internationalization possible, with nation-states autonomously agreeing to tie their own hands. The extent to which national states have been pushed into denationalized policy-making, or have jumped into it, remains a controversial matter. But this does not change the fact that some policy options become more difficult at the national level due to internationalization, be it voluntary or forced.

Today, mobile economic actors are more able to impose fiscally conservative policies and greater openness to foreign trade and investment, and to preclude generous social policies (Sassen, 2006: 224). In Eurozone states, monetary policy lies with the independent European Central Bank based in Frankfurt outwith national political control, even though central banks prioritize low inflation over the struggle against unemployment – a political view indeed. This does not mean that convergence towards more liberal policies is not restricted by previous national paths regarding both the reorganization of national economies (Hall and Soskice, 2001) and the retrenchment of welfare systems (Pierson, 1994), where significant cross-national variation persists.

Less attention has been paid to the possible effects of internationalization on the domestic decision-making processes of our democracies. The major claim in that respect is that internationalization increases relative governmental influence in decision-making (Moravcsik, 1994). Executive dominance occurs at the expense of legislatures, which we know suffer also because of other changes such as the 'presidentialization' of parties. With internationalization, governments benefit from the 'two-level game' (Putnam, 1988) across the domestic and international scene, as they are the only domestic actors able to play such a game. Governments perform a gatekeeper function between the national and international scenes. They can reinforce their bargaining position in international negotiations by threatening that the parliament in their country will veto a compromise too remote from national preferences. They can avoid being treated like 'bad guys' by their partners if they convince them that they can reasonably make no further compromises because of domestic pressures. At the domestic level, governments can persuade their audiences – usually poorly informed about intergovernmental negotiations conducted behind closed doors – that they had no other choice but to accept unpopular measures, shifting blame to unaccountable spheres beyond the national level. Therefore, being present at both levels simultaneously generates informational asymmetry, and as a result confers the advantage of blame-shift strategies.

The 'executive bias' is not the only bias. This chapter first deals with the multiple forms of internationalization in rule-making and their repercussions on democratic control. International regulatory bodies are often characterized by a lack of balanced representation and deficient accountability, which is aggravated by the existence of many less formal regulatory agents at transnational level. Many consider the increasing number of NGOs to be a countervailing power; however, there are obvious limits to influence of NGOs and the accountability processes they can trigger and, what is more, NGOs are not immune to representation and accountability deficits. Important trends towards the privatization of regulation are also detected, which further amplifies the problem of deficient democratic input in rule-making, and the problem of deficient accountability of rule-makers for the outputs that they produce. Interestingly, such deficits do not seem to be the outcome of conscious design. Rather, they seem to result from the primacy, both among designers of and participants in regulatory bodies, of concerns about effectiveness and efficiency, with a lack of awareness of issues of democratic control as a correlate.

Thereafter, the chapter focuses on the particular case of supranational integration in the European Union, and discusses the often-criticized 'democratic deficit' of European institutions. On the one hand, the executive bias of European integration strengthens domestic trends towards power concentration, such as 'presidentialization' or 'court' government (see Chapter 1). On the other hand, parliaments are becoming increasingly aware of their marginalization, so that a process of 'reparliamentarization' is occurring in a number of countries. This, however, generates its own accountability problems, because parliamentary influence is primarily exercised informally. Executive bias has been relativized by studies of European integration that emphasize its 'multilevel' aspect, and rehabilitate the role not only of subnational public actors, but of non-public actors as well. However, representation and accountability problems are not solved: multilevel governance structures are often characterized by limited pluralism, weak codification, and deficient transparency.

## Internationalization of governance: limits to inclusiveness and accountability

The conventional 'realist' reading of international relations is characterized by states competing with each other for power under conditions of interstate anarchy: no rules matter, only states' interests and the power balance among them. In reality, however, there is a long-term trend towards the 'legalization' of international relations (Goldstein *et al.*, 2001). International relations are increasingly institutionalized and codified in international 'regimes', which can be defined as 'social institutions consisting of agreed-upon and publicly announced principles, norms, rules, procedures, and programs that govern the interactions of actors in specific issue areas' (Zürn, 2010: 80). International organizations serve as the material infrastructure of sector-specific regulatory regimes: the WTO, for instance, is the entity serving as the material infrastructure for the international trade regime. The reason such forms of international cooperation have emerged is simple: 'Without reciprocal cooperation, governments cannot reach domestic goals such as slowing global warming, liberalizing the international economy, integrating communication systems, combating terrorism, and regulating multinational corporations" (Keohane *et al.*, 2009: 4). Such functional regimes can even restrict the decisional autonomy of a supranational system like the European Union, as the WTO does in the field of trade policy. It follows that EU member states are not only constrained by EU regulation, but also by WTO law derived from accords in the World Trade Organization. Therefore 'Europeanization' ought to be viewed as part of the broader process of internationalization of politics (and also of economies and culture).

Quantitatively, more institutions beyond nation-states influence people's lives now than in the past; and, qualitatively, regulations issued beyond the national level have deeper consequences on social life (Grande and Pauly, 2005: 286). Governments are represented in boards and decisional forums of international institutions, but in many of them a small group of powerful states has the upper hand in the formulation of internationally agreed rules through a combination of formal and informal influence (Woods, 2007: 27). Considering only formal influence in the World Bank, for instance, the United States is able to veto an expanding number of decisions requiring a supermajority (Woods, 2006: 27; Zweifel, 2006: 91, 105–6). The vast majority of developing countries, in contrast, command only a small proportion of voting rights, even though these are the countries primarily affected by WB policy. Africa is a continent strongly affected by the policies of the International Monetary Fund, but as of July 2008, 44 African states controlled no more than 4.4 per cent of the votes in this institution of global governance (Sperling, 2009: 40). As a possible remedy to representation deficits, Ramachandran *et al.* (2009) propose that states accounting for at least 2 per cent of the world's GDP, or comprising 2 per cent of the world's population, currently 16 states, form the core of global governance systems, while states that meet neither of these standards – which currently comprise about one-third of the world's population – should be represented indirectly by delegates from the region they belong to, so that minority rights remain protected. However, even if a weak country has a voice in decision-making, it will not necessarily be heard in international forums (Slaughter, 2004: 229). Not only are more than the three-quarters of the member states of the IMF and the WB not represented on the board of executive directors of each institution, they are also absent from senior management, and many have virtually no nationals working on the staff (Woods, 2006: 190). It is often argued that international institutions are legitimate if those who finance their policies, not those who are subject to them, control them, but Woods (2006: 199) found that the burden of costs is now increasingly borne by borrowing countries. The 'congruence' principle is overtly violated: the most affected are the least represented.

An additional problem is that the accountability of officials participating in international regimes is, to a large extent, fictitious, because those who have the power to hold them accountable seldom possess the necessary information to do so. International rules are prepared by top-rank administrators and officially negotiated by members of the executive board, with government officials forming transnational government networks, for example in trade policy (in the WTO) or in financial policy (in the IMF). These networks are sectoral, and their members are engaged in cooperative relations (Slaughter, 2004). Thus networks imply a view of international relations that is both more complex and disaggregated, and less adversarial than the 'realist' view of unitary states in competition for power in the international arena. However, the interplay between network members of this global elite and the public at large is weak, so that control of networks by affected groups becomes illusory.

Accountability problems are accentuated by the fact that most international organizations are hybrids, incorporating a global body acting autonomously and a negotiation system comprising representatives from national governments (Mayntz, 2008: 52). Even though he observes significant variation between global governance organizations (GGOs), Koppell (2010: 112–13) asserts that, depending on sector specificity and technicality of tasks, 'The permanent staff of the GGOs does seem, in many cases, to possess the true ability to "make things happen" and understand "how things work" in a way that the "legislators" do not.' Traditionally, international organizations were not considered actors in their own right, but only as arenas where mostly states acted. 'What these organizations did after creation, and whether their behavior conformed to what states wanted, provoked very little curiosity', note Barnett and Finnemore (2004: viii), who treat them as bureaucracies with significant leeway for autonomous action. For example, the accountability chain in the IMF is 'tortuous' (Sperling, 2009: 42): from administrative staff, to the executive board, to the board of governors, to the government of member states represented by a governor, and finally to national voters. In addition, members of the IMF executive are not bound to follow the instructions of their state of origin, they cannot be removed before their term has expired, they are not subject to formal reviews or evaluation, and their actions are not made public (Woods, 2006: 192). Further, hybrid organizational character is even more pronounced in the case of specialized bodies jointly created by several international organizations instead of an intergovernmental treaty-building process, such as the Joint United Nations Programme on HIV/AIDS (UNAIDS) established by several agencies of the United Nations system including UNHCR, UNICEF, UNDP, UNESCO, WHO, and the ILO. In these cases the link with national governments is very weak, because the new organization has multiple 'masters', and decisional autonomy is greater for both the 'mother' international organization and the secretariat of the newly created body (Wessel, 2007: 4).

The existence of international regimes shows that the international arena is the realm of cooperative *governance among governments*, in spite of the absence of a global government able to issue collectively binding decisions. Cooperative governance at the international level takes place not only in international organizations and functional regimes such as the UN and the WTO, but also, notably, in the field of regulation, in less formalized, specialized instances such as the Basel Committee on Banking Supervision (BCBS), the International Organization of Securities Commissions (IOSCO), the International Association of Insurance Supervisors (IAIS), and the International Competition Network (ICN). These organizations 'tend to operate with a minimum of physical and legal infrastructure; most lack a foundational treaty, and operate only along a few agreed upon objectives or bylaws' (Slaughter, 2004: 48), so that the concept of 'club-type rulemaking' (Koppell, 2010:. 172) seems to adequately describe their *modus operandi*. They do not have the capacity to issue binding decisions, but it is hardly questionable that their national members – who do have the capacity – are strongly influenced by their debates and resulting exchanges of information. Such transnational networks of experts produce norms of 'best practice', and thus act as sites of socialization for their national members (Eberlein and Grande, 2005). The latter tend to follow these soft norms of conduct because they become convinced of their relevance, or perhaps because they fear a loss of reputation by their peers.

Reference has been made, for example, to a global 'mercatocracy' (Cutler, 2003) engaged in unifying, harmonizing, and globalizing private international trade law, and comprising a mix of private and public actors including transnational merchants, international law firms and their associations, government officials, and international organizations. Considering their influence in cross-national policy coordination and convergence, the fact that such networks are composed of transnational elites raises accountability questions similar to those raised about formal international regimes. But the fact that informal networks operate in a sort of 'grey zone' and are not necessarily composed of formally authorized representatives is a supplementary source of concern.

The fact that transnational elites stand remote from the public at large does not mean that the members of this elite always display strong cohesion, or that they collude with one another. Members of policy networks can be connected by strong or weak ties, and share the same interests or values to varying degrees. For example, environmental policies can be very controversial, and the insurance industry has occasionally even allied with environmentalists out of fear that huge ecological disasters would do enormous damage to its reputation (Halliday and Osinsky, 2006: 461). Yet the fact remains that the institutionalization of rules governing the right to participate in networks is insufficient: no institutional framework guides decisions on inclusion or exclusion of territorial communities or functional interests in a satisfying way, and there is no institutionalized political competition that would ensure a pluralist representation of interests and values. For example, not all nations have an equal probability of being represented in circles of influential transnational elites. Most nations become rule-takers rather than rule-makers (Braithwaite and Drahos, 2000: 3), whereas in national polities there is in principle territorial congruence between elected decision-makers and their constituencies. Therefore a 'disjunction' (Held, 1996) occurs, perceptible not only in organizations with weighted voting, but also in knowledge inequalities across nations. Shifting power to technocrats, as is often the case in transnational governance, 'means privileging the views of those nations that *have* technocrats – notably the most developed nations', writes Slaughter (2004: 221; emphasis in the original). In technocratic policy-making, expertise is a key resource of legitimacy, but a resource which is very unevenly distributed.

## Global civil society: the solution?

'Governance' contrasted with 'government' also means the increasing importance of international NGOs and advocacy networks as a countervailing power to weakly accountable transnational bodies

(Keck and Sikkink, 1998; Khagram *et al.*, 2002; Della Porta and Tarrow, 2004; Tarrow, 2005; Della Porta *et al.*, 2006; Smith, 2008). There were 985 international NGOs in 1956, about 14,000 in 1985, and 21,000 in 2003 (Reimann, 2006: 45). Today more than 30,000 operate internationally, but only about 1,000 have members from three or more countries (Vogel, 2008: 266). NGOs 'bemoan global sins, and certify competence and righteousness' (Boli, 2006: 113); they base their legitimacy on generalized trust and on the public resonance of their claims. Some, such as Amnesty International, Transparency International, and the World Wildlife Fund, have an undisputed 'principle-based' (Avant *et al.*, 2010: 13) authority for very diverse populations. NGOs benefit nowadays from stronger financial and organizational support by international organizations – which may, however, generate dependencies – and from better access to them (Reimann, 2006). Not only do NGOs 'serve important epistemic and legitimation functions' (Hall and Biersteker, 2002: 13), but they may also have the capacity to set the problems that preoccupy them on the political agenda. At the same time, control by NGOs tends to be considered the functional equivalent of the disciplining power of elections upon decision-makers at a national level. NGOs thus induce the establishment of a transnational public sphere where public policy-makers, as well as global private firms, face justificatory burdens. Both are pressed by NGOs to engage in issues that they would otherwise ignore, and to give reasons for their choices. NGOs are often the only actors obliging transnational policy-makers to provide justifications for their activities (Dryzek, 2010: 192–3). Critical scrutiny of the justifications advanced and a deliberative exchange can then take place (Nanz, 2006: 80–81). As described by Steffek (2008: 2):

> Organized civil society is instrumental in exposing current governance to wider public scrutiny and in detecting and denouncing pathologies of governance that some of the actors involved would prefer to silence; in translating the highly technical and specialized discourses of regulatory policies into a language accessible to lay people; in flagging new issues and formulating alternatives to the choices made by policy-makers.

In the case of the European Union, for example, Kohler-Koch (2008: 5) points out that NGOs have been successful in establishing an 'accountability regime', whereby accountable behaviour is defined as virtuous and desirable, and power holders are pressured to conform to it. In a nutshell, NGOs are proactive agenda-setters as well as reactive watch-dogs, and their claims force the international system to become more self-reflective. The increasing participation of NGOs and transnational activist movements has indeed changed the debate, not only on substantive decisions – by favouring the inclusion of minority exper-tise, or of stakeholders' concerns – but also on the policy process (Zürn, 2003: 248–52). International regimes and organizations are opening up to groups concerned with peace, the environment, human rights, consumer interests, feminist issues, and the like (Jönsson and Tallberg, 2010). For example, the World Bank has established a formal NGO–World Bank committee, and in fiscal year 2003, 72 per cent of all projects funded by the WB involved NGOs (Steffek and Nanz, 2008: 19). NGO pressure in the 1990s forced the IMF and the WB to revise their debt strategy and move towards more transparent practices (Woods, 2007: 36). There are, however, important limits to the impact of NGOs, be it in regards to their policy influence through 'input' formulation, or their role in evaluating critically policy 'outputs' at transnational level.

As regards NGO influence on 'input' formulation, it is true, for instance, that under NGO pressure international organizations now pursue more open information policies, but dissemination of more information does not mean that such institutions are more transparent in their internal deliberations (Barnett and Finnemore, 2004: 170). It also appears that, even when an institution like the WB makes some effort under external pressure to be more accountable to the people it affects – such as in setting up an inspection panel, a sort of internal court of appeal – the people affected are usually not aware of the possi-bility of holding the WB accountable (Zweifel, 2006: 92–3). Moreover, this panel can issue only non-binding recommendations for bank policy improvements; there are no sanctions if the WB does not comply with them, and the WB has not substantially altered its policies on the basis of feedback from the panel (Dijkstra, 2007: 284).

In addition, the participation of NGOs representing civil society in instances of global policy-making remains weakly codified, so the selection of participants matters. In that respect, international organi-zations remain the gatekeepers, and to a large extent the shapers, of what is officially labelled as the 'global civil society' (Woods, 2007: 38). Although a structured intermediate system now exists at the EU level composed of party federations and European lobbies, nothing similar has emerged so far at the international level. For example, one does not encounter the kind of sectoral monopoly of representation enjoyed by some associations at the national level, which makes them negotiation partners that cannot be ignored by public authorities (Mayntz, 2008: 50). An exception is the International Labour Organization (ILO), to which business and labour interests have traditionally enjoyed privileged access through 'tripartism', but in which they use this privileged position to oppose the integration of other civil society organizations (Thomann, 2008). Overall, one should not idealize the global civil society, or paint it as an idyllic world in which competition is absent.

Furthermore, due to the lack of robust sanctioning of decision-makers at the transnational level through an electoral mechanism, public surveillance by NGOs appears to be a necessary-but-insufficient condition for effective accountability. As Steffek (2008: 15) puts it:

> In the international setting there is no mechanism of electoral accountability in the background by which the public could force unresponsive power holders out of office. The synergies between public and electoral accountability.... are significantly weakened. Therefore, transnational public accountability remains a rather soft mechanism of holding international network governance to account.

In some situations, the public sphere operates as an accountability 'forum' (Bovens, 2007) that critically evaluates the performance of international bodies. But such a forum lacks the formal capacity to sanction decision-makers if they prove to be unresponsive. In sum, the interests of many policy-takers are still not duly considered, despite the NGO 'boom'. As a result, the outcomes of decisions by international bodies are often viewed as negative, so that not only 'input' (democratic) but also 'output' legitimacy – based on a positive evaluation of policies – is lacking (Verweij and Josling, 2003: 7–8).

In contrast, not only do corporations and economic associations influence international governance directly, but their interests are also considered more by national governments, thereby allowing them to profit from a 'double voice' (Woods, 2002: 27). It is also doubtful if corporations are effectively checked by NGOs. It is argued, for instance, that NGOs press global firms to comply with norms of corporate social responsibility, and today approximately 300 voluntary codes of conduct govern most major global economic sectors (Vogel, 2008: 262). As stated by Hirschland (2006: viii), 'Into this vacuum of waning government capacity and interest to regulate the parameters of acceptable business behavior, have stepped global public policy networks made up largely of non state groups'. NGOs threaten firms that are reluctant to apply social or environmental standards – such as in the footwear or apparel sector – with consumer boycotts, sanctions by investors motivated by 'ethical' concerns, and 'branding' prejudice (or loss of reputation). However, the effective impact of self-restraining practices is limited; for example, 'The reach of western [labour] codes is limited to small enclaves of employees in developing countries' (Vogel, 2008: 274), and the lack of enforcement mechanisms leads to credibility problems (Bexell *et al.*, 2010: 95). In addition, NGOs face strong organizational incentives to move on to new topics even when the need for monitoring private regulation persists (Büthe, 2010: 21).

We also know that 'advocacy' democracy – which prevails even more prominently at the transnational level with the role of 'civil society' representation – is no real substitute for the more egalitarian, traditional mechanisms of electoral representation. Although NGOs act as 'watchdogs' and are considered the most efficient channel for democratization of global policy-making, they may also suffer from their own democratic deficits (Erman and Uhlin, 2010; Steffek and Hahn, 2010; Scholte, 2011; Tallberg and Uhlin, 2012). NGOs do not escape problems of opacity, elitism, lack of representativeness and accountability. On the one hand, the projects manager of the Global Accountability Project of One World Trust announced that several important international NGOs, including Oxfam International and Greenpeace International, had engaged in self-reflective processes to define to whom, for what, and how they are accountable, leading to adoption of an INGO Accountability Charter (Lloyd, 2008: 207). On the other hand, a comparative study by One World Trust assessing transparency of '30 of the world's most powerful' IGOs (international governmental organizations), firms, and NGOs, and leading to the establishment of a 'Global Accountability Index', came to the conclusion that NGOs perform best in terms of stakeholder participation, but less well than IGOs regarding information disclosure about their activities, and score even lower than transnational corporations in the availability of 'feedback' mechanisms for complaint and response (Blagescu and Lloyd, 2009).

NGOs often speak in the name of groups not represented in the organization, and to whom organizational leaderships do not have to justify their options (Sperling, 2009, chapter 6). In addition, the internal accountability of NGOs to their members may be weak. A well-known phenomenon is that of so-called 'suitcase NGOs', 'made up of one person who travels from conference to conference' (Jordan, 2007: 152). Urbinati and Warren (2008) claim that, although the problem of self-authorized representation is not new, the novelty now lies in the number and diversity of self-proclaimed representatives. A multitude of representatives 'claim to represent a wide variety of goods: human rights and security, health, education, animals, rainforests, community, spirituality, safety, peace, economic development, and so on' (Urbinati and Warren, 2008: 403). They typically seek to influence not only power-holders – lobbying is relevant here – but also the media and public opinion – here the strategic option is 'going public'. The authors note that such alleged representatives 'function beyond borders' and 'in areas where no electoral democracy exists'. Needless to say, in a context of high mediatization (see Chapter 2), the media largely contribute to the 'labellization' of self-imposed representatives, especially when established channels of representation are lacking (Hajer, 2009: 183).

There are, however, a number of important problems with this kind of representation. A formal initial authorization to represent – mandated in representative democracy by success in competitive elections – fails. This results in a representation bias; therefore, the extent to which NGOs act as a genuine 'transmission belt' (Steffek and Nanz, 2008) for expression of the concerns of the global citizenry is questionable. For instance, 87 per cent of the 738 NGOs accredited to the WTO Ministerial Conference in Seattle were based in developed countries. Woods (2007: 38) and Vogel (2008: 263) claim more generally that virtually all 'public participation' is by western activists. Urbinati and Warren (2008: 404) suggest, a bit too optimistically, that 'it is up to those who are claimed as "represented" to say yes or no or to offer alternative accounts'. Yet there is no guarantee that they will be asked or will do that, or that this is really an option available to them. The authors also claim that the 'represented' can exit if they are dissatisfied, yet, as we have noticed, internal accountability of NGOs to members who theoretically have an 'exit' option may be low. More importantly, the same applies to the 'external' accountability NGOs have to populations for whom they speak, and for whom talk of 'exit' is meaningless. It may well be that an NGO's definition of what is good for a population is not necessarily shared by that population. A well-known problem is that of environmental standards being viewed as a nontariff trade barrier, rather than a global common good, by governments and segments of the population in less developed countries. Vogel

(2008: 274), for example, suggests that 'Many labour codes essentially empower NGOs, rather than developing country workers, and the two's priorities can often conflict', and concludes that 'To the extent that voluntary labour codes replace rather than supplement state regulations, developing country governments are essentially ceding their sovereignty to the demands of western activists'. It may even happen that the 'represented' are not informed at all about the action of NGO activists 'in their favour', or may ignore the sheer existence of such alleged representatives of their cause. True, organizations may be held accountable by rival organizations or by the media; however, no institutionalized mechanism ensures that. Consequently, one should take Vibert's (2007: 180) reservation seriously: 'The idea that the unelected can confer democratic legitimacy on the unelected is simply misconceived.'

Given these problems, one should consider the option of conferring an oversight role of global governance on directly elected representatives. Beyond the EU nothing similar to the European Parliament exists, and proposals such as that of a United Nations Parliamentary Assembly may be normatively attractive, but lack realism. Yet an organization like One World Trust promotes at least greater accountability of governments to national parliaments in relation to their actions at the global level (Blagescu and Lloyd, 2009: 273n). Moreover, networks of parliamentarians have emerged with the aim of checking on the activity of international organizations, such as the Parliamentary Conference on the WTO, or the Parliamentary Network on the World Bank and the International Monetary Fund. For the time being, legislators remain laggards with respect to their international networking activity; it has a low priority in terms of re-election, turnover rates are higher, and the degree of expertise is lower among parliamentarians than among bureaucrats and regulators (Slaughter, 2004: 105). Further, networks of legislators rarely acquire an official role, or receive formal recognition, as is now the case in the EU with the COSAC (Conference of Community and European Affairs Committees of Parliaments of the European Union), which is formally recognized. Even COSAC's influence on European matters remains marginal for lack of binding decision-making capacity (Bengtson, 2007). Yet European integration remains the governance process beyond the nation-state that is subject to the closest 'multilevel' scrutiny by parliaments.

Let us take the case of the open method of coordination (OMC) in the EU, a soft governance method implemented through non-binding instruments such as recommendations and voluntary compliance based on benchmarking and cross-country learning. OMC applies in domains, such as employment or pensions policy, where harmonization of national legislations through the traditional and more demanding 'community method' is not feasible. Initially both the European Parliament and its national counterparts had a weak role in the OMC, but parliaments became increasingly aware that, in spite of its non-binding character, the OMC leads to the reframing of policy norms and entails important policy choices, generating winners and losers. This awareness led to cooperation among standing parliamentary committees. Such cooperation took the form most notably of the establishment of joint committees, and co-chaired meetings of representatives of the relevant committee of the European Parliament, and of national parliamentary committees in charge of specific OMC issues. Such a learning process was 'mainly due to the efforts of the European Parliament and at least some of the more active national parliaments, which have taken it upon themselves to take a more active role within the limits that the formal rules permit' (Tsakatika, 2007: 554). Given these limits, this enhancement of the parliamentary dimension of the OMC can be depicted only as a 'half step', yet it goes in the right direction (on the parliamentary dimension of European integration see also later in this chapter).

It would indeed be a promising avenue if networks of legislators came to challenge the frequent monopoly on expertise held by technocratic governance networks. For example, a code of best practice promulgated by an international network of securities regulators would have to compete with another code on the same subject formulated by an international network of specialized parliamentary committee representatives. As pointed out by Slaughter (2004: 255), who is the source of this idea: 'The determination of what a best practice is and whose interests it is most likely to serve would likely be different. Certainly such a possibility would provide a counterweight to the consensus of professional technocrats.' Such a counterweight would introduce a welcome politicization of issues of collective interest and a welcome 'reparliamentarization' of policy processes. This is also suggested by Braithwaite and Drahos (2000: 608), who propose that international committees of parliamentarians 'oversee the work of international organizations like WTO, IMF, and ITU and [...] hear complaints against them by citizen groups'.

## The democratic deficit of private governance: invisible and by stealth

Parliamentary monitoring would also counteract, to some extent, the negative consequences of trends toward privatization of governance. The global level appears to have the most 'islands' (Stone Sweet, 2004) of private governance, giving a key policy role to democratically unaccountable entities. Each policy sector regulated at this level has its own distinct decisional architecture where the role of public and private actors, the divisions of competences across territorial levels, and the intensity of regulation vary (Mayntz, 2008: 53). To this must be added variation across countries; for example, the role of non-public actors in the formulation of national positions for intergovernmental negotiations differs from one country to the next. However, despite some diversity, the trends towards privatization of global governance ought not be obscured by an excessively formalistic or legalistic view of international relations (Hall and Biersteker, 2002: 24).

One first observes various forms of unequally codified public-private partnerships (PPPs) (Hirschland, 2006: 86–113), which are also *en vogue* at the national level (see Chapter 4). Such partnerships lead to a blurring of the public–private divide and challenge the classic realist conception of international relations being the realm only of states. Partnerships are established for the primary purpose of service provision, but also with aims of standard-setting and rule implementation. A prominent example is the World Commission on Dams, which incorporated national governments, the World Bank, NGOs, and construction firms to make the construction of large dams compatible with sustainability requirements (Börzel and Risse, 2005). Other examples are the Roll Back Malaria Initiative – based on cooperation between the WHO, the World Bank, UNDP, UNICEF, several large corporations and NGOs – and the UN Global Compact, in which more than 7000 firms – voluntarily and in the absence of sanctions – agreed to comply with principles of corporate social responsibility, a partnership set up by corporations, a few large NGOs, and several specialized agencies of the United Nations. It is hard to assess the governance capacity and the effective impact of PPPs, especially when they issue non-binding recommendations and thus produce 'soft' law based on moral suasion and mutual learning, but these may be non-negligible.

Some PPPs have been designed explicitly to ensure balanced representation of affected parties, as well as accountability to them. In international settings, where classic representative mechanisms do not exist, this can be considered a second-best option in terms of democratic quality. Conzelmann and Wolf (2008: 102–3) cite as an example the Forest Stewardship Council (FSC), 'an independent worldwide non-profit initiative bringing together a broad set of different stakeholders, including environmental NGOs, the timber industry, traders, indigenous peoples' organizations, and forest product certification organizations'. The objective of the FSC is to promote sustainable commercial forestry through a voluntary code of conduct. The FSC General Assembly is based on a checks and balances logic: it consists of three chambers – economic, social, and environmental – whose representatives have equal voting rights. To add to its institutional sophistication, representatives of the North and South also have equal voting rights in each chamber to guarantee adequate representation of sectoral and territorial interests. However, it seems that the inclusive structure of the FSC does not make it attractive to business, and this may be an impediment to its effectiveness. The FSC model was emulated by the Marine Stewardship Council (MSC) in charge of natural fisheries management, and the Sustainable Tourism Stewardship Council, among others (Bernstein and Cashore, 2007: 351), but it should be noted that the market share of FSC-certified wood remains small, with only 2 per cent of the world's commercial forests covered by FSC norms, and those largely the ones least in need of regulation (Dryzek, 2010: 129).

Besides, not all PPPs perform as well as the FSC in the areas of stakeholder representation and accountability. Although there is no systematic research, case studies reveal that 'mechanisms through which affected actors can control the decision making in the supreme governance bodies of PPPs are largely absent' (Beisheim *et al.*, 2010: 377). PPPs often also raise problems of lack of transparency and accountability, which are more serious when their outputs have a binding effect. Joint forms of policy-making can be more or less conflictual – think of possible clashes between firms and NGOs, or about sensitive issues for authoritarian governments – and making decisions behind closed doors helps solve such problems. Besides, private actors are less habituated to transparency exercises than public actors, who must periodically provide justifications for their actions (Hirschland, 2006: 144–5). In addition, although their institutional set-up varies, PPPs often have an informal structure, sometimes deliberately to raise business confidence, and most are not registered anywhere (p. 106). In the case of the – now discontinued – World Bank's Business Partners for Development program, Hirschland (2006: 99) notes 'little is revealed about how particular projects or partners were chosen, or the nature of the engagements themselves'. He adds the more general problem of provisions that complicate or even inhibit the observation of PPP activities: crucial information such as who sat at the table, what was discussed, who was cooperative, and which programs failed is not disclosed (pp. 106, 146). In that respect, Hirschland makes an eloquent comparison with a parliament, for which it would be unimaginable to shield debate from public scrutiny and share only the positive results of legislative activity. He goes on to argue that 'If the recipients of partnership goods are dissatisfied with outcomes, they have limited recourse. It is difficult for affected parties to unseat unelected companies or NGOs acting on their behalf. Few if any mechanisms for this are built into the process' (p. 99). Moreover, accountability in partnership ventures is more difficult not only because sanctions are not available, but also because of 'blame-shift games'. In case of failure, each partner can shift the blame to the other (Hood, 2011: 81–83), and this can work especially well if PPPs remain 'black boxes' for outsiders.

To the development of PPPs should be added the thorough delegation of global governance functions to private bodies. One can speak of the emergence of privately-driven, as opposed to publicly-driven, arrangements (Ronit, 2007), or of 'the construction of many public policies as a result of what are essentially private efforts' (Hirschland, 2006: 12). This means either a transfer of decision-making capacity to non-public actors, or that such a capacity autonomously emerges outside public organizations. However, for lack of democratic authorization and accountability, private authority can be found wanting in terms of legitimacy (Cashore, 2002; Quack, 2010; Take, 2012), and therefore be confronted with compliance deficits. A specialist in private forms of governance (Cutler, 2002: 32) maintains:

> Only public authorities are entitled or empowered to prescribe behavior for others because only public authorities are accountable through political institutions. Private entities, such as corporations or business associations, are not entitled to act authoritatively for the public, because they are not authorized by society and are thus not subject to mechanisms of political accountability. Indeed, their accountability (legally and financially) is to their private members. Thus, under democratic theory, only elected representatives and their delegates may function authoritatively in prescribing and proscribing behavior.

To be sure, private governance can be delegated public governance, but, as mentioned, the chain of delegation is so lengthy that linkages for *ex ante* democratic authorization and *ex post* democratic accountability become fictitious when norm-making is privatized. In principle, public endorsement of private rules is reversible, but public actors often depend on expertise provided by private actors for endorsement decisions. This is the case for the endorsement by the European Union of accounting standards set by the (private) International Accounting Standards Board (IASB). The EU Commission is advised on its endorsement decisions by another private organization: the European Financial Reporting Advisory Group (EFRAG), itself 'an umbrella network of organizations representing European employers, banks, accountancy professions, insurers, stock exchanges and financial analysts' (Perry and Nölke, 2006: 576).

Private international regulatory regimes exist today in fields as diverse as regulation of the internet and intellectual property, international minerals, insurance, maritime transport industries, and industrial production standard-setting (Hall and Biersteker, 2002: 30). In the latter field, for instance, 'thousands of standards were authorized for thousands of commodities and productive processes by autonomous and non-governmental organizations well before quasi-state bodies became involved in monitoring and implementing the standards' (Rosenau, 2002: 82). Together with the International Electrotechnical Commission (IEC), the International Standardization Organization (ISO) accounts for about 85 per cent of all international product standards (Büthe and Mattli, 2010: 456). ISO was little known, and issued few standards, until the 1980s. Then, it worked under the shadow of powerful national standardization organizations such as those of Germany and Great Britain. The situation changed, however, with market globalization, which gave ISO a prominent role.

The annual output of ISO has almost doubled since the beginning of the 1980s (Mattli and Büthe, 2003: 7). Since then, the ISO has expanded its offerings to include standards on quality control, the environment, food safety, and corporate social responsibility. So far it has developed more than 16,000 standards (Prakash and Potoski, 2010: 75), and has 107 members. (IEC has 59 members: Büthe and Mattli, 2010: 464.) Although membership is by country, ISO funding is private, and states cannot be members. Such an international nongovernmental organization is best described (Mattli and Büthe, 2003: 4) as a global network:

comprising hundreds of technical committees from all over the world and involving tens of thousands of experts representing industry and other groups. The institutional backbone of these networks is formed by private sector standards bodies at the national level. Domestic bodies are thus part and parcel of the international institutional architecture.

The ISO comprises about 180 technical committees, 550 subcommittees, and 2,000 working groups involving several thousand representatives selected by national organizations, mostly from industry. ISO standards are decided by majority vote on the basis of the principle of one country, one vote. Even though there is strong emphasis on consensus, only technical objections are admissible (Büthe and Mattli, 2010: 464–5). The standards are voluntary, and the organization has no formal capacity to enforce them; however, countries increasingly adopt this form of soft law, which tends to be hardened by the fact that if states stick to their own standards despite international norms this can be found to constitute an unnecessary obstacle to trade and thus a violation of WTO law (Mattli and Büthe, 2003: 2). Interestingly, WTO law itself may be influenced by the activity of private governance bodies; for example, the Intellectual Property Committee, a multinational grouping of the largest pharmaceutical companies, 'developed a set of shared normative understandings that gave it remarkable influence in the adoption of intellectual property provisions in the Uruguay Round of international trade negotiations' (Porter, 2005: 222). Though consumers are affected by that kind of norm-making activity, their organizations often lack the money, time, and expertise to compete with business influence within the global circuits where technical standards are set and assessed; representatives from developing countries face the same problems (Graz and Nölke, 2008: 22; Büthe and Mattli, 2010: 466).

A similar mode of regulation has emerged in the field of transborder construction projects, where *lex constructionis* is a private, self-governing regime in an economic sector dominated by a small number of large firms preferring to regulate their field autonomously (Sassen, 2006: 246). International trade relations are also governed by a private regime of commercial law, considered a kind of resurrection of the medieval *lex mercatoria*: 'Today, traders increasingly govern themselves, and the institutions that traders and their lawyers have created are substantially insulated from, while being parasitic on, state authority' (Stone Sweet, 2004: 144, 122). In fact, the designation of *lex mercatoria* as private international *trade* law becomes increasingly inaccurate 'because it extends well beyond regulation of exchange to include a full range of international productive relations, including, for example, the regulation of international licensing, distributorships, joint ventures, construction contracts, and the extraterritorial application of tax, antitrust, and securities laws' (Cutler, 2003: 34). Although national courts and public international law can still be used formally, a self-organizing social order emerges in parallel because long-distance traders seek to retain control over their own interactions, and to increase their autonomy vis-à-vis national jurisdictions. Conflict among national orders, and the possible bias in favour of locals, generates an intolerable unpredictability; therefore, international commercial arbitration is a core component of that increasingly codified private regulatory system. Partners involved in trade disputes 'may by contract agree to exclude the application of national law and national judicial systems, invoking perhaps the application of general business customs and practices, thus *delocalizing* the transaction and methods for enforcement and dispute resolution' (Cutler, 2003: 40, emphasis in the original). Proliferating private arbitration bodies – mainly large multinational, but above all Anglo-American, legal firms – compete with each other for the adjudication of international commercial disputes (Dezalay and Garth, 1996). Cutler (2002: 30) thus emphasizes a paradoxical evolution: 'The juridification of international commercial relations is intensifying, but at the hands of predominantly non-state, corporate actors.'

In 1910 there were only ten arbitration houses; today there are more than 150. The activity of the largest among them has tripled in the past three decades (Stone Sweet, 2004: 135). The annual rate of filings with the world's largest arbitration institutions has increased from 1,148 in 1992, to more than 3,700 in 2008. As of 2009, 144 out of the 192 United Nations member states had ratified the 1958 New York Convention on the Recognition and Enforcement of Foreign Arbitral Awards, stipulating that states recognize the validity of arbitral judgments and use their coercive resources to enforce them (Whytock, 2010: 6 and 10). Though exceptions are admitted if public policy reasons are invoked, these exceptions tend to lose their practical relevance in most states. As a result, several possibly politically sensitive matters, such as competition, securities, tax regulation, intellectual protection, and consumer protection disputes, are removed from public supervision and control by national courts (Cutler, 2003: 26–7). However, the latter retain a non-negligible role in the enforcement procedures that follow transnational commercial arbitration. This makes private actors incorporate judicial enforcement in their calculations so that, in reality, private and public modes of governance support each other (Whytock, 2010).

It should also be noted that corporate actors are not the only non-public actors to be involved in transnational regulation. As we have seen, NGOs play a central role in the origination of voluntary norms that aim to 'civilize' globalization by making corporations more socially responsible, and this is yet another recent manifestation of privatized norm-making. In fields like workers' rights or agricultural production for instance, NGOs function as regulatory actors themselves in the framework of the privatization of certification. In the field of environmental regulation they serve as sources of 'eco-labelling' certification, and establish standards of 'sustainable forestry' recognized by firms (Hall and Biersteker, 2002: 13–14). It would, then, be misleading to attribute the privatization of governance only to the diffusion of neoliberal values and recipes. Privatization mainly aims to increase regulatory efficiency; the establishment of private norms can be less costly, and these norms can be implemented more easily. Proximity to rule-takers is deemed to favour the knowledge pooling necessary for effective regulation, as well as increasing trust in rule makers, which enhances compliance.

Clearly, the shift of authority to private hands does not have much to do with a deliberate attempt to hollow out democratic procedures. Most probably, such a hollowing out is an unintended side-effect; the designers of private forms of governance simply prioritize efficiency and do not put issues of participation and democratic control high on their agenda. Despite efficiency gains made by private governance, there is a clear trade-off in terms of loss of accountability. Such a loss is hardly visible, because few are acquainted with the subtleties of transnational private governance. Not only is the loss of accountability problematic on normative grounds, but we cannot exclude the possibility that sooner or later it will be denounced and exploited instrumentally by strategic-minded political movements.

We know, for instance, that the alleged role of a remote bureaucratic 'Eurocracy' nourishes not only Euroscepticism – see Taggart and Szczerbiak (2008) on its expression in party politics – but also contributes to populist and cynical attitudes towards public officials. What voters, and, arguably, most members of national parliaments, do not see (yet?) is that the 'democratic deficit' at the transnational level is much larger outwith the EU. Braithwaite and Drahos (2000: 3) write about Australia:

[...] for years some of Australia's air safety standards have been written by the Boeing Corporation in Seattle, or if not by that corporation, by the US Federal Aviation Administration in Washington. Australia's ship safety laws have been written by the International Maritime Organization in London, its motor vehicle standards by Working Party 29 of the Economic Commission for Europe and its food standards by the Codex Alimentarius Commission in Rome. Many of Australia's pharmaceutical standards have been set by a joint collaboration of Japanese, European and US industries and their regulators, called the International Conference on Harmonization. Its telecommunications standards have been substantially set in Geneva by the International Telecommunication Union. The Chair (and often the Vice-Chair) of most of the expert committees that effectively set those standards in Geneva are Americans, the Motorola Corporation has been particularly effective in setting telecommunications standards through its chairmanship of those committees. As a consequence, Motorola standards have been written into many of the ITU standards that we all must follow.

This trend has not been reversed; rather, it has been amplified, and globalization combined with privatization of regulation affects the entire world. What if people became more aware of the details and amplitude of such a power shift? It is very likely that the accountability gap would become broader; the limited supply of democratically accountable decision-making beyond the nation-state would be challenged by more demands for accountability. To be sure, the globalization of regulation can improve its procedural quality; for instance, Braithwaite and Drahos (2000: 507–11) identified significant gains in transparency in nearly all sectors they scrutinized, enough to refer to a 'triumph' of transparency. These authors also found that even if globalization erodes national sovereignty by removing decisional competences from national authorities, access of critical NGOs to international regulatory bodies can be easier than access to their national counterparts, which are also more likely, according to them, to be captured by private interests (Braithwaite and Drahos, 2000: 606–7). Although such improvements should be acknowledged, there is hardly any doubt that the *de jure* or the *de facto* internationalization of authoritative policy-making also entails a formidable potential for contestation by those who feel they are dispossessed from their power at the profit of unauthorized, unaccountable, and thus at best weakly legitimate policy-makers.

## Europeanization and multilevel governance

The European Union is probably the most sophisticated supranational organization, with extensive competences and a complex institutional architecture. This architecture has become increasingly similar to that of the democratic nation-state, with a government (the Commission), a parliament, and a judiciary power with a significant role. It would nevertheless be an exaggeration to postulate that decisions by EU member states are 'made in Brussels'; significant areas of national competence remain – think of the variety of pension systems in Europe – and national administrations retain room for manoeuvre when implementing European directives. On the other hand, national systems have become increasingly 'Europeanized', which means that a large number of policies are now downloaded from the EU to the national and lower levels. Is European integration yet another source of danger for national democracies?

We know that the circular relationship based on the congruence principle between policy-makers and policy-takers is the cornerstone of democratic legitimacy. It has been argued that European integration does not negatively affect that circular mechanism of democratic accountability (Moravcsik, 2002). European treaties have been ratified by democratically elected national parliamentary assemblies, and, increasingly, by referendum votes. As governments are accountable to their electorates for domestic policies, they are also accountable to them when they participate in intergovernmental negotiations in Brussels, where, after all, they seek primarily to upload national preferences on policy matters. In addition, the European Parliament – directly elected by the citizens of the 27 EU-member states – has increasingly become a key player in the EU decision-making system, through the mechanism of 'codecision' that placed it on equal footing with the intergovernmental institution of the Council. In addition, the European Parliament has acquired further competences as a consequence of the Lisbon Treaty.

In a recent publication, Bovens *et al.* (2010) convincingly show that different EU institutions are subject to different accountability regimes, so we can say that accountability in such a complex system is composite. However, these nuances do not negate the democratic deficit of the EU. For instance, the influence of the European Parliament has undeniably increased, but it has not yet acquired formal competences equivalent to those of national parliaments, nor has it gained sufficient political legitimacy, though its members have been directly elected since 1979. Although the EP is democratically elected, European elections are seen as 'second-order' elections; they are popularity tests for the national incumbent parties rather than opportunities for real public deliberation on European issues. Though the EP's powers have steadily increased, turnout in European elections has steadily decreased – turnout was less than 20 per cent in Slovakia in 2009! In several policy sectors subject to the ordinary legislative procedure, the EP has the same legislative role as the Council of Ministers, in a system not dissimilar from bicameralism involving two separate legislative bodies at the national level. Nevertheless, despite expansion of the EP prerogatives, within the framework of the so-called consultation procedure the Parliament's role remains weaker than that of the Council. If we compare the latter with a chamber of states in a federal system, such as the *Bundesrat* in Germany or the Senate in the United States, the 'quasi-federalist' institutional architecture of the EU (Schmidt, 2006: 47–54) presents the peculiarity of having a universally elected first chamber (the European Parliament) that is still relatively dominated by a second chamber (the Council). Further, the EU is not a fully fledged parliamentary system. Though the competences of the EP have increased, its influence on the composition of the European executive, the EU Commission, is weaker than that of national parliaments on the process of government formation in parliamentary systems. True, the EP must now approve the nomination of the Commission president and agree on the composition of a new Commission. A few years ago, proposed commissioners who generated significant opposition from the EP had to be removed from the Barroso Commission. However, the commissioners are still proposed by national governments. Moreover, a supermajority of two-thirds is required in the EP to censure the Commission, which is extremely high by national standards. Finally, regarding policy-making, the Commission still retains a monopoly on initiating legislation – also a strength vis-à-vis the Council – and its input is formulated in consultation with a vast array of organized interests, experts, and national civil servants, which marginalizes elected representatives.

Supranational institutions such as the Commission and the European Court of Justice are key actors in the integration process:

but, crucially, the Commission enjoys more autonomy with respect to the European Parliament than national governments do with respect to elected assemblies in parliamentary systems, and the ECJ is an independent branch of government similar to national supreme or constitutional courts (see Chapter 6). The European Central Bank is yet another independent supranational institution, in charge of monetary policy in the euro area. It appears, then, that in reality, 'National executives have delegated to a range of EU institutions authority over policy areas that used to be sovereignty-defining tasks of the nation-state, whether in monetary policy or international trade' (Schmidt, 2006: 55). Accountability linkages are even weaker for technocratic back-stagers in EU governance, such as the numerous committees – 233 in 2010! – of the so-called comitology system. These committees are composed of national experts and are in charge of the implementation of European legislation. Comitology meetings serve to discuss and vote on measures drafted by the Commission to implement EU legislation decided by the Council and by the European Parliament. Such measures may have important Europe-wide implications on social life – broad constituencies may be profoundly affected. Comitology committees are an important governance tool for the EU system; they handle nearly 50 per cent of all European acts, and release more than 2,000 implementation measures per year (Brandsma, 2010: 17 and 49). However, their transparency is not satisfactory; membership lists do not contain information about the identity of participants other than the number of representatives per country, summary records contain only very brief information about committee discussions, and though nearly all votes are registered, only 5.5 percent of the draft measures decided are publicly available (Brandsma *et al.*, 2008: 836).

Even in areas where national authorities retain the upper hand, accountability is not satisfying. Consider ministers making decisions at Council meetings: they belong to government parties accountable to national electorates, but many European issues debated in this arena are not crucial for party competition within member states, and the Council as a whole is not accountable to European voters. Voters are not well informed about their government's conduct in Brussels because intergovernmental negotiations lack visibility. The outcomes of such negotiations are compromises, and governments can claim credit for the positive aspects as they shift blame to negotiation partners for the negative aspects. The accountability of governments to their electorates on EU issues is thus often fictitious.

The title of an article on Europeanization nicely depicts the risks described above: 'The Commission Made Me Do It' (Smith, 1997). The same applies in the European Union to the Council, where the increased use of qualified majority voting, instead of unanimity across member-states, induces the governments of minority countries to present themselves domestically as victims, although in practice voting seldom takes place and compromises are sought under the shadow of possibly negative votes that Council members try to avoid. International weakness thus becomes an asset in domestic power struggles, what Edgar Grande (1996) aptly called the 'paradox of weakness'. Raunio, for example, argues that European integration increases leadership autonomy within national parties, which has to do with the structural properties of the EU that provide party leaders of incumbent parties, such as cabinet members, with an arena for intergovernmental negotiation where 'the party organization exercises little if any control over party representatives' (Raunio, 2002: 411). The author provides evidence that European integration 'consolidates the centralization of decision-making through strengthening the agenda-setting powers of party leaders' (p. 406). Through their regular participation in Council meetings as ministers, high party officials have considerable discretion in making agreements, even though they are constrained by their electoral pledges. This happens because of 'informational asymmetries resulting from the uneven participatory rights of national politicians in the EU political system' (p. 411). Two basic problems exist here: 'hidden information', which means that party organizations do not know their leaders' actual preferences; and 'hidden action', meaning that party organizations are not able to see what party leaders are actually doing in the EU. In sum, the transformation of parties into electoral machines, mediatization, and European integration all contribute to the centralization of national party organizations.

What is a handicap for party organizations vis-à-vis party leaderships is also a handicap for national parliaments vis-à-vis national executives. European integration has been depicted as a process that switches the power balance to the advantage of territorial interests represented by national governments and corporate interests represented by interest groups, to the disadvantage of the electoral channel incarnated by parties and parliaments (Bartolini, 2005: 382). For example, recent comparative research in seven EU member states – Denmark, the United Kingdom, Austria, Slovenia, Spain, France, and Poland – concludes that the Lisbon strategy has been advancing centralization of EU policy coordination at national level, empowering core executives. This is caused by the Lisbon strategy's goals being highly visible politically, and by organizational requirements that put national administrations under stress (Borras and Peters, 2011). As suggested by Schmidt (2006: 63–4):

> The contribution of national parliaments in areas of EU competence has become primarily one of transposing into national law EU directives elaborated in the EU Commission and approved by national executives in the Council of Ministers.... National parliaments have been ill-informed, if they have been informed at all, not only of government positions before the decision but also of what stance they took in the negotiations, given the secrecy rule that forbids even minutes being taken during the meetings.

In fields delegated to the EU, the legislative function of parliaments is limited mostly to transposition and downloading of EU legislation. Yet not all member states are equally zealous in that respect; Falkner *et al.* (2005) show distinct 'worlds' of compliance with EU regulations among member states, from a legalist approach in the Nordic countries, to neglect and a lack of administrative capacity – if not sheer corruption – in the European south. There is also cross-country variation in the capacity of parliaments to control their governments in the uploading process. Government leadership and autonomy should be greater when parliamentary scrutiny of EU affairs is weak; the latter is a function of factors such as domestic salience of issues related to European integration, and the amplitude of domestic conflict associated with them. Media scrutiny of government action in Brussels and the presence of Eurosceptic parties may thus play a role.

Parliaments are also able to undergo learning processes that are probably broader because they also occur in reaction to the shift of power to governments in domestic issues. Alarmed by their lack of influence on European legislation negotiated in the Council, several parliaments reorganized themselves – namely, by establishing European affairs committees and involving their specialized standing committees in greater scrutiny of European matters – in order to monitor the actions of national governments in the EU arena more closely. Thus parliaments tend to fight back (Raunio and Hix, 2000), and some reparliamentarization of decision-making occurs. In addition, the Lisbon Treaty foresees an early-warning mechanism that allows each national parliament to indicate when the subsidiarity principle is in danger of being violated by the EU. If negative opinions from national parliaments reach one third, or one quarter in the area of justice and internal affairs, the Commission must reconsider its proposal. This mechanism also includes the possibility that national parliaments could turn to the European Court of Justice for violations of the subsidiarity principle. It is, however, uncertain if such a mechanism will produce any substantial changes, as it is unlikely that a sufficient number of national parliaments would agree on what constitutes a violation of subsidiarity by a single legislative proposal (Raunio, 2009: 325).

Moreover, comparative research shows that the degree of reparliamentarization strongly depends on the broader pattern of executive–legislative relations in each country. For example, in the Westminster system of the United Kingdom, where the government controls the parliamentary majority through strong party discipline, the parliament generally cannot credibly threaten to veto the government's position; hence, it hardly influences national positions on European issues and must content itself with a control function, forcing the government to provide more public justification of its behaviour (see Auel and Benz, 2005: 380–83). Besides, parliaments are reluctant to be too intrusive since they know that 'rigid positions are seen as counterproductive in pursuing national goals, because the government representatives must be able to negotiate compromises with their counterparts' (Raunio, 2002: 413). To avoid the risk of stalemate, parliamentary influence is usually exercised through informal negotiations with the government, elaborating its positions to be defended in Brussels (Auel, 2007). A trade-off then appears: governments and party leaders become more accountable to parliaments, but MPs are not accountable to voters regarding the quite invisible influence they successfully exert on EU matters. There might be another problem, too, with respect to the quality of democratic control: rather than strengthening the autonomy of parliaments, indirect parliamentary influence on government positions 'might further undermine the checks and balances between executive and legislature, creating additional problems of democratic legitimacy instead of solving them' (Börzel and Sprungk, 2009: 371).

In general, internationalization affects the power balance not only among, but also, more subtly, within, national actors. Administrations are not unitary actors and are often characterized by bureaucratic infighting and competition for resources between ministries; hence, some segments of national administrations are empowered as a result of Europeanization, while others are weakened. For instance, ministries involved in intergovernmental negotiations not only gain a strategic advantage in terms of informational asymmetry, their arguments also gain weight because the ministries enjoy cognitive advantages in terms of knowledge pooling. Thus, they not only enhance their influence through the two-level game, but also thanks to the advantages of 'two-level arguing' (Risse, 2006). We know that domestic factors influence implementation of European policies at national levels; therefore, the ability of administrative and other domestic 'norm entrepreneurs' to disseminate norms and justifications borrowed from debates in the external scene becomes crucial in convincing domestic actors of the need to adjust to new recipes imported from outside.

Interestingly, informational asymmetry even benefits ministers in charge of weakly Europeanized portfolios (Raunio, 2002). Moreover, the empirical evidence regarding differential empowerment within parties is more nuanced than one might expect. Poguntke *et al.* (2007) assumed that two groups of party actors would be most likely to benefit from the process of Europeanization of national political parties. First, the executive bias of EU decision-making is likely to work in favour of party elites in general, as predicted by Raunio (2002). Second, party officials who specialize in EU affairs are likely to have greater access to resources and more control over policy decisions within national parties because of the growing importance of European integration. An empirical analysis compared 30 parties in six countries – Austria, France, Germany, Spain, Sweden, and the United Kingdom. The authors found rather weak support for their hypotheses. Although party leaders were indeed empowered, it was difficult to disentangle the effects of the EU from the effects of domestic factors leading to party presidentialization. The EU had an effect on party leaders' power beyond governmental parties, something that qualifies the advantages of playing a two-level game. Regarding the second hypothesis on the empowerment of EU specialists, there is little evidence in support of it, largely because EU specialists within parties are still few in number. In short, the authors of that cross-national study found only limited Europeanization of national party organizations (Poguntke *et al.*, 2007: 212).

All this colours the assessment of the impact of Europe on national democratic governance. Considering executive dominance for instance, and the intergovernmentalist view of integration as a process driven mostly by summit negotiations among national executives, one can see things quite differently. Schmidt (2006: 56) and several others maintain that national governments are no longer the core actors in decision-making, a situation that does not only benefit supranational institutions: 'National executives have not only lost autonomy in consequence of the shift of decision-making upward to the EU but they have also lost control as a result of the shift of decision-making power downward to subnational authorities, through processes of devolution and decentralization, and outward to independent regulatory agencies.' The amplitude of downward decentralization varies across nations, but 'Europeanization has increased regional authorities' autonomy from the national executive, by providing them with new access to EU-level policy formulation processes and resources' (Schmidt, 2006: 57). In addition, vertical movements of power diffusion are supplemented by horizontal trends – at national, European, and transnational levels – to involve non-public actors in policy-making (see Chapter 4). According to the intergovernmentalist perspective, internationalization leads to governments gaining power not only with respect to national legislatures but also with respect to organized interests; however, such a view tends to neglect the fact that organized interests are now often associated with the policy process at all decision levels. In fact, this view may be adequate to describe decision-making about major events such as the elaboration of treaties in the EU, but it is misleading in relation to everyday policy-making, in which actor constellations are more complex.

As a matter of fact, the role of the EU and the influence of transnational bodies on policy-making can lead to so-called multilevel governance (MLG) structures, the vertical version of a cooperative form of governance (see Chapter 4). MLG involves 'a large number of decision-making arenas ... differentiated along both functional and territorial lines, and ... interlinked in a non-hierarchical way' (Eberlein and Kerwer, 2004: 128). It implies the formulation or implementation of public policies by networks of public agents (politicians and administrators) at different decision levels, along with non-public participants such as economic agents, interest representatives and stakeholders, and experts. Skelcher (2005: 90) defines the crucial role played by networks in MLG: 'Networks engage mainstream state, federal, regional, and local governments in interactions with arm's length public bodies including quasi-governmental agencies, single-purpose boards, public–private partnerships, and multi-organizational collaborations.' In the complex system of EU governance in particular:

> self-organized networks have developed around specific policies. These consist of actors who are mutually dependent on one another

for the delivery of their goals and who cross-cut the branches and levels of Union governance as well as the divide between public and private interests.... Since *ex hypothesi* all members of networks are necessary for the delivery of the goals of all other members, there is no other basis for collective decision than an outcome that leaves each at least as well off as before. (Lord, 2004: 113)

With regard to the particular issue of the EU's structural funds policy, Kohler-Koch (2003: 21) notes that many authors attribute its successful performance to:

the formation of cross-cutting networks, which bring together public and private actors from the national, the sub-national, and the EU level. These networks are considered to be ideal breeding grounds for learning processes and the emergence of policy communities, which share interpretations of problematic situations, agree on common objectives and consent on problem-solving strategies.

In order to understand how multilevel processes are set up and how they operate in the EU quasi-federal system, one can rely on the expertise drawn from federal states. It is of note that although large European democracies have traditionally been centralized, with the exception of Germany after World War II, they have all recently been subjected to pressure to decentralize, and have tended to react positively to that pressure to varying degrees. Spain's asymmetrical federalism, which was set up in the 1970s after transition to democracy and gives more-or-less extended competences to regions, is constantly evolving. Devolution and regionalization have been part of the agenda in the traditionally unitary UK and in Italy over the last few years, and even strongly centralized France underwent phases of a significant decentralization process. Among small West European states, Belgium is under constant federalization pressure to reduce linguistic tensions, and some regional variety and local experimentation are now tolerated, if not encouraged, in the traditionally homogeneous Nordic countries. This is happening as a corollary of the success of neoliberal approaches emphasizing the benefits of competition across regions or municipalities (Loughlin, 2007: 397), and of New Public Management doctrines that view customer proximity as a condition for optimal service delivery (see Chapter 5).

In federal polities, competences are usually formally distributed across various decision levels: national, regional, and local. The formal division of competences notwithstanding, these levels are interdependent in several ways; for example, a situation where the central level provides financial resources while necessitating the knowledge of local actors. This leads to a 'competence mix', and to horizontal and vertical cooperation schemes even in systems of formally pure dual federalism characterized by a clear division of competences between the national and the subnational levels (Thorlakson, 2003). As several actors are involved in these schemes, each possessing a fraction of the power, there is a risk of policy blockade. Fritz W. Scharpf (1988) calls this a 'joint-decision trap', and its management necessitates negotiations that are more likely to succeed if they are conducted under conditions of discretion. Scharpf's work on German cooperative federalism compared with the European Union has shown that so-called *Politikverflechtung* is a core feature of MLG: diffusion of resources across decision levels makes negotiations inescapable and informality a condition of successful conflict resolution.

Europeanization adds yet another level to the multilevel system. For instance, the EU Commission may circumvent national authorities and establish partnerships directly with regional-level government (Egeberg, 2008: 239). The latter may now deal directly with EU authorities and with national and subnational governments in other member states. This kind of direct connection between domestic and European actors challenges national governments' monopoly in representing domestic interests beyond the nation-state (Hooghe and Marks, 2009: 2). In some cases, such as in EU regional and cohesion policy using structural-fund instruments, 'multilevelness' is accompanied by cooperative governance at the horizontal level. The establishment of partnerships is a condition for funding, and subnational governments have an interest in showing they stand close to civil society to prove the authenticity of their representational claims (Piattoni, 2009: 174). In multilevel governance, policy formulation and implementation involve 'Commission, national, regional, and local officials as well as the social partners at all levels and stages of the policy process' (Schmidt, 2006: 67). Further, subnational governments are not the only domestic actors able to bypass national authorities by going directly to the EU level; organized interests lobby the Commission, and courts have direct links to the European Court of Justice (see Chapter 6).

Nowadays, multilevel forms of governance are no longer confined to federal states. Even in centralized states, the dispersion of material and immaterial resources necessary to govern, including local knowledge and trust on the part of those affected by policy, requires negotiation and cooperation across levels. This can be illustrated by the case of France where 'downward' decentralization beginning in the early 1980s, coupled with 'upward' Europeanization, led to a shift from the traditionally French tutelary state to more horizontal relations, and to decision-making negotiated in policy networks (CEPEL, 1996; Duran, 1999). This general trend towards MLG has to do with functional pressures for adjustment of:

> the scale of governance to the scale of collective problems. Where the externalities that arise from a problem such as providing clean air, minimising transaction costs of monetary exchange, or reducing trade barriers, are transnational in scope, the most efficient level of decision-making is similarly transnational. Where the externalities are local or regional, as for garbage collection or land-use planning, the most efficient level is subnational. (Hooghe and Marks, 2008: 114)

This should not be seen too mechanistically; in order to translate pressure into change in governance structure, political, business and other actors must frame it convincingly. These 'norm entrepreneurs' often have to engage in struggles with opponents who do not share their conception of the most efficient (or legitimate) level of governance; the debates on the breadth and depth of European integration are typical of such controversies. MLG thus appears to be a device for the management of fragmegration, that is, of 'simultaneous, diverse, and contradictory forces that can be summarized in the clash between globalization, centralization, and integration on the one hand, and localization, decentralization, and fragmentation on the other' (Rosenau, 2004: 34). As regards partnership logic, for instance, Bache emphasizes that 'in the context of globalisation and marketisation, it provides a mechanism for coordinating governance in complex and uncertain areas. In this difficult context it offers the potential to draw on the knowledge capacities of an array of actors to provide the most effective response to public policy dilemmas' (Bache, 2010: 58).

Although viewing policy-making in the EU as multilevel governance implies acknowledging that executives and government bureaucracies are not the only key players, MLG is not immune to democratic accountability problems. These problems will be scrutinized in the next chapter on cooperative forms of government, but let us mention here the crucial problem of 'many hands', or shared responsibility. If decisions are the outcome of negotiations between a large number of actors, who can be judged responsible for them? This problem is aggravated by the frequent informality of negotiations that inhibits public scrutiny, similar to the informal influence exerted by national parliaments on their governments in EU policy-making that cannot be checked. Accountability problems are exacerbated by the multilevel structure. The often-informal negotiations between decisional units not only lack visibility, but also tend to involve participants who are subject to administrative, rather than democratic, accountability, such as European, national, and subnational bureaucracies. Furthermore, in governance networks, even elected politicians who are in principle subject to citizens' control, are in reality subject to a two-level accountability process: they must account for their actions not only vertically to their constituencies, but also – or even primarily – horizontally to their peers, who are their negotiation partners (Papadopoulos, 2007).

As the preferences of negotiation peers may differ from those of voters, responsiveness to the latter's preferences is weakened. 'Europe has given us a vote of confidence', asserted former Greek prime minister Papademos back from Brussels in the beginning of March 2012 (Athens News, 2012) – a revealing formulation indeed for those who thought that votes of confidence are the prerogatives of parliaments! With MLG, the proportion of rulers' democratically accountable actions is diminished. In the next chapters we shall see that this is a more general trend, also induced by other processes such as administrative reform, the diffusion of independent agencies, and the empowerment of the judiciary (see Chapters 5 and 6).

## Overall assessment and prospects

Through the electoral mechanism, citizens in a sense authorize *ex ante* the incumbents to issue collectively binding decisions, and those affected by government policies can *ex post* vote the government party or parties out of office if they are dissatisfied. With the globalization of regulation, this circular relationship that generates a feeling of congruence between policy-makers and policy-takers is broken. Also, several sites of transnational decision-making are not sufficiently pluralist, visible, and formalized. The increasing involvement of NGOs in transnational governance has generated changes in policies at this level as well. However, NGO impact on international bodies should not be overestimated, and 'civil society' organizations do not escape representation and accountability deficits.

As regards the European Union, its democratic deficit is less acute than in other sites of governance beyond the nation-state, but it remains multifaceted. In addition, the internationalization of decision-making and Europeanization both seem to increase the domestic influence of the core executive observed with presidentialization (see Chapter 1). They have led to a strengthening of bureaucracies, and have accelerated the weakening of parliamentary institutions, whose influence on the policy process is in decline because of a number of factors, from a lack of knowledge of complex problems to the parliamentary discipline of governing parties that subordinates parliaments to the executive. True, some elected assemblies are becoming aware of their marginalization, and seek to stop deparliamentarization by increasing their influence on the executive. However, this often occurs behind closed doors, so that it is the public that is marginalized. The influence of policy-making bodies beyond and below the nation-state also leads to multilevel governance structures. This means that the formulation or the implementation of public policies takes place in networks that involve public agents who belong to different decisional levels, together with non-public participants. This is a more pluralist image of decision-making, but one should not forget that multilevel governance often implies informal negotiations among decisional units conducted, or at least largely prepared, by technocrats. They are seldom the object of media scrutiny and thus lack visibility. Figure 3.1. summarizes these developments.

In relative terms, the role of democratically accountable political action is diminished. Decisions resulting from European integration are criticized because they are produced in insufficiently legitimate processes. For example, a survey of frequently visited political websites and blogs during the European Parliament election campaign of 2009 concluded that the majority of contestation focuses on the institutional setup of the EU, and that negative evaluations are often justified with concerns for democracy (Wilde *et al.*, 2010: 8). European integration is also criticized because it negatively affects the condition of 'modernization losers'. Thus a new structural cleavage generated by the dynamics of internationalization began to reshape the political life and the partisan landscape of our democracies: the cleavage between a politics of supranational integration supported by winners and a politics of national demarcation supported by losers (Marks and Wilson, 2000;

Figure 3.1. *Internationalization of policy-making and the subsequent loss of democratic control*

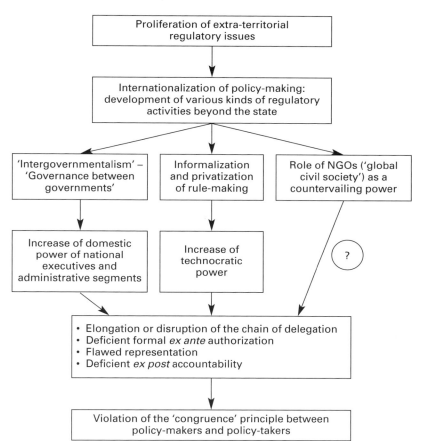

*Note*: The question mark refers to the fact that the positive or negative contribution of NGOs to democracy is a variable

Bornschier, 2005; Kriesi *et al.*, 2006). Those who benefit most from the mobilization of losers are the anti-establishment parties that present themselves as defenders of national identities and an alternative to a mostly pro-European political class that is insensitive to losers' concerns. Therefore, Europeanization reinforces distrust, populism, and the divide between citizens and elites, as discussed in Chapter 1.

However, what voters do not see (yet?) is that the democratic deficit is much larger at the transnational level beyond the EU. In transnational governance, the traditional features of a democratic polity are even less discernible than in the EU (Benz and Papadopoulos, 2006). Most notably, nothing reminiscent of a democratically elected assembly exists. When national democratically elected legislatures – if they exist – are asked to ratify international treaties, they have no latitude to influence their content. Their only option is take it or leave it, and states with no international influence have 'no practical way of excluding their people from the effects of the regime' (Braithwaite and Drahos, 2000: 609). Beyond the European level the chain of delegation is lengthier and more complex, and most people often ignore that important decisions affecting them are adopted at a global level. What is more, rules are increasingly formulated, or at least prepared, by informal or private regulatory bodies that do not enjoy legitimate public authority. People attached to democratic values would have good reason to be concerned about the poor democratic quality of policy-making procedures at this level of governance, yet they are hardly aware of their existence. The appeal of both sovereignist parties and anti-globalization movements is increasingly broad, but these political entrepreneurs have not yet seriously attacked these governance arenas. One may reasonably hypothesize that there is potential here for more contestation: 'the democratization of global governance will undoubtedly emerge as a defining feature of the twenty-first century' (Flinders, 2012: 24).

# Chapter 4

# Collaborative Governance and Cooperative Policy-Making

This chapter shows that cooperative forms of governance discussed in the context of 'multilevelness' in the previous chapter are part of a more general trend whereby the state loses 'its monopoly on collectively binding decision-making and on the production of public goods' (Pauly and Grande, 2005: 15). Thus, the nation-state's loss of centrality is related not only to 'multilevelness' but also to policy-making in networks that include non-state actors:

> In recent decades, we have witnessed the strengthening of international organizations; the establishment of new, regional levels of political decision-making; the emergence of new forms of governance and new types of interaction and cooperation between public and private actors; and the emergence of new roles for private actors in the production of public goods. (Pauly and Grande, 2005: 15)

The non-state actors' participation in the decision-making process can reach far beyond their traditional lobbying role. As discussed in the previous chapter, sometimes the production of public decisions and goods is entirely delegated to non-public actors. This is the case in so-called 'PIGs' (private interest governments) mostly composed of interest-group associations; they do not confine themselves to the narrow self-regulation of a specific sector such as vocational training, but produce decisions that affect broad and diffuse interests, such as those of consumers. Such decisions may even acquire the force of law through governmental 'imprimatur'. This is demonstrated by negotiated agreements between business and labour unions regarding economic and social policy matters, and by standards set by professional associations; in those cases, the authority of PIGs is not truly distinguishable from that of the government (Rudder, 2008).

Another, currently widespread, illustration of cooperative forms of policy-making is offered by various forms of durable joint ventures such as public–private partnerships (PPPs; see also Chapter 3), and by the creation of hybrid quasi-governmental organizations that have gained in importance over the last few decades in fields such as public transportation, health care, network industries, and educational infrastructures. Partnerships 'combine the resources of government with those of private agents (business or not-for-profit bodies) in order to deliver societal goals' (Skelcher, 2005a: 348), thus transcending the boundaries between public and private interests. Not only resources are shared between public and private actors, but also the risks and costs related to service delivery. In the United Kingdom, which is the European leader in the development of PPPs, between 1987 and April 2005, 665 contracts were signed between the central government and private actors, all in the framework of the 'private finance initiative'. These contracts generated private investments worth 62 billion Euros (Marty *et al.*, 2006: 4, 10).

More generally, the OECD (2002) defines 'distributed public governance' as 'the great number of "fringe bodies", extra-governmental organizations, independent non-majoritarian institutions and quasi-autonomous non-governmental organizations that form a significant and administratively dense component of modern governance structures' (quoted by Flinders, 2004: 520). As Haas (1992: 31) points out, such an enumeration denotes the fragmentation of power arenas that is linked to cooperative forms of governance:

> Decision-making, rather than being centralized, occurs within an amorphous set of subgovernments. Whether the parties involved are characterized as interest groups, iron triangles, advocacy coalitions, issue networks, or policy networks, the point is the same: small networks of policy specialists congregate to discuss specific issues, set agendas, and formulate policy alternatives outside the formal bureaucratic channels, and they also serve as brokers for admitting new ideas into decision-making circles of bureaucrats and elected officials.

Much has been said about the contribution (or lack thereof) of so-called 'new' forms of governance to policy effectiveness, but less about their overall impact on democratic governance. This is what this chapter is about: after explaining the reasons for preference for collaborative forms of governance, it discusses why and how these forms can cause representation and accountability problems that can be harmful to democratic policy-making. Non-majoritarian institutions will be treated distinctly (see Chapter 6); even if their diffusion is part of the general trend towards power fragmentation, unlike other institutions or procedures, they do not imply stronger cooperation with stakeholders. Rather, subjected to a more technocratic rationale, they rely on their own expertise, and their credibility is a function of their independence not only from public authorities but also from stakeholders such as members of the regulated sector.

## A move from 'government' to 'governance'?

Even though changes in policy styles can be driven by concerns about the crisis of state finances and by the managerialist paradigm that focuses on efficiency in the delivery of public goods, they should not be considered simply as the embodiment of neoliberal beliefs, neither should they be assimilated to marketization. Nowadays, there is indeed a common suspicion about the efficiency of top-down state action, but if privatization relies on market-based reforms, then cooperative policy-making relies on the role of networks, which provide a different means of regulation.

Collaborative forms of governance are also an embodiment of the 'subsidiarity' doctrine, according to which the production of public goods should, as much as possible, involve the private actors who are affected by their allocation. PPPs for instance are even welcomed by part of the Left when they have a communitarian or participatory orientation, and they have been considered part of a reflexive state that is committed to learning, especially when their designs contain provisions for monitoring and evaluation that are intended to foster continuous improvement of service delivery. On the other hand, tensions may appear between cooperative policy-making and other simultaneously implemented reforms in state action. According to Peters (2007), 'The New Public Management (NPM) has tended to influence government in the direction of utilizing markets more than political influences such as networks to make and implement policy', and this is likely to reduce the effectiveness of network-based forms of governance (p. 70). Whereas neoliberal inspiration encourages actors into competitive relations, PPPs rely on a collaborative logic (Bevir, 2010: 184–5), and advocates of regulation through trust-based networks fear that competition may destroy them (Olsen, 2005: 7). Nevertheless, it has also been asserted, in the United Kingdom at least, that marketization boosts network governance, albeit as an unexpected consequence. According

to Bevir and Rhodes (2007: 78), Margaret Thatcher's government tried
to reduce the power of long-standing networks:

> by using markets to deliver public services, bypassing existing
> networks and curtailing the 'privileges' of professions, commonly
> by subjecting them to rigorous financial and management controls.
> But these corporate management and marketisation reforms had
> unintended consequences. They fragmented the systems for deliver-
> ing public services, creating pressures for organisations to co-oper-
> ate with one another to deliver services. In other words,
> marketisation multiplied the networks it intended to replace.

It is often claimed that cooperative policy-making represents a shift
from government's vertical steering of society to the more horizontal,
network-based form of 'governance'. Here, 'government' refers to the
textbook image of public regulation, whereby the political system has
a legitimate monopoly over issuing collectively binding decisions and
employing coercion in order to enforce them. Apparently, in many
policy fields this *modus operandi* is no longer the rule. Many recent
studies focusing on different policy sectors in diverse national and local
environments have found a broad convergence toward a cooperative
policy-making style. This style of governing refers to 'sustaining coordination and coherence among a wide variety of actors with different
purposes and objectives such as political actors and institutions, corporate interests, civil society, and transnational governments' (Pierre,
2000: 3–4). The quote from Pauly and Grande in the beginning of this
chapter emphasizes the novelty of the situation. Nevertheless, one
should avoid an evolutionist bias; neither the amplitude of the shift nor
the novelty of cooperative forms of governance should be overstated.

The trend towards collaborative governance is most perceptible in
highly centralized polities with traditions of strong states. France is a
prime example thereof: in this 'textbook' case of state centralization,
the decentralization that began in the 1990s led to the emergence of
network forms of governance at urban and regional levels. These
networks formulated contracts that were negotiated between various
public and non-public actors (Le Galès, 1995; Gaudin, 1999).
However, one may ask if the conventional image of French centralization is not excessively guided by a formalistic reading of the policy
implementation process, which passes under silence the compromises
and arrangements that state agents had to make with powerful groups
locally, well before the first wave of decentralization reforms began in

the early 1980s (Crozier and Friedberg, 1977; Padioleau, 1982). Thus, perhaps the changes observed more recently are of degree, but not of nature.

In Anglo-American literature about political science, several works – written decades ago – have identified *de facto* 'subgovernments' playing a major role in policy formulation, and composed of cohesive 'policy communities' in which public and private actors closely cohabit. As reminded by Haas (see above), 'iron triangles', comprising specialized politicians, bureaucrats, and interest representatives, used to control decision-making about key issues (such as agricultural policy) in which especially large economic interests were at stake. Several small European countries have been characterized by collaborative forms of governance for decades, if not centuries. In so-called 'pillarized' countries (culturally heterogeneous societies segmented along religious or linguistic groups, such as Belgium or the Netherlands), service delivery in the field of education or health care has been widely delegated, in a logic of 'subsidiarity', to nonprofit organizations subsidized by the state and closer to the Protestant or Catholic religious 'pillars'. In countries such as Austria, Germany, and Sweden, 'corporatist' arrangements between peak associations that represented business and labour interests used to prepare political decisions in economic or social policies, and the same organizations often managed their implementation (see Pierre and Peters, 2000: 199).

Collaborative governance translates into *de facto* power fragmentation, even in formally majoritarian systems of government. For instance, a comparative study of three policy sectors in seven European democracies showed that even in the United Kingdom, which 'constitutes Lijphart's paradigmatic case for a majoritarian democracy, its policy networks have a fragmented character which actually resembles the characteristics of Swiss networks, the paradigmatic case of a consensus democracy' (Kriesi *et al.*, 2006a: 350). 'Governance was pre-eminent at the turn of the century, obsolete in the 1960s, and reinvented in the 1980s', notes R.A.W. Rhodes (2003: 71), the political scientist who introduced the 'governance narrative' – also called the 'differentiated polity narrative' (Bevir and Rhodes, 2008) – in the United Kingdom. The traditional Westminster model of British politics, which is dominated by the prime minister and the core executive and characterized by the absence of checks and formal 'veto points', is today challenged by this 'differentiated polity narrative'. This view depicts the Westminster narrative as a 'smokescreen' that has 'distorting' effects on the public's comprehension of the system (Bevir and

Rhodes, 2006: 671). According to this line of thinking, the British core executive is not unified under a strong leadership; rather, prime ministers act under constraint, co-ordination is rather unrealistic, ministries are segmented in 'baronial politics' and have to engage in bargaining with the sectors under their jurisdiction, and the implementation of laws at street-level is problematic. In addition, there is much scholarly agreement today on the description of the United Kingdom as a system of multilevel governance due to institutional devolution. Scholars also emphasize that through EU cohesion policy, the process of Europeanization led to the development of single-issue jurisdictions, agencies, partnerships, and networks in this country, including the voluntary and community sectors at the subnational level (Bache, 2008: 17–18).

The reader may however reasonably object that this trend contrasts with the executive face of the 'presidentialization' of politics (Chapter 1). It seems that this happens only on the surface: 'While enhancing its coordinating power in the domain which it regards as particularly critical, the core executive attempts to reduce the scope of its direct responsibility for government', as acknowledged by the proponents of the 'presidentialization' thesis (Poguntke and Webb, 2005: 14). More radically, the proponents of the 'differentiated polity narrative' consider the centralization process within the British cabinet not as a sign of leadership strength but as a sign of leadership weakness: 'The center grabs desperately for new levers of control precisely because it finds its efforts at control are frustrated' (Bevir, 2010: 255). In any case, interpretations accentuating 'court' government (strong prime ministerial leadership and concentration of power; see Chapter 1) may not be suitable for generalization to countries remote from the Westminster majoritarian model, in which prime ministers must negotiate with the leaderships of parties forming the governmental coalition. More generally, those interpretations probably overstate the strategic capacity and latitude of political leaders, since cooperation and power delegation may not be a matter of choice but rather a decision made under constraint.

As the proponents of the presidentialization thesis themselves assert, 'Leaders may have more control over policy decisions than in the past, but they will not necessarily have improved their ability to achieve desired policy objectives' (Poguntke and Webb, 2005: 22). Numerous works on implementation deficits and failure now confirm this. The difficulties involved in steering under conditions of power fragmentation are also apparent in attempts at administrative reform.

It seems that after a first period in which politicians granted more autonomy to managers, they want to regain control over the administration through political appointments (see Chapter 5). Additionally, the creation of formally independent regulatory agencies did not necessarily imply that they are *de facto* autonomous from government (see Chapter 6). Not only, as suggested before, may cooperative forms of governance not be new, but hierarchical forms of governance may not have declined (Hill and Lynn, 2005): these are limits to the validity of evolutionist accounts of governance 'shifts'.

However, policy networks tend to become denser and more intricate along with the growing awareness of problem complexity and along with the growing social fragmentation that is reflected in the increasingly varied groups that claim to have influence in political decisions. In a paradoxical sense, despite the decline of membership in the social organizations mentioned in Chapter 1, 'More and more associations, movements, and foundations are chasing after members and funds to support ever more specific definitions of collective interests and passion' (Schmitter and Trechsel, 2004: 55). The consequence for political systems is that more interest groups and associations are (in one form or another) involved in the decision-making process, and more experts are now called upon to give advice – simply because interest pluralism tends to be reflected in the heterogeneity of experts' views as well.

## Why collaborative governance?

The older literature on 'iron triangles' or 'policy communities' would consider such manifestations of collaborative governance, at best, as the sign of a commonality of thought among policy-makers coming from diverse universes, and, at worst, as the consequence of the collusion between public officials and powerful private groups, leading to private interests' capture of public decisions. It did not treat networks as the product of reflection by public authorities, who are basically animated by two kinds of concerns: the concern to take appropriate decisions that solve complex social problems by relying on sound technical knowledge, and the concern to implement these decisions smoothly in a context of social fragmentation in which it is likely that various groups find good reasons (in their view) to object to them.

Modern societies are split along various cleavages, such as those related to class divisions and to functional specializations; for example, the interests and worldviews of lawyers or medical doctors are not the same as those of artists or scientists. Increasingly, our societies are also fragmented along lines of cultural identities and particular lifestyles. Thus, societies experiencing centrifugal forces are likely to suffer from a lack of solidarity and cohesion. It is wise to assume that individual and collective actors are often short-sighted because they are motivated by their self-interest or because it is cognitively difficult for them to include others or the future in their considerations. Free-riding (in which one benefits from the allocation of collective goods while evading contribution to their production costs) and exiting (in which one moves to settings where the cost–benefit ratio of collective goods is more profitable) are options available to individuals, firms, groups, organizations, or even entire nation-states that are eager to maximize their narrow interests. Often, these actors are not very concerned about the diffuse costs (to taxpayers, consumers, or future generations) of the policy options that they are keen to see implemented.

German sociologist Norbert Elias (1991: 187–91) showed that, paradoxically, along with the growth of inter-individual interdependence the valuation of individualism rises. A similar paradox is observable at the collective level; for example, the scientific community is jealous of its independence, even though, in reality, scientific research is heavily dependent on external (public or private) funding. Moreover, the social consequences of scientific discoveries may be negative, which pleads for some form of supervision over scientific activities. Private rent-seeking or simply the rational pursuit of sectoral interests can generate negative externalities. This kind of interdependence, in which one causes harm and the other suffers it, is common in interstate relations (consider cross-border pollution). But the same problem exists when parts of society are obliged to suffer the costs of decisions made by other segments. For example, the problem of stress at work is generated by (understandable) goals of economic performance; nevertheless, it affects not only the labour force but also the country's health system, the costs of which increase explosively. It is unsurprising that governments are under pressure to deal with this kind of problem. This can be depicted as the need to regulate competition between autonomous social spheres and their organizational embodiments, eloquently portrayed by Olsen (2005: 15–16):

> Within a common set of values and morals in society, modernity involved an extensive differentiation among spheres with different organizational patterns, norms and values, roles, vocabularies,

resources, and dynamics.... There are intrusions and attempts to achieve ideological hegemony and control over other institutional spheres, and institutional imperialism may threaten to destroy what is distinct about other institutional spheres. However, there is also institutional defence against the invasion of alien norms.

There is thus a social demand to combat externalities caused by the self-referential operation of autonomous social spheres and, more generally, to counteract the centrifugal dynamics of fragmentation among sectoral, territorial, class, or lifestyle communities. However, such a task cannot be carried out only through coercive public intervention; it also requires interactive coordination among the interdependent actors (Leca, 1996: 340). Public authorities are required to ensure the 'management of interdependence' (Mayntz, 1997: 272), but they are themselves in a situation of interdependence when they perform this role. It is this kind of paradox that drives the advent of collaborative forms of governance in which the state is a *primus inter pares*. The diffusion of these forms of governance is driven by the view that public steering is desirable, but the state's steering capacity is relatively low. Cooperative policy-making styles derive from the perception of limits on the effectiveness of vertical steering of social life by the state. As suggested again by Olsen (2005: 7):

It is argued that no single political center can legitimately claim to represent the public and the common good, issue commands, and expect compliance. Attempts to command are likely to generate withdrawal of cooperation, noncompliance, and a loss of trust, and a defining activity of administration is building support and mobilizing resources. Popular elections and majority government are not the only source of legitimacy. Demands and support are not channelled solely via the institutions of representative democracy, and citizenship involves more than voting.

Pierre and Peters (2000) attribute the (probably increasing) awareness of state limits to globalization, state financial crises, policy failures, market-focused ideology, and the diffusion of New Public Management reform (see Chapters 3 and 5). In complex and highly differentiated – sometimes even deeply culturally fragmented or strongly individualized – societies, state bureaucracies seldom control all the resources required to provide adequate and effective responses to social problems. Hood (1983) identified four 'tools of government', all of them necessary for effective and efficient policy-making: nodality (that is location in a strategic or 'nodal' position in a communication network), authority, treasure, and organization. State bureaucracies must resort to some form of external cooperation in order to acquire some of these governing tools, such as knowledge (learning how to handle problems whose causes are complex, uncertain, and unstable), authority (in order to avoid blackmail by groups that are able to block decisions, and generate compliance by policy-takers), finances (needed to provide services and to conduct redistributive policies), and organization (required to achieve sufficient capacity to implement policy choices effectively).

Financial resources are needed to implement most policies that are intended to enhance collective welfare and well-being, and an efficient bureaucracy is needed in order to produce appropriate regulations and monitor their implementation. But the extractive capacity of the state (its ability to raise public money through taxation) depends on a flourishing economy and on the presence of large corporate taxpayers who find no reason to emigrate to more favourable fiscal environments. Furthermore, to produce effective policies, public agents must possess specific kinds of knowledge. In a complex society, the targets of public intervention are often 'black boxes' for public agents. Adequate technical knowledge of the causes of social problems is needed to avoid policy mistakes, but this knowledge must often be pooled from actors close to the policy sector or local territory to which public regulations apply.

In addition, governments require knowledge about the degree of policy acceptance demonstrated by those affected by public regulations. Authority itself features prominently among the resources that a state may lack; as a result, target groups' compliance with public decisions can be deficient. Actors may contend that the state should make decisions favourable to their interests, but at the same time, resist state intervention that they consider unfavourable. Because the mere issuance of formally binding decisions does not always implicate compliance with them, governments are obliged to resort to 'softer' instruments of persuasion, and they seek to convince policy addressees that their decisions are necessary and wise. Hence, governments must not only be sensitive to knowledge input, but must also persuade and diffuse knowledge output; indeed, they must locate themselves in 'nodal' points of communication flows.

State agents thus become embedded in a complex web of interdependence with other organizations, groups, or even with private actors such as powerful firms. In such a context of interdependence, policy efficiency appears to be a function of coordinated intervention under public leadership. The establishment of policy networks is considered an adequate way to promote integration because within networks, actors communicate and exchange with each other. Networks are an arena of mutual deliberation (under the force of others' arguments, actors may change their preferences and include considerations initially ignored by them) or at least a negotiation arena in which bargaining actors seek to work out policy solutions, taking into consideration a broader array of concerns and interests. In the United Kingdom, for instance, 'joined-up' forms of government are devised to favour communication between the various actors involved in service delivery, such as non-profit organizations, public agencies attached to different territorial levels, and the private sector. Such forms have developed in areas as diverse as school management, community policing, watershed policy, land planning, and community health (Ansell and Gash, 2007).

'Good governance' and 'the deliberative imperative' have now become core ingredients of what is advertised as an adequate policy-making style that involves civil society in collective deliberation (Blondiaux and Sintomer, 2002). The number of non-state actors who enjoy a *de facto* veto power in policy formulation or implementation (business, trade unions, residents, and so on) is non negligible, and they are especially eager to exert this power if they distrust governments or bureaucracies (Tyler, 1998). Bureaucracies seek to secure consent to their policies and restore trust to themselves through closer stakeholder involvement in the policy-making process. This kind of involvement, though somewhat valuable in its own merits, is above all deemed to bring policies more in line with the wishes of their addressees. This has been referred to as a quest for 'output legitimacy' (Scharpf, 1999) or, to use a classic distinction by David Easton (1965), as a quest for 'specific support' of policies, which can then spill over into 'diffuse support' of the whole political system.

Thus, engaging non-public actors in more horizontal policy-making is not a voluntaristic attempt to democratize decision-making, but rather a piecemeal strategy that primarily results from the pragmatic and instrumental concerns of policy-makers. According to Wolf (2002: 40), 'The primary normative guideline for governance is not democracy but legitimacy'. Gbikpi and Grote (2002: 23) also emphasize the functional rationale of cooperative policy-making:

> Participatory governance is definitely less a matter of democracy in the sense of institutionalizing a set of procedures for electing those

in charge of the policy-making, than it is a kind of second best solution for approaching the question of effective participation of the persons likely to be affected by the policies design.... [P]articipation can be effective in the realisation of policy objectives because it can help to overcome problems of implementation by considering motives and by fostering the willingness of policy addressees to comply as well as through the mobilisation of the knowledge of those affected.

As noted before, social fragmentation makes state intervention simultaneously necessary and delicate. In fragmented societies, all sorts of groups claim that their interests should be protected; in other words, they express 'intense' preferences on particular policy issues that deserve, according to them, to be given high priority by policy-makers. Even though public authorities can claim that they are authorized to act by the electoral legitimacy they enjoy, majoritarian power is not sufficiently authoritative in situations of social fragmentation. A prominent illustration of such a limitation is offered by policies that have spatial consequences. For example, the development of the railway system may be considered beneficial for a community as a whole, but these benefits are too dispersed among a large constituency to be visible, or they only become visible in the long term. On the other hand, residents of neighbouring areas will tend to emphasize the costs that such a development generates at their expense, such as noise pollution or damage to the landscape. Infrastructures ranging from highways to nuclear plants are often viewed as public 'bads' – not public goods – by those whose quality of life or environment is thereby deteriorated or even merely threatened. This gives rise to the so-called 'nimby' syndrome ('Not in my backyard!'); those who are subject to high concentrated costs will not agree to balance any global benefits of the policy. The electoral legitimacy of the government that opts for the measures that affect those people so negatively does not make them feel more positive.

   This is but one example showing how much public actors' exercise of their power is dependent on resources held by non-public actors, including the capacity to resist state intervention (Papadopoulos, 1995; Pierre and Peters, 2005). Further, regulatory efficiency requires contextual adaptability. Hence, there is a need for regulation to be frequently adjusted in the light of changing needs. Experimentation, 'trial and error', provisional 'sunset laws', and policy evaluations are considered to be learning and reflexive mechanisms that ensure, thanks to their flexibility, that legislation adequately solves changing complex problems. The practice of policy evaluation, for example, has increasingly moved from a purely top-down approach, in which what counted was whether the goals set by the legislators were attained, to a more horizontal and pluralistic approach, in which a consensus on goals and means is sought amidst the most relevant stakeholders.

Collaborative governance also leaves its mark on policy instruments; 'hard' law is losing its grip as an instrument of political regulation, and is increasingly replaced by 'soft' law. Soft law is defined as regulation that aims to change the behaviour of targeted groups, even though it does not entail any formal obligation and is not accompanied by legal sanctions for non-compliance. It takes the form of recommendations, guidelines, gentleman's agreements, professional and ethical codes, standards, and so on. Compliance is no longer based on coercion but is rather (more or less) voluntary, relying on mechanisms such as peer pressure and naming and shaming. Yet there is often an obligation to report one's efforts to adjust to non coercively enforceable regulations. We know that soft law plays an important role at the transnational level, and the same increasingly happens at European level, most notably with the open method of coordination (OMC). The role of soft law in domestic settings, such as environmental policy, is not negligible either. It has the same origin as the shift to collaborative governance; it stems from the state's inability to impose regulations in a top-down manner. Whereas the shift to collaborative governance mainly refers to the changing constellation of agents involved in policy-making, the shift to soft law refers to a change in policy instruments. In a context of strong interest differentiation coupled with resource fragmentation, emphasis is placed on influence and persuasion rather than on command because decision-makers know that if powerful actors object to state policies, it may be impossible to force compliance.

It is true that soft law may not be the outcome of negotiation with non-public actors; public agents can decide by themselves to regulate through persuasion and the dissemination of information. Similarly, hard law may be the outcome of negotiated agreements or delegated regulation; non-public agents such as professional associations obtain delegated authority from the state to issue standards or codes of conduct, which, in a second step, may receive public endorsement and thus become binding. However, soft law is also better accepted when it is produced in agreement with – or even directly by – the kind of non-state participants who are involved in governance networks; in such a case, the trends towards soft law and network governance are related. One problem with 'soft' law, however, is its tendency to be 'fuzzy' law (Chevallier, 2004); negotiated agreements, for instance, are almost inevitably formulated vaguely. The margin for law interpretation is broadened, and that strengthens the influence of the judiciary, which simultaneously increases for other reasons too (see Chapter 6). This causes a loss of influence for the traditional representative circuit of party-parliamentary democracy – unfortunately not the only negative impact of collaborative governance on the quality of democracy, as argued in the next part of this chapter.

## Collaborative governance, representation, and accountability

Collaborative governance appears as a correlate of policy-making under the combined constraints of problem complexity, the pluralism of social forces and resource interdependence. Problem-solving and compromise-seeking are the rule in governance arenas, which are characterized by cooperative relationships rather than top-down regulation. Accordingly, the proper functioning of governance networks demands the accommodative orientation of their participants, who are expected to demonstrate an inclination for compromise and possibly even a shared willingness to learn from each other. The problem with such an 'irenic' conception of networks is that it obscures power relations among their members and between network members and outsiders.

In principle, the inclusion in policy-making of stakeholders and 'civil society' organizations through network governance may be seen as a promising step towards a more horizontal, open process of decision-making that is politically less coercive and socially more pluralistic. However, determining whose claims are legitimate or who can be considered a credible 'stakeholder' and hence deserving of recognition is, in reality, often the outcome of a power struggle. Moreover, those with a presence in policy networks, and thus influence, are likely to erect barriers against the participation of newcomers. Lord (2004: 114) writes:

> Instead of balancing and checking one another, networks or their members may collude to suspend competitiveness between themselves, to reduce prospects of challenge from the constituencies to which they are supposedly accountable, and to freeze new entrants out of access to the benefits of engagement with the political system.

Even without adhering to this perhaps cynical view, there are clear structural barriers to participation in governance networks. These barriers first affect the capacity of interests to undertake collective action. Paradoxically, broad interests find it harder to organize them-selves than narrow interests because peer pressure is lower and the benefits of collective action more diffuse (Olson, 1965). Further, in order to be included in networks, actors must possess resources that are unevenly distributed. For instance, a crucial resource is organiza-tion; no one would include neighbourhood residents in a policy process unless they had formed some type of association. Selectivity flows not only from inequalities but from imperatives of governability; the costs of bargaining and consensus building increase with the number of participant actors, and network designers or managers consider that 'overcrowding' complicates the policy-making process. Another complicating factor is heterogeneity of views. Hence, networks may be reluctant to include non-mainstream actors who are unwilling to 'play the game'. Some groups are thus excluded, while others might not wish to join networks likely to forge compromises, thereby further reducing their pluralism.

Even if organizational pluralism is safeguarded, this is not tanta-mount to democracy: stakeholders and advocacy groups are coopted because of the intense preferences they manifest on policy issues, but they cannot be equated with the *demos*. The opening up of policy processes to civil society depends on the principle of affectedness and thus on the inclusion of particular interests. It replaces the egalitarian principle of 'one person, one vote' by the principle of stakeholderism, whereby actors who are eligible for participation can credibly claim that they fight for causes that are of vital interest to them. In a sense, collab-orative governance can be considered as the output facet of advocacy democracy, in a period where – as noted in previous chapters – parties appear to be in decline as effective agents of governance. However, in practice, weaker advocacy groups often face a dilemma between enter-ing networks, at the cost of watering down their claims, or staying outside, at the cost of losing policy influence. For instance, while study-ing the restructuring of the Canadian welfare regime, Jenson and Phillips (2001) pointed to crucial problems raised by 'partnerships', such as the alteration of some NGOs' natures and the creation of hier-archies among them (pp. 85–6). NGOs focused on service delivery were privileged while those focused on advocacy and social change were considered irrelevant. As noted previously, those stigmatized as extrem-ists are likely to be excluded from collaborative governance.

After emphasizing the risk of limited 'horizontal' pluralism in networks, the risk of a bias in 'vertical' representation relations must also be mentioned; the existence of sufficiently tight links between actors involved in networks and the constituencies that they claim to represent should not be taken for granted. The network partners of public officials may be no more than self-proclaimed interest representatives, or even 'professional advocates', according to Stoker (2006: 107). Having carefully scrutinized partnerships in France, Gaudin (1995: 92) considered them to be the domain of 'established spokespersons of elusive populations'. Civil society actors involved in collaborative governance may suffer from external accountability deficits (see Chapter 3). Even when organizations claim to represent broad interests, they are seldom accountable to the populations whose concerns they allegedly voice. The leadership and membership of public-interest NGOs such as those concerned with environmental issues often have an upper- or new middle-class bias.

Another problem has to do with the possible internal accountability deficits of advocacy groups; the link may be too weak not only between representatives and those whom they claim to be their constituencies, but also between organizational leaderships and the rank and file. Representation and accountability problems can be aggravated by the proximity of civil society organizations to decision-makers. The attribution of a public status may necessitate both concessions to the goals of state bureaucracies and compromises with the demands of other interests that may not be supported by the basis of organizations (Offe, 1981). This points to possible contradictions between the 'logic of influence' and the 'logic of members' (Schmitter and Streeck, 1999). The more an organization cedes to the logic of influence for efficiency reasons, which requires a capacity of its leaderships to negotiate freely with partners whose preferences differ, the more the internal gap between elites and the rank and file tends to increase. State recognition or public funding (in the case of the European Union, by the Commission) generates additional problems. Coopted organizations are expected to provide expertise, so they often must rely on professional staffs whose connections to militants are tenuous. True, since the state depends on the resources provided by the coopted organizations (such as expertise or trust among regulatees), it also risks being subject to blackmail and capture by particular interests. Yet the balance may be tipped in the reverse direction too; the attribution of public status consolidates the influence of an organization, but it is likely to reduce its independence from the state. This creates a grey zone of uncertainty regarding the winners of such 'games'.

If organizational elites are remote from organization members or from the groups they claim to represent, then there is clearly a problem with their accountability; elites or organizations are not under sufficient pressure to inform those they should keep informed, nor to justify their options to them. Those who should be kept informed then have few opportunities to impose sanctions. Accountability problems of network governance are not only related to representation (Papadopoulos, 2003; 2007). They can also derive from weak coupling between governance arenas (committees, working groups, round tables, and the like) and the institutions of representative democracy (most notably parliaments), which are formally authorized and legitimized to make collectively binding decisions on behalf of populations.

We know that the legitimacy of decisions made by the representative democratic system is grounded on the circular relation between policy-makers and policy-takers: through the mechanism of competitive elections, policy-takers authorize *ex ante* a governmental team to produce, in their name, decisions that affect them, and governments in turn operate under the shadow of *ex post* sanctions by policy-takers in forthcoming elections, if the latter are not satisfied with their record. With the internationalization of politics, the congruence between policy-makers and takers is disrupted. Chapter 6 will also explain that the circular relation between policy-makers and takers may be deliberately broken if some governmental elements, like regulatory agencies, are uncoupled by design from the democratic process on the grounds of efficiency. As regards network governance, the decreasing importance of parliamentary institutions at the national, the European and, above all, the transnational level impacts the degree of its coupling with the representative circuit (Benz and Papadopoulos, 2006). Nevertheless, even in the presence of fully fledged parliamentary bodies, governance networks may emancipate from them. This generates yet another problem of accountability – not of network participants to their basis or to affected populations, but of networks as a whole to official decision-making institutions.

Research on this kind of coupling is an emerging field. Studies of network forms of governance have long been dominated by managerial considerations regarding efficiency, and they have mainly focused on the quality of output delivery. Yet the consequences of these forms of governance for the democratic quality of the policy process are significant. 'Governance *with some of* the people', writes Vivien Schmidt (2006), cannot make up for 'the lack of government *by* and *of* the people' (pp. 28–9; emphasis in the original). There are few empirical works addressing this problem with a comparative framework that allows for the assessment of variation across cases. They offer, however, some first insights on how collaborative governance schemes perform with respect to democratic authorization, representation, and accountability.

Some years ago, a comparative overview of policy network studies in Germany, the United States, Japan, and Switzerland suggested that in most cases, the influential actors were not parties or parliamentary bodies, but rather executive bureaucracies and corporations (Schneider, 2000: 253–5). A more recent comparative study concludes that state agents are the most powerful group in policy-making (Kriesi *et al.*, 2006a: 354). This qualifies the idea that governance means a 'hollowing out' of the state, yet is not necessarily good news for representative democracy and political parties. Although it is not clear from the text who the state agents are, their influence in the policy-making process is (according to the study) stronger than the influence of parties, the traditional sources of preference aggregation and policy formation. A recent study by Skelcher *et al.* (2011) comes to less pessimistic conclusions. It found substantial cross-national variation between the United Kingdom, Switzerland, the Netherlands, and Denmark in the relationship between governance networks and representative institutions, depending on patterns of democracy (majoritarian or consensual) and on the vibrancy of the associational nexus. There are stark contrasts between countries regarding the presence of elected officials in local partnership boards (Skelcher, 2009: 168–9). Nevertheless, this does not seem to be a sufficient indicator of politicians' influence. Another comparative study (Bache and Olsson, 2001), which showed that elected officials participated in partnership bodies in Sweden but not in the United Kingdom, also suggested that this hardly made any difference because even in Sweden the influence of politicians was negligible. Kübler and Schwab (2007) analysed 20 schemes of policy coordination in five Swiss metropolitan areas in the fields of water supply, public transport, social services for drug users, and cultural amenities. They found that contextual factors account for differences even within a single country. Overall, their evidence is mixed: according to them, the shift from government to governance does not intrinsically imply democratic drawbacks. The results suggest that 'governance' is indeed superior to 'government' in terms of inclusiveness, but it cannot be seen as significantly linked to the fostering of deliberative decision-making, and it has serious flaws in terms of accountability.

Since the available evidence is anecdotal, and probably can only be anecdotal because there are countless governance arrangements characterized by large variation, it is hard to formulate general conclusions with regard to the degree of power of elected officials. What can be asserted for certain is that in the complex processes of network governance, elected politicians are not necessarily at the core of policy-making, even though they are highly visible as decision-makers thanks to media attention (Klijn, 2008: 25). To be more precise, with mediatization politicians may have become less dependent on public managers as regards knowledge pooling (Chapter 1), but they may have ceded power to them through the tasks of administering the governance networks that they perform. We may hypothesize that the consolidation of cooperative forms of governance has first been facilitated by the weakening of partisan organizations, and that it now further undermines parties' functions in a self-reinforcing process. This does not only apply to the OECD world; in the rhetoric of global institutions such as the World Bank, which bandies about 'good governance' as a catchword, it is primarily the involvement of civil society organizations that is praised, whereas political parties are suspected to be part of the corrupt world of illegitimate rulers.

The presence of elected politicians may be marginal in policy networks, but are authorized bodies such as parliaments able to oversee the operations of collaborative governance bodies effectively? Do parliaments constrain network members to deliberate or bargain under the threat that their decisions will be overruled, thus forcing them to anticipate their objections? Can the lack of direct influence be compensated for by this kind of indirect influence through the 'shadow of hierarchy'? We can only make conjectures on that. For instance, it may make a difference whether mechanisms of collaborative governance are established in the process of law-making (that is formulating the principles, norms, and rules of a policy) or in the process of implementation (that is making policy decisions on how to interpret and implement what is in the law). In the first case, it is more likely that the preferences of elected politicians will be taken into account, because they are the target group that must be convinced. In the second case, however, it is mainly segments from the administration (often at the local or regional level) that cooperate and deliberate with civil society actors, and this happens remotely from the politicians who made the decisions.

Yet another problem is that governance networks seldom operate under public scrutiny. Collaborative governance is usually based on less formal modes of decision-making, within structures that are hardly visible from the mass public. Hence, not only the problem of deficient coupling with democratically authorized institutions, but also problems of opacity undermine accountability. A study of business-improvement districts charged with revitalizing, through various devices, commercial districts in the United States and the United Kingdom sought to assess their legitimacy grounded on authorization, the degree of consent on the process, account-giving, and sanctions. The authors (Justice and Skelcher, 2009: 750) emphasize their 'club' characteristics and conclude that 'it is noticeable how wider notions of a "public" are generally absent from these forms of private, third-party government. This introduces questions about how the public interest is assured.'

Accountability was also systematically analysed in a study of two 'mega' projects entailing network forms of governance in Nordic countries (the building of a bridge across the Fehmarn Belt between Germany and Denmark, and the application of the Norwegian city of Tromsö for the Winter Olympics). The authors (Aarsether *et al.*, 2009) scrutinized whether participants in the network felt constrained to justify their options, and also if accountability operated 'upward' to political authorities with the latter being then able to control the network, 'outward' with the development of contacts with the affected stakeholders, and 'downward' to the citizenry at large with the existence of public debate on the issues. In spite of a favourable context due to the presence of a vivid democratic culture in Nordic states, evidence is mixed again: the Fehmarn Belt forum showed a high degree of accountability on two of these dimensions, but the Tromsö network showed accountability on none of them.

Public–private partnerships exemplify the possible addition of delegation and accountability problems. In order to keep the upper hand in designing and monitoring the partnerships – in other words, to be an effective player (Skelcher, 2005a) – public authorities must have resources in terms of knowledge or negotiation skills that are not always available to them. This is especially true since the decision to set up PPPs may precisely result from a lack of state resources. Problems related to delegation are aggravated by the fact that PPPs often operate remotely from democratically elected institutions. Skelcher *et al.* (2005) studied 26 partnerships, covering the issues of economic development, crime reduction, health improvement, and educational enhancement for preschool children, in two medium sized local government areas in the United Kingdom with contrasted characteristics ('Mid Town' is a compact urban area within a large metropolitan region, while 'West Shire' is predominantly rural). The evaluation is, once again, mixed: they found that delivery of public policy outcomes was privileged over due process norms, and more specifically delivering gains in public welfare mattered more than the respect of norms ensuring legitimacy, consent, and accountability. The authors conclude that partnership governance offers flexibility at the cost of conventional notions of democratic performance. In addition, the professional staffs of NGOs, which form a significant part of partnerships' board members, operate quite independently. They autonomously decide whether to confer with their organizations about matters discussed in board meetings. This is clearly a manifestation of the more specific internal accountability deficit identified above.

## More horizontal governance, less democracy?

Figure 4.1 summarizes the social origins and the political consequences of collaborative governance.

As noted in regard to forms of governance beyond the democratic state of which the mass public is unaware, those forms' accountability gap would increase if they became more visible. The same applies to network forms of governance within the nation-state that lack visibility: often amorphous and informal, policy-making through networks is not visible to outsiders. Peters (2007: 71), for instance, sees no reason why collaborative governance should be unaffected by the consequences of decreased faith in public action, even though it is considered by policy-makers, experts, or academics as an alternative to more conventional and dirigist forms of state action. What still prevents the diffusion of negative views on collaborative governance is the fact that ordinary citizens ignore not only what happens (even the decisions that affect them) in networked forms of governance, but also even the sheer existence of such policy-making arenas.

It would, however, be wrong to adhere to a conspiratorial view of politics: governance by networks is not the outcome of a usurpation of power. Rather, it emerges for functional reasons, because effective steering and efficient regulation in the face of wicked problems cannot only rely on the limited public resources. In addition, the properties of policy networks that are incompatible with the requirements of democratic representation or accountability are structural, not the result of deliberate action on behalf of malevolent rulers. At this point, one can

Figure: 4.1.    *Social origins and political consequences of collaborative governance*

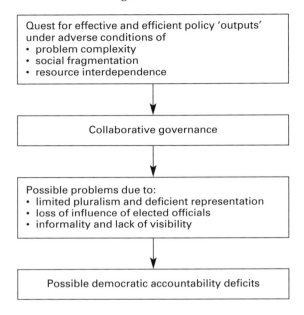

only conclude that through collaborative governance (this chapter) and internationalization (Chapter 3), the proportion of activities that affect ordinary people's lives but escape public scrutiny is increasing despite mediatization (Chapter 2). This clearly prejudices democratic accountability. The lack of visibility of governance networks is not the only problem. Collaborative governance requires 'metagovernance' and this task is often delegated to bureaucracies enjoying considerable discretion, or even to private experts in conflict management. Not only the direct, but also the indirect influence – the 'shadow of hierarchy' – of elected officials in collaborative governance schemes is limited.

Governance networks often include stakeholders with intense preferences to satisfy the requirements of pluralism. With networks, we observe a *de facto* fragmentation of power, even in systems of government where power is held to be concentrated in the head of government; policy 'coproduction' may thus be seen as a counter-trend to presidentialization. Concentration of power in the core executive can, paradoxically, go hand in hand with a diminishing autonomous policy-making capacity of the government. However, this does not necessarily benefit the citizenry, but rather the best-organized segments thereof. In governance through networks there is no room for the exercise of policy influence based on the egalitarian principle 'one person, one vote'. Although it is possible that participatory governance relying on citizens-as-stakeholders supplements representative government relying on citizens-as-voters (Skelcher and Torfing, 2010: 76), the interplay may not only lead to a win–win situation but to trade-offs as well (Skelcher, 2009: 169). Besides, nonprofit organizations and civil society groups whose inclusion in networks is considered as a sign of democratization may suffer from representation and accountability deficits. The organized pluralism of collaborative governance is not tantamount to democratic policy-making. This provides fertile soil for critique because democratic ownership, defined as the 'feeling of being an integral part of the formulation and implementation of policy solutions' (Skelcher and Torfing, 2010: 84), is weakened. Of course, the extent to which governance networks are decoupled from the public sphere, or are disconnected from the official representative institutions, the extent to which voting in elections remains a crucial input for the formulation of policy outputs, and to which networks are pluralist and representative, are all empirical matters. But the available evidence, although admittedly so far insufficient, makes us relativize the democratizing potential of collaborative governance, which is not necessarily a plus for democracy.

# Chapter 5

# Empowering the Citizen or the Customer?

Reforms driven by a concern to involve citizens more directly and more closely in the policy process take place in parallel to the closer involvement of organized interests under the label of collaborative governance, as discussed in the previous chapter. We know that collaborative governance is primarily triggered by the need to increase the expertise of public authorities and support for their policies. This chapter first discusses deliberative and participatory experiments which, by contrast, appear to reflect a will to make citizens become more interested and competent in public matters, as well as allowing them to express their preferences on policy-making. Although concerns about increasing the legitimacy of policies through participation are not absent, one common characteristic of many participatory experiments is that neither elected officials nor well-established groups should, at least in principle, be the key players.

Varieties of experiments in participatory forms of policy-making are proliferating across the globe today. Some of them have found international resonance and, in addition, participants can now interact and deliberate over the internet. Does this challenge our previous conclusion that changes in modes of governance may be inimical to the quality of democracy? This clearly applied to the internationalization of governance, but it seems that even the more promising trend of collaborative governance is likely to undermine democratic control. What about participatory experiments then? Do they represent more effective forms of democracy, and is it possible to counterbalance through them the negative trends observed before?

This chapter also discusses administrative reforms inspired by New Public Management (NPM) doctrines and their derivatives. Although NPM reforms have their origin in economic thinking and are inspired by heavily idealized market principles, they can also be seen – to some extent at least – to be part of an accountability agenda. They imply closer attention to the needs of citizens receiving public services, and embody a quest for greater responsiveness to these needs. But how does this operate in practice? Two questions spring to mind: does account-ability operate 'downwards' effectively, and – as in the case of partici-patory experiments – does authentic citizens' empowerment indeed take place?

Another crucial question is to what extent administrative reform has altered the degree of 'upward' accountability of the bureaucracy to elected officials. With respect to the democratic quality of public deci-sion-making, more direct involvement of affected populations may be welcome but, initially at least, NPM reforms were also intended to give more autonomy and discretion to the administration: public authori-ties should 'steer' but not 'row'. Could there be a risk of a technocratic drift thereby, which would add to the influence of technocrats in policy-making through its internationalization, or also through collab-orative forms of governance, in which the steering has largely been delegated to bureaucracies?

## Deliberative and participatory experiments: do they matter?

A democratic accountability agenda, which 'seeks to make administra-tive agencies accessible, accountable, and transparent by ensuing direct participation or representation of citizens in administrative affairs' (Ansell and Gingrich, 2003: 165), seems to guide a number of changes in policy-making processes. In that sense, political elites seem to have learned from the critiques and claims articulated by social movements of the 'New Left' during the 1970s (Blondiaux, 2008). Interestingly, along with reforms in policy styles involving collaboration with orga-nized interests, there are also reforms driven by a concern to involve people on the ground. The two reform streams do not completely over-lap. They seem to differ not only in the nature of the involved actors, but also partly with regard to their objectives.

As already noted, collaborative forms of governance primarily result from the need to increase the expertise of public authorities and the legitimacy of their policies. In the case of participatory experiments, an important motivation is to educate citizens to become involved in, and express informed opinions on, public matters, in a context with a growing bottom-up demand for participation, related to the general climate of distrust with established politics (see Chapter 1). However, more instrumental concerns about enhancing policy legitimacy through participation are not absent either, and this appears, for example, in the fact that it may be necessary to be recognized as a 'stakeholder' to be eligible for participation. This kind of resemblance to collaborative governance makes Mark E. Warren – a leading specialist in these devices and in the role of associations – speak about 'governance-driven democratization' (Warren, 2009).

Participatory experiments can be divided into two categories. There are those that are initiated by experts or civic organizations, that seek to remedy political apathy and to improve the quality of citizens' involvement in public affairs. Thus, they have primarily expressive and educative functions, such as the 'deliberative opinion polls', where a sample of the population meets in person, or now also online, to deliberate over specific issues, assisted by experts. The intention of their proponents is primarily to induce – thanks to exposure to information and to deliberation – changes in the attitudes of lay individuals with respect to public issues, though it has also been claimed that in some cases, their outcome did influence the policy process (Fishkin, 2009: 150–58). On the other hand, there are experiments initiated by public bodies with more instrumental goals: to contribute to the acceptance of political measures, even though in a merely consultative form, as part of the process of policy formulation or implementation. Conflict management is, then, an important function, and in that case, it makes less sense to select participants randomly just 'because they are citizens, rather than because they claim expert authority or are the representatives of an organized group within society' (Smith, 2009: 2). The aim is rather to include key players, such as stakeholders or those claiming to represent them, or 'brokers' capable of bridging the differences between conflicting viewpoints. In that case, it is the representation of, broadly speaking, partisan interests and deliberation between their advocates that is privileged (Hendriks *et al.*, 2007).

Participatory forms of policy-making are proliferating in developing countries as well as in OECD states (for an overview, see Gastil and Levine, 2005). Some of these exercises have found international resonance, such as the participatory budgeting process first established, with some mythical references to the French *Commune,* in the Brazilian city of Porto Alegre (1.3 million residents) in 1989 by the Workers' Party local government in the aftermath of its electoral victory (Abers, 2000; Avritzer, 2002; Baiocchi, 2005; Sintomer and Gret, 2005). The participatory budget lived on after the party's loss of the office of mayor in 2004, but was somewhat emptied of its radical content, and participation declined (Sintomer *et al.*, 2008: 239–40).

On the one hand, it has been suggested that, despite the proliferation of idealized accounts of the Porto Alegre experiment, bureaucratization of the process and co-optation of civil society organizations impeded its sustainability (Cleuren, 2008). On the other hand, the principle of participatory budgets has aroused worldwide interest in the last decades, including local authorities in communist China (He and Warren, 2011). The participatory budget has been widely emulated, especially as the World Social Forum has repeatedly met in Porto Alegre. In the state of Rio Grande do Sul, with a population of ten million, attempts have been made to apply the design principles of the participatory budget on a larger political scale. Though the figure should be treated with caution, it is claimed that in a four-year period, not less than 16 per cent of the electorate participated in the process. This is interesting in that limitations due to large scale are a persistent challenge to participatory experiments (Smith, 2009: 29 and pp. 67–8).

Participatory budgeting currently adopts diverse forms in different parts of the world, but remains most popular in Latin America. Approximately 1200 out of the 16,000 Latin American municipalities have established such budgets, especially the larger ones (Cabannes, 2006). In Europe, it is estimated that about five million people live in approximately 100 cities or districts – mostly under left-wing local governments – with participatory budgets (Sintomer *et al.*, 2008: 38). Spain is a case in point: about 5 per cent of the population lives in cities with a participatory budget, and these may be quite large, such as Seville with 700,000 residents. However, one also finds participatory budgets in districts of the capital cities of Paris, London, Berlin and Rome (Sintomer *et al.*, 2007). Even the World Bank promotes this kind of budgeting process now as an example of best practice with respect to 'good governance', especially in Eastern European countries, and in 2007 it issued a *Report on Participatory Budgeting* (Sintomer *et al.*, 2008: 66; Talpin 2008: 112–13; Pateman, 2012: 7). Diffusion, however, has led to heterogeneity; Sintomer *et al.* (2008) distinguish between six types of participatory budgets, each with very different characteristics and implications.

Similarly, in general, participatory experiments are so numerous that it is simply not possible to draw any generalizations on their implications, although they have now generated a considerable number of studies. First, most experiments take place locally and are not widely publicized beyond this level. Second, variation among these experiments is considerable; 57 techniques of participatory deliberation have been listed in a report on democratic innovations (Smith, 2005).

Significantly, there is only partial overlap in the lists produced by the field's specialists. In 2000, John Dryzek referred to 'public inquiries, right-to-know legislation, citizen juries, policy dialogues, impact assessment with public comment, regulatory negotiation, mediation and other kinds of third-party-facilitated conflict resolution' (Dryzek, 2000: 164). The list, in a more recent co-authored article, contains 'citizen's juries (invented in the United States but used most widely in the United Kingdom, especially under the New Labour governments), consensus conferences (invented in Denmark, widely copied elsewhere), planning cells (invented in Germany), deliberative polling (invented in the United States, applied there and elsewhere), citizen's panels (used by the UK government to test policy proposals), the '21st Century Town Meetings' organized by America Speaks, and one-off exercises (...)' (Dryzek and Tucker, 2008: 864). Urbinati and Warren (2008: 405) include in their account 'experiments with citizen juries and panels, advisory councils, stakeholder meetings, lay members of professional review boards, representations at public hearings, public submissions, citizen surveys, deliberative polling, deliberative forums, and focus groups'.

For example, one may distinguish between deliberative opinion polls and devices involving smaller groups. In the former, the participants form a randomly selected representative sample, a sort of 'microcosm' of society. Deliberative polls were even established to advise on local issues in communist China, with public authorities, surprisingly, following their recommendations (Fishkin, 2009: 106–11). In set-ups that involve only a few individuals, such as focus groups, consensus conferences, or citizens' juries, the representation of diversity is ensured by less rigorous means (Weale, 2001: 416–17). Moreover, labels vary; consensus conferences are quite similar in design to citizens' juries (and the same applies in part to German *Planungszellen*); policy dialogues in Germany are frequently called '*Risiko Dialogen*' because they mainly deal with the assessment and treatment of collective risks; mediation procedures are called 'alternative dispute resolution' or 'public conflict resolution', and so on.

Urbinati and Warren emphasize in their text that, notwithstanding their differences, these experiments privilege the participation of ordinary citizens and not of professional representatives. The fact that this type of deliberative device is considered as participatory does not mean, however, that the representation relation is absent. Therefore, it would be improper to consider them as mechanisms of direct democracy, even though affectedness may be a condition for participation.

Only a very small proportion of the citizenry is involved therein, and they frequently have only an advisory status. Nevertheless, one common characteristic is that neither elected officials nor large, organized collective actors – unlike in the forms of collaborative governance considered previously – should, at least in principle, be the key players in these bodies. Although what is usually emphasized is that these are sites of deliberation, this should not obscure the fact that their innovative aspect is related to their participatory properties. As a matter of fact, what characterizes them is neither their deliberative nor their participatory component as such, but the combination of the two: the fact that deliberation over policy issues is extended to people who normally do not participate in the policy-making process. Most of these innovations can be subsumed under the label of 'democratic experimentalism' (Dorf and Sabel, 1998), which is a complement to traditional parliamentary and administrative procedures of policy-making.

Empirical studies of such innovations have significantly contributed to the reflection on the virtues and limits of deliberative democracy in the real world (Parkinson, 2006). Most of the empirical work on collective deliberation deals with issues related to its quality and its contribution to the improvement of democracy, by scrutinizing such aspects as the openness and degree of inclusiveness of deliberative sites, the nature of exchanged arguments, or the possibly transformative effect of deliberation on preferences and collective will, leading to a citizenry that is more enlightened, and perhaps also more other-regarding and consensus-oriented. This is not surprising, considering that many deliberative experiments have at best a tenuous relationship to public decision-making, defined as the process of the authoritative allocation of goods and values. Often, their primary goal is to contribute to the collection and dissemination of information by public authorities or, even less related to decision-making, simply to reinvigorate civic participation in a context of distrust for established politics.

However, deliberation is also an instrument for complexity management. When it involves a plurality of adequately selected actors, it copes better with problem complexity because it allows for the grounding of decisions on more accurate 'insider' knowledge. As a remedy to uncertainty regarding the causes of public problems and their solutions, it is expected that deliberation by a wide range of participants will contribute to more competent policy-making and is, in that respect, a necessary ingredient for the technical improvement of public decisions. Deliberation is also expected to enhance mutual respect, recognition, tolerance and empathy. It is seen as the appropriate anti-dote to the fragmentation of complex societies; as a component of contemporary 'management of interdependence', deliberation is deemed to lead to less controversial decisions, thus reducing the risk of 'pluralized ungovernability' (Warren, 2009: 5). Therefore, deliberation is considered as a necessary ingredient for the political feasibility of policy measures too. An example of this kind of function is when delib-eration is used to cope with 'political conflicts surrounding develop-ment projects, sitting decisions, new technology, risk, environmental impacts, and the distribution of the associated burdens and benefits' (Holzinger, 2001: 71).

In scientific and technological policies, for instance, participatory mechanisms are part of the 'public discussion' of science and are inte-grated in technology assessment. In a context of scepticism about the risks for health and the ethical problems generated by scientific and technological development, public participation is expected to make expertise more responsive, on the one hand, and to make the public more 'enlightened' on the other; both changes are deemed to enhance the acceptance of policy choices (Callon *et al.*, 2001; Weale, 2001). Deliberative mediation techniques are thus used in the case of decisions that encounter opposition from social groups which can credibly threaten with a policy blockade. In policies generating costs – negative externalities, such as air and noise pollution – that are geographically concentrated, participatory governance schemes or mediation proce-dures are established in the implementation phase to overcome local protest (Renn *et al.*, 1995). The aim is to combat the so-called Nimby – 'not in my backyard' – syndrome against public 'bads'. The idea is that a number of projects that contribute to the collective well-being – such as the construction of roads or railway lines or the creation of sites for the deposit of toxic waste – can become annoyances to those living in their neighbourhood, whose opposition (either through legal or more radical means) might jeopardize the whole project. In France, for example, the *Commission nationale du débat public* (CNDP) has been established as an autonomous administrative agency with the task of organizing public debates on crucial issues related to the environment and to land planning. In issues where the spatial-territorial aspect is important, designers of deliberative procedures may confer an impor-tant role on local associations and other groups opposed to policy implementation, with the hope that through deliberation and the promotion of 'advocacy' forms of political expression contentious policy choices will be immunized from 'irresponsible' (for example, narrowly partisan) manipulation. However, this is not the sole reason; collaborative and inclusive decision-making is also privileged for the management of natural resources because short-term selfish behaviour and lack of self-limitation can lead to disputes or to the depletion of the resource, and thus to a collectively suboptimal outcome (a problem that is known as the 'tragedy of the commons').

Not only has the scope of participatory experiments been extended to numerous policy areas, but new information technologies enable the involved parties to proceed with online and partly interactive consultations. No doubt this leads to more pluralism in consultations, given that not only organized lobbies, but ordinary citizens can express their views. However, given that 'e-government' methods may lead to an overload of information directed at public authorities, it is most likely that the authorities will continue to weigh the status and power of the source of the information, and that they will tend to undervalue flows of emails addressed to them, at virtually no cost for their senders, as 'cheap talk' (Chadwick, 2006: 121). More importantly, this type of technological progress does not solve the problem of the weak interface between public deliberation and decision-making, if the outcomes of participatory procedures are not binding for legislators.

Hence, part of the empirical work on deliberation focuses on the policy relevance of participatory devices (see among others Papadopoulos and Warin, 2007). Dennis Thompson (2008), one of the major theorists of deliberative democracy, pleaded for better knowledge of how deliberation relates to other decision-making modes. Are official decision-makers responsive to the concerns expressed in deliberative procedures, and do such concerns impact the content of collectively binding decisions? Or is public deliberation simply a form of symbolic politics, promoted because 'battles over public policy and political influence are in part a matter of whether or not one used a good decision technology or not' (Parkinson, 2004: 390–1)? Is participatory deliberation just 'window-dressing' in order to acquire procedural (or so-called 'throughput') legitimacy?

Participatory procedures may be instrumentalized by policy-makers who use them as public relations strategies in order to 'sell' decisions made in other places. The proposals made by participatory bodies may not be seriously considered, and may be filtered through complex or opaque decision-making circuits. Hence, the establishment of such bodies is insufficient to alleviate distrust and perceptions of a democratic deficit because they do not, in fact, act as countervailing powers (Sintomer *et al.*, 2008: 295). If such mechanisms are perceived as mere window-dressing or, worse, as part of elites' manipulation strategies, there is a risk that the evils they are expected to alleviate, such as distrust and cynicism, may grow instead. The larger the gap between participatory rhetoric and political reality, the larger the discrepancy between words and deeds, the more numerous the unfulfilled promises of 'empowerment', and the more likely it is that participatory reforms will not reduce but instead increase cynicism.

However, some evidence demonstrates that participation can result in bifurcations in individual trajectories that do not mean more apathy or resignation, but a genuine increase in civic competence. Talpin (2008) shows, on the basis of three case studies of participatory budgeting in European cities, that participants acquire different types of skills. These can include learning how to speak in public, and, for some, learning how to organize and manage debates, or how to conduct negotiations. It can also be acquiring knowledge of technical matters, which reduces the gap between experts and lay people. It can also mean achieving a better understanding of the complexities of the administrative machinery, or being able to handle political conflict. Through participation, people acquire expertise on public matters and are thus more likely to become critical, with a desire to change the system internally. They may join as militants in local civil society organizations. In Porto Alegre, for instance, there has been increasing associational density due to the participatory budgeting process, particularly in those areas where the associational tradition was low (Smith, 2009: 47). Alternatively, participants themselves become political professionals, as party machines are badly in need of competent people for elective mandates.

As for the policy effects of participatory devices, their assessment requires careful empirical scrutiny. As stated before, generalizations are very difficult to make, given the extreme diversity of these devices. A precise identification of effects requires a meticulous reconstruction of policy processes because participatory devices are one input among others, and their effects may have an indirect, 'diffuse and temporally dispersed character' (Hendriks *et al.*, 2007: 375). Anecdotal evidence can be provided both in support of and against the argument that these devices are influential. On the basis of a cross-national case comparison, Dryzek and Tucker (2008) suggest, for instance, that the impact of deliberative devices depends on 'macro' features of national political systems – notably, their degree and mode of inclusiveness. More specific aspects, however, may be relevant as well, such as the organizer's authority, media coverage of deliberative events, their location in physical spaces of decision-making such as parliamentary assemblies, or their connection to elections and issues put to referendum votes (Hendriks, 2005: 90–3). An example of an indirect impact is the effect of media coverage (Parkinson, 2005). If deliberative events are mediatized, their discussions can alter the preferences of decision-makers or generate an interest among broader publics and organized actors, thus exerting pressure over those making decisions. However, mediatization requires that deliberative mechanisms address high-salience issues producing news values that are compatible with the 'dramaturgical' media logic (see Chapter 2).

Overall, it would be exaggerated to speak of generalized positive effects on the vigour of democracy. Mudde (2004: 558) suggests that participatory experiments do not alleviate populist pressure (see Chapter 1), because they are inspired by the populist demands of the New Left, whereas the demands of the more powerful 'silent counter-revolution' are 'more leadership and less participation', as evidenced by the hierarchic structure of conservative populist movements under a charismatic leader. The success of anti-establishment political entrepreneurs may well be a result of lack of trust in politicians, but there is no reason why offering more places in citizen panels and similar steps would solve this problem (Pollitt and Bouckaert, 2004: 155). In spite of that, organizers of participatory experiments repeatedly assert that increasing citizens' trust in politics is a core motivation; worse, although the social segments that traditionally do not participate in politics are often absent from participatory experiments, their absence is not questioned by those in charge.

Thus, the empowerment of dominated segments is very relative. Within participatory procedures, it is contingent on procedural rules, which can make a difference in the degree of inclusiveness or in terms of equality among participants. When questioning who participates (Fung, 2006), in the cases where participants are not selected randomly, then the answer often points out imperfections in representation caused by the 'Schattschneider bias': 'The flaw in the pluralist heaven is that the heavenly choir sings with a strong upper-class accent' (Schattschneider, 1960: 34–5). In addition, the deliberative quality of these procedures may not be satisfactory; phenomena of domination are not absent, and sheer presence is not a sufficient condition to have one's voice heard. Speaking in public can be intimidating, and those not intimidated but unfamiliar with the prevailing communication codes may be marginalized. A moderator or a facilitator can help less self-confident people to express their views and ensure that there is a balance in the expression of various standpoints. However, more importantly, even when genuine empowerment takes place, it often remains circumscribed to narrow populations. It obviously matters, for example, if participants in experiments are just a 'mini public' of about a dozen – as in citizens' juries or consensus conferences – or several thousands, as in citywide participatory budgeting.

There are only a few experiments, such as those of the participatory budget, where collective deliberation clearly aims for the democratization of the decisional process and leads to the formulation of policy options endorsed by public authorities. Let us have a closer look at the procedures of this kind of budgeting in Porto Alegre. Regional assemblies in the 16 city districts, open to all, elect delegates to the regional budget Forums and to the Council of the Participatory Budget. Interestingly, the number of Forum delegates is a function of the turnout in each assembly, a clever incentive for participation. In addition, participation is not plagued by the usual pattern of over-representation of the wealthiest and better-educated, because participatory budgeting addresses public problems that are most crucial for the poor, such as sanitation, basic urban infrastructure, or housing. Thus there are structural incentives for the disadvantaged to participate (Fung, 2006: 72). Approximately 8.4 per cent of the adult population of Porto Alegre reported having attended assemblies at some point over the previous five years (Goodin and Dryzek, 2006: 240). In 1999, there were over 20,000 participants, and 16,600 in 2001. This may be a tiny proportion of the city population, but, among the positive features of participation, one notes that there is considerable turnover from one year to another, and that 'demonstration effects' act positively; citizens in neighbourhoods with lower participation realized that neighbourhoods with higher participation levels attracted considerable investments, and this induced them to become active too (Smith, 2009: 1 and 40–4).

The budget Forums often make difficult choices between different demands and subsequently monitor the implementation of the decided measures. The Council sets rules for the distribution of resources and, in cooperation with the administration, applies them in order to set priorities between the measures decided by the Forums. The Council then presents the budget to the city mayor, who has to gain approval from the legislative body (the City Council). Although the elected mayor and legislature retain the formal power to veto the budget, this never happens because of the popular legitimacy of the participatory budget (Smith, 2009: 49–50). There are also six thematic assemblies dealing with issues that are not neighbourhood-specific, such as education, and social and health services. They elect delegates in the budget Forums and two members of the budget Council. Nonetheless, they attract less participation than regional assemblies because the direct relevance of the issues they deal with is less visible to people, something that may be a structural limitation for participation opportunities (Smith, 2009: 37 and 47). Overall, with this process between 9 per cent and 21 per cent of the budget (Baiocchi, 2005: 14) is more or less directly decided by ordinary citizens, who thus become *de facto* co-decision makers (Sintomer *et al.*, 2007: 121). 'Co-decision makers' is the right term because, as noted above, representation is not absent from the participatory budget. However, there seem to be enough safeguards to prevent representatives distancing themselves from their constituencies: terms of office are limited to one year, delegates and Council members are subject to recall, and the latter cannot serve more than two consecutive terms (Smith, 2009: 51). The high degree of turnover of representatives prevents the formation of a local political class with its own interests. There is, however, a negative facet: the low degree of professionalization leads to dependence on bureaucratic expertise. As Smith (2009: 53) remarks: 'the time constraints that councillors work under and their reliance on information from the administration make it difficult for them to fully scrutinize the administration's proposals, which include highly technical reports on the distribution of resources among agencies, agency investment plans, calculations based on the distributional criteria, and so forth'. Despite this, participatory budgeting has acted against endemic corruption in Porto Alegre and has led to a reorientation of policy measures towards the primary needs of the poorest segments of the population.

In European cases, municipalities have more limited competences, and the social problems they seek to solve are less acute than in the South (Talpin, 2008: 113–16). This reduces the incentives for broad participation, and as a result, the legitimacy of the participatory budgeting process. Even if open to all residents, participation is limited: as low as between 1 and 5 per cent in the three cases in France, Italy and Spain surveyed by Talpin (2008). Moreover, several devices in Europe suffer from the usual participation bias in favour of the better-educated or the more politically active. They are less inclusive than in Latin America because the popular classes have deserted institutional politics. One may reasonably question the legitimacy of a handful of the most highly committed residents, who have sufficient time to invest and possess the necessary cultural capital, deciding part of the budget of a collective. In addition, participatory budgets are less frequently initiated by a bottom-up dynamic than in Latin America. For example, they have often been diffused by anti-globalization militants, who are not of popular extraction (Sintomer *et al.*, 2008: 68–9).

Participatory mechanisms are not designed as alternatives to traditional mechanisms of electoral representation; rather, their advocates claim, they are intended to supplement them. However, this poses the problem of their coupling with the overall institutional (representative) architecture or, stated slightly differently, of 'the macro-political impact of micro-political innovations' (Goodin and Dryzek, 2006: 220). As advocates of participatory devices themselves admit, direct influence on decision-making is the exception (Goodin and Dryzek, 2006: 225). Porto Alegre is a case of positive coupling of direct participation with the representation principle, but the broad diffusion of the concept of participatory budgeting introduced heterogeneity in that respect as well. Participatory budgets differ on their principles of actor inclusion (individual or collective), but also on their binding or advisory character, on the degree of top-down control and of formalization, and on the importance of the topics and resources at stake (Sintomer *et al.*, 2008: 33).

Another interesting example of a deliberative and participatory experiment tightly coupled to the formal decision-making process is provided by the case of electoral reform in British Columbia (Lang, 2007; Warren and Pearse, 2008), which relied on a combination of non-electoral – thus lacking formal authorization – and electoral representation. To reform the electoral system of this Canadian province, the authorities established a citizens' assembly composed of 160 individuals selected on the basis of a quasi-random process, and set them the task of drafting a reform proposal. The assembly met several weekends for 11 months and organized numerous broadly attended public hearings. The proposal that was the outcome of its deliberations was thereafter submitted to a referendum vote, as initially promised by the provincial government. The assembly proposal failed by a narrow margin to reach the qualified majority of 60 per cent of the votes, which is probably related to the fact that the assembly deliberations had not been widely publicized (Pateman, 2012: 9). Yet what is important here is that there was a formal commitment to enact the assembly proposal, if endorsed in the referendum. Urbinati and Warren (2008: 406) correctly maintain that 'because it combined authorization by an elected government, random selection, a deliberative format, and accountability through a referendum, the BC Citizens' Assembly was designed as a counterbalance to both electoral representation and self-authorized representation. Its democratic credentials stemmed from its initial constitution by elected representatives, its statistically representative makeup (so as "to look like the people of BC"), and its submission of its final recommendation directly to the people'. The experiment was replicated on the same topic in the province of Ontario (Smith, 2009: 75). Effects of participation are thus stronger in the presence of genuinely influential participatory instruments, such as referendums; it is known that even when referendums are formally advisory, politicians cannot easily afford to ignore their outcome. However, even if institutional reforms were carried out in this direction in a number of countries, this does not mean that the use of the new referendum instruments would become widespread, and again, such innovations often remain confined to the local (or at best the subnational) level. Ultimately, Scarrow (2003: 57) concluded in her study on this topic that 'outside Switzerland and some U.S. states, referendums still play only a very limited role in the political life of established democracies'.

Both cases of Porto Alegre and British Columbia show that, paradoxically, the success of participatory mechanisms requires a top-down commitment by those in power to take them seriously (Blondiaux, 2008). Recent research on participatory governance institutions in Brazil has come to similar conclusions: in the area of housing policies, the incorporation of municipal housing councils into decision-making is associated with an increase in pro-poor program adoption across municipalities, regardless of whether a strong civil society is in place (Donaghy, 2011). At the other end, there are cases such as that of the deliberative poll on *Tomorrow's Europe*, organized by the Foundation *Notre Europe* in October 2007, on pension matters and on the enlargement of the European Union (Fishkin, 2009: 175–89). Such devices, even when they deal with controversial topics, display no influence at all on elite decisions about the fate of the European Union and its citizens.

Usually, influence lies somewhere in between and can take more subtle forms. Sintomer *et al.* (2008: 297) noticed that, with the proliferation of public participation devices, claims from elected officials that they should enjoy a decisional monopoly become less credible; lack of responsiveness to citizens' demands becomes illegitimate; and the question of what are the most efficient channels for participation becomes an important issue. On the basis of several observations in France, a country where the idea of representative democracy is well-entrenched and direct participation is often considered with suspicion by elected officials, Blondiaux (2008) concluded that it is impossible to annihilate the emancipatory potential of participatory deliberation. The existence of participatory mechanisms encourages contestation of the way political debates are organized and conducted; in other words, the 'throughput' legitimacy of the policy process is put into question. In the name of the democratic principles that power-holders themselves advocate, participants can force them to take their commitments seriously, and not use them simply as rhetoric. It can happen that the perceived lack of genuine commitment on behalf of power-holders becomes the major source of contestation. Such mechanisms are akin to Elster's (1998: 12) 'civilizing force of hypocrisy': Once commitments to participation or to the general interest are formulated by political actors, they are bound by them and must adhere to them, even if they do not sincerely believe in them, for fear of being discredited. By multiplying *Ersatz* forms of participation, those in power run the risk, not only of inducing cynicism, but also of politicization by reaction. Further, participatory devices can oblige political leaders to appear in public to account for their policy choices; the same applies to experts, whose conclusions are challenged. Their 'softer' role as 'rituals of justification' should be considered too. Consequently, participatory mechanisms can be exploited by those who have an interest in radicalizing them, even if their designers had an interest in taming their effects. Public discourses too closely focusing on personal experience or on the defence of private interests are subject to severe criticism, and those producing them risk losing their reputation.

On the other hand, owing to the commonly local level of deliberation, even public interest is likely to be defined in rather narrow terms. More importantly, the limits of participation at the local level are important. 'The use of such procedures is piecemeal, and with few exceptions it depends primarily on the resources and initiatives of individual local governments', according to Ansell and Gingrich (2003: 188). Consequently, if their outcomes have an impact on political decisions, the affected groups mostly remain restricted to local populations. Moreover, experiments that are more democratic and representative – such as citizens' juries – tend to have little decisional influence. They may even be viewed with scepticism by parties and associations, whenever they are perceived as a threat to their interests – for example, if they feel they cannot use them to improve their image or to propagate their views (Hendriks, 2006). By contrast, the most influential procedures, such as mediation arrangements, are often populated by leaders of organizations who count by reason of their opposition potential, without necessarily being representative. They are thus more likely to have an impact on decisions through the presence of key players in them. Hence, there seems to be a trade-off between democratic quality and policy influence. This is problematic because any direct or indirect form of influence on collectively binding decisions of procedures, whose participants enjoy no formal authorization like the electoral one, poses genuine accountability problems.

Overall, it would be wrong to argue simply that participatory devices do not matter. This is a list of the major functions that are more or less explicitly ascribed to them by scholars and practitioners:

- multifaceted educative effect on individual participants;
- conflict management and policy acceptance;
- citizens' empowerment and direct influence on policy content;
- indirect effects on the political 'division of labour';
  - challenge to the decisional monopoly of professional politicians, and public debate on decision-making procedures;
  - contestation of lack of responsiveness, coupled with pressure for public commitment to pledges and justification of choices.

These functions differ across participatory devices, and the same device can generate diverse, or even conflicting, expectations. Furthermore, all ascribed functions are properly fulfilled only infrequently, and with respect to policy impact, it is reasonable to think that in most cases it is at best indirect. More importantly, in order to assess *how much* participatory devices impact on the transformations undergone by contemporary democracies, they should be put into context. Assessing the relevance of these forms of policy-making in the decisional process requires taking into account the broader context of governance changes in our democracies. This leads to rather pessimistic conclusions.

The growth of participatory forms of policy-making is not general – it applies to single policy fields – and does not take place in a vacuum, but in a context of emergence or development of new modes for the production of collectively binding decisions, most of which are not genuinely participatory or even not participatory at all. This judgment applies to changes discussed in the previous chapters of this book – such as transnational or collaborative governance – and to changes that will be discussed later, such as administrative reform, regulation through independent agencies, or the role of courts. The innovations that seem to count most do not go in a participatory direction. This goes much further than suggesting, as is often the case in empirical works on the types of experiments reviewed in this section, that participatory bodies are insufficiently representative. In quite a number of policy-making procedures, representation and participation are seriously flawed, and in others, they are not sought at all for deliberation on public issues.

As a matter of fact, participatory experiments of 'deliberative democracy' are introduced at the same time as other deliberative but non-participatory policy-making modes, with greater direct or indirect influence on policy, and probably in more crucial policy areas, beyond the local or subnational 'micro-political' level. Therefore, it may not only be observed in participatory devices that 'people find themselves deliberating about topics that are constrained by larger forces over which they have no control' (Parkinson, 2004: 392), but these uncontrolled large forces also undermine popular participation. Stated differently, not only do participatory deliberative devices have limitations, but their undeniable development is offset by counteracting trends in policy-making. These trends are characterized by limited inclusiveness of the decision-making process, weakness of democratic modes of accountability, and in the cases of collaborative or privatized governance, lack of formal authorization as well.

## New Public Management and subsequent reform layers: who are the winners?

Cooperative and participatory forms of governance are thus not the only major changes in policy modes experienced by our democracies. Other changes, inspired by 'new public management' (NPM) doctrines and their derivatives, equally imply a closer involvement of policy addressees, while being primarily guided by concerns about the efficiency of service provision. Paradoxically, these changes originating in a quest for better public performance appear on the agenda at the same time as obstacles to the effectiveness of public policy seem to abound (see Chapter 4). NPM reforms have an individualistic tone, as they rely less on the cooperation of organized segments and are targeted on bringing services closer to the expectations and needs of individual users. As noted by Hammerschmid *et al.* (2006: 1):

Highly centralized, hierarchical organisational structures have increasingly been replaced by decentralised management environments where decisions on resource allocation and service delivery are made closer to the point of delivery. Constraints in financial and HR management are removed. Managers and organisational units are given greater freedom in operational decisions and then held accountable ex post. Such reforms have become a ubiquitous feature of public management reform.

Unlike collaborative governance, these reforms are not primarily motivated by the fact that organized interests have the capacity to resist state regulation and blackmail the state with their veto power. In spite of their dissimilarities, however, there are also linkages between collaborative governance and NPM. For example, the establishment of public–private partnerships (see Chapter 4) is guided by the same doubts about the performance of public bureaucracies with regard to cost efficiency (value-for-money) as the NPM principles that aim to introduce in these bureaucracies operational rules imported from the private sector. With NPM, the inefficiencies and failures due to public monopoly on service provision should be remedied by the introduction of market principles and competition. A client-orientation, privatization of public companies, use of market mechanisms for service delivery, or the introduction of private management tools in the public service – such as flexibility in hiring and firing or performance-related pay – are all features characteristic of what Christensen and Laegreid (2001a: 14–17) describe as the 'supermarket state model'.

The proposed recipes changed but, as with cooperative forms of governance, the beliefs that the quality of public service can (and should) be improved are not new and probably part of the broader trend towards the 'rationalization' of the world, as depicted in the seminal work of German sociologist Max Weber. As early as the beginning of the twentieth century, 'Taylorism' was presented as a mode of scientific management of industrial production, and later post-war attempts to create more rational budgeting systems – such as the PPBS (Program-Planning-Budgeting System) in the United States or the RCB (Rationalization des choix budgétaires) in France – were all manifestations of the obsession with the optimization of organizational efficiency. Similarly, the focus on 'outputs' is not new either; as early as the 1920s, the famous French public lawyer Léon Duguit, one of the founders of the administrative principles of *service public*, stated that 'public authority cannot be legitimized by its origin, but only through the services it provides in conformity with the rule of law' (cited in Rosanvallon, 2008: 69). Duguit perceived the state primarily as the locus of coordination of a multitude of autonomous and functionally oriented public services (Rosanvallon, 2008: 70), a vision that seems eminently modern in the era of quangos and autonomous agencies (see Chapters 4 and 6). As a matter of fact, the focus on continuity and change depends on the conceptual lens employed (see Lynn, 2006, Chapter 8).

Although the will to reform public services in order to increase efficiency and produce better services is by no means new, specialists estimate that the amplitude of the reform trend and its cross-national diffusion in the last decades has been exceptional (Pollitt and Bouckaert, 2004: 24). It has been suggested that the bulk of NPM reforms became a 'new administrative orthodoxy' in the last decades of the twentieth century (Christensen and Laegreid, 2001), and complying with NPM reform targets largely became a norm of appropriate behaviour on behalf of administrations. It became increasingly difficult for administrations to ignore the sirens of modernization, so that the diffusion of reforms has been compared to a 'pandemic' (Pollitt and Bouckaert, 2004: 1). What is its aetiology?

Ansell and Gingrich (2003: 166) suggest that administrative reforms 'derive from a lack of citizen trust in government'. We know that such a lack is currently pervasive (see Chapter 1), but this assertion deserves some qualification. A significant proportion of distrustful citizens opt for 'exit' strategies, such as abstention from elections. They withdraw more broadly from politics, therefore it is not very likely that decision-makers are receptive to the complaints of this segment. Another portion of critical citizens opt for 'voice' strategies, to the benefit of anti-establishment parties who formulate their claims in an excessively vague manner – in the form of general criticisms of an allegedly parasitic bureaucracy – to convert them into policy measures. Besides, as these parties are usually not in office, they have no direct grasp on policy-making. Therefore, although NPM-inspired reforms have better chances of resonating among a public which is critical of politics and displays diffuse feelings of distrust that include the state bureaucracy in a global negative appreciation, these reforms are driven more by supply than demand.

NPM reforms are primarily the result of elite beliefs, mainly on the neoliberal Right but also in part of the Left, forged by works of 'management gurus' like Osborne and Gaebler, whose widely diffused *Reinventing Government* was published in the United States in 1992. Reforms are also related to the increased influence of external consultancy on administrative action (Saint-Martin, 2004). The international dimension is present too, even though external input is not formally binding, unlike in the case of Europeanization through EU rules. The role of recipes promoted by international organizations such as the OECD has been important, in particular its Public Governance Committee (PUMA), which issues recommendations for reform and evaluates 'good' and 'bad pupils' in regular public management reviews. Significantly, PUMA has been portrayed as an international 'community of discourse' on public management reform (Pollitt and Bouckaert, 2004: 20).

As regards the intellectual origin of NPM reforms, it lies in economic thinking – an 'economics-of-politics' approach (Hood and Peters, 1994) – and fits well with the neoliberal agenda that demonizes public bureaucracies and idealizes the operation of private firms. To a large extent, reforms originate themselves in a critique of public bureaucracy, which is often portrayed by politicians or journalists as 'too big, powerful, hierarchical, rule-bound, indifferent to results, inefficient, lazy, incompetent, wasteful, inflexible, unaccountable, and inhumane; it is harmful to democracy, economic efficiency, and individual freedom' (Olsen, 2008: 14). According to this line of thinking, adherence to formal rules is viewed as excessively formalistic, a source of rigidity, and an obstacle to efficiency. What is more, bureaucrats are primarily motivated by self-interest and tend to maximize their own personal utility, or at least that of their administrative territory, instead of serving the public good. For example, although they do not necessarily seek to maximize their budget, bureaucrats occupying executive positions seek to improve their working conditions, maximize their political influence and work in proximity with the decision-making spheres: they are interested in 'bureau-shaping' (Dunleavy, 1991).

In view of these problems, NPM advocates demand not only more flexibility for public bureaucracies to improve service delivery, but also more responsibility for them regarding the way they operate. NPM aims 'to restore access, accountability, and transparency by imposing market (or market-like) discipline on administrative agencies' (Ansell and Gingrich, 2003: 165). Rehabilitating service users as actors whose views should count in the day-to-day operations of the bureaucracy is no doubt crucial to the appeal of NPM. However, the quest for greater accountability to service users cannot be reduced to its market-line dimension, and it is sometimes difficult to distinguish the 'client orientation' from concerns at the origin of the development of the participatory procedures described previously in this chapter. Part of the European social-democratic Left supported NPM reforms, because of a concern with the accountability of the administration and the quality of service delivery by the state, rather than because of a fascination with the market.

The quest for 'accountability by results' exemplifies these types of expectations from public bureaucracies: 'Supported by quantitative techniques of evaluation, managerial accountability focuses on cost-effectiveness, output efficiency, results, and customer satisfaction, rather than institutional processes and formal procedures' (Considine and Afzal, 2011: 376). The focus on 'outputs' and the so-called derived 'output-legitimacy' were convincingly presented as core rhetorical innovations in the NPM mainstream discourse, and were embodied, for example, in the development of 'management by objectives'. Compliance accountability that focuses on rules and procedures to be followed is replaced by performance accountability. It is no longer the question to monitor in detail the formal process by which inputs are transformed into outputs; rather to monitor outputs and outcomes (Hammerschmid *et al.*, 2006: 19), because the provision of satisfactory outputs is expected to contribute to the legitimacy of public authorities. Emphasis is thus put on instruments to evaluate performance, such as the setting of standards, benchmarking, reliance on indicators facilitated by progress in information technologies, and the development of audits to evaluate outputs. Such instruments are part of an 'emulation' logic; one can think of the role of publicity in rankings of schools or hospitals, with 'naming and shaming' of those who are not performing well serving as a disciplinary device. It is frequently assumed that the focus on outputs will generate a virtuous circle: If citizens come to view themselves as rational and utility-maximizing consumers, they will increasingly require value for money and formulate more demands, and this will put more pressure on politicians and on the administration to 'deliver' and care about 'output-legitimacy'.

To put it in a nutshell, NPM 'grants agencies greater autonomy to manage their own affairs while providing them with market-like incentives to perform on the "output" side. NPM restores sovereignty to consumers with a variety of techniques that seek to make agencies responsive to citizen "demand" .... One of the central themes of NPM is making bureaucracies more "customer"- or "client"-oriented' (Ansell and Gingrich, 2003: 166). Novel devices are coined for that purpose, such as the design of charters stipulating the rights of service users and the obligations of service providers in countries including Belgium, France, Italy, Portugal and the United Kingdom (Pollitt and Bouckaert, 2004: 19). Furthermore, feedback techniques are valued, such as complaints and suggestion schemes, or customer surveys aiming to assess satisfaction with services, increasingly labelled as 'products'. According to Ansell and Gingrich (2003: 165–6), 'the common sense of (administrative) reforms is the desire to make the relationship between citizens and government more *direct* by streamlining or eliminating the layers and complexities of government' (emphasis in the original). Recent experiments in 'e-government' – the use of new information technologies in communication between governmental services and citizens – pursue the same objective and go in the same direction.

In principle, the clienteles of administrations are supposed to gain influence through more direct channels of expression. Usually, such channels are made available to the specific segments of the population that are personally affected by administrative action and service delivery. This may present advantages with regard to the degree of state responsiveness to public needs; given that they are directly affected, these segments may have better knowledge of what appropriate public action should be, and whether the latter truly meets their needs. However, not all the affected have the same chances to make their voice heard. Peters (2003: 124) rightly maintains that this produces a middle-class bias because less-educated people are less effective in expressing their grievances. Furthermore, it is also likely that reforms reinforce the trend towards 'advocacy' democracy, as some forms of organization may be necessary to become a credible spokesperson for the interests of clients. After all, for client feedback to become effective, it must be recognized as legitimate and decoded by bureaucrats and politicians. This often leads to conflicts over the appreciation of the clients' will, and it certainly reduces the real empowerment of ordinary people. Another noticeable evolution is that with administrative reform giving priority to street-level interactions as a feedback mechanism, the 'abstract' citizen loses part of the influence she traditionally exercized through her vote. Hence, there is no guarantee that the demands expressed by people as customers, service users or clients through NPM tools for service improvement find much resonance, while citizens' influence through their right to vote on concrete service delivery becomes increasingly fictitious.

On the other hand, one should avoid too-hasty generalizations. If NPM discourses found such a broad resonance, it was also because they are not devoid of ambiguity. NPM is a loose and multifaceted concept: a 'shopping basket' (Christensen and Laegreid, 2001a: 19) or a 'chameleon' (Pollitt *et al.*, 2007: 5). For instance, NPM is not completely of neoliberal inspiration; it also rests on the widely shared belief that decentralization allows for the improved exploitation of local knowledge, and it borrows from traditional tools of administrative rationalization as well, such as the introduction of management by objectives. However, the potentially contradictory expectations that coexist in NPM discourse risk undermining goal attainment. Neoliberals require NPM to cut costs for the delivery of public goods in the name of efficiency, but this objective may conflict with that of responsiveness, which is also present in NPM and implies being receptive to a variety of social demands. Reforms are often deemed to lead to an increase of 'both productive efficiency (costs and service quality in general) and allocative efficiency (the match between citizens and services)' (Van Slyke and Roch, 2004: 192). However, reconciling both goals may be hard, and the quest for efficiency that often prevails in the end is not politically neutral (Peters and Pierre, 2004: 285).

Ambiguity also lies in the fact that reformers criticize bureaucracy, but they simultaneously criticize political interference in administrative operations, opting for devolution and delegation that free management from the pressure of cumbersome compliance rules. It is argued that politicians delve too much into the details of day-to-day administrative activities and suffocate any creativity that may exist among public servants. The proposed remedy is a functional differentiation between politics and the administration; politicians should provide only general guidelines regarding public decisions (steering), while rowing – the concretization of such guidelines – should be more generously delegated to the administration. However, not only is the demarcation between decision-making and the conduct of policy implementation often illusory in practice, but devolution of tasks to managers implies a significant level of trust in them, which tends to invalidate the critiques of bureaucracy. Politicians considered traditional bureaucracies as an impediment to policy change but hoped that the coupling of reforms making them more efficiency-oriented with reforms leaving more discretion to them would be a positive bargain. They were soon disillusioned by the fact that, ultimately, bureaucracies gained power from reforms. A simple reason for that was that reforms led to the hiring of new civil servants from the private sector who themselves distrusted politicians (Peters and Pierre, 2004)!

To original ambiguities should be added the fact that concrete NPM reforms are extremely heterogeneous. The wide diffusion of NPM conceals considerable variety, and further affects the coherence of the paradigm. It is precisely ambiguity coupled with heterogeneity that generated support across nations for the reform agenda. NPM was progressively de-ideologized (Sahlin-Andersson, 2001: 56) and benefited from a 'contradictory consensus' (Palier, 2003: 177) that encompassed both right- and left-wing forces around the values of what may be called an 'efficiency state'. A distinction has been made, for instance, between a 'hard' and a 'soft' version of NPM, and each has different implications regarding the exercise of accountability and the relations between politicians, administrative managers, street-level bureaucrats, and service users.

Hard NPM is characterized by 'a rise of audit, performance measurement, performance management, and performance-related finance. This new paradigm assumes (1) performance identification through measurement and (2) a reward or punish strategy, using hard numbers and performance indicators as the basis of judgment' (Ferlie and Geraghty, 2005: 431). Whether hard NPM ensures better accountability of civil servants to elected rulers or simply more hierarchical control by management over street-level bureaucrats who are under increased pressure to deliver, remains an open question. In soft NPM, by contrast, 'professionals are drawn into newly developed managerial processes based on principles of joint learning, high commitment and culture change, rather than measurement, audit and external regulation' (Ferlie and Geraghty, 2005: 436). Though this description may be overly idealized, in soft NPM, the voice of customers and stakeholders is supposed to count more, as these actors are consulted to render the bureaucracy more responsive to their needs.

NPM diffusion was thus achieved at the price of reinterpretations and concessions. Local reforms have been packaged after the event with an NPM label to enhance their chances of acceptance. Comparative research shows that the content of NPM often had to be differentially 'acclimated' (Eymeri-Douzans, 2008) to persisting national administrative traditions (Painter and Peters, 2010), or reinterpreted in light of prevailing norms and values. It also reveals that the importation of reforms has been relative, filtered by the domestic institutional context and the power balance between actors. Genuine cross-national convergence is limited, and it is highly likely that apparent convergence in terms of discourse or formal decisions remained higher than operational convergence, 'a further step down the road, because it would mean that hundreds or thousands of civil servants had changed their day-to-day behaviours, and were converging on a single set of new routines' (Pollitt, 2007: 14). NPM has undergone 'hybridization' in the transnational diffusion process: editing, translation, blending

(Christensen and Laegreid, 2006: 7) or selective shopping (Homburg *et al.*, 2007: 2) are the terms used to portray this phenomenon. In spite of cross-country imitation and rhetorical convergence, the resonance of NPM has been stronger in Anglo-American cultures than in continental or Northern European countries (Olsen, 2008: 26).

Countries have followed quite different trajectories and reform paths. For instance, traditional German legalism has proven resistant to reform, especially because reforms often necessitate a broad consensus, the second federal Chamber (the *Bundesrat* where *Länder* governments are represented) being frequently controlled by opposition parties. More generally, it is harder for reforms to be comprehensive in federal states because power is fragmented among territorial levels, and not all public authorities at these levels are animated by the same reformist fever (Pollitt and Bouckaert, 2004: 43). In Scandinavian countries, obstacles to NPM resulting from the *Rechtsstaat* culture are accompanied by obstacles to substantial reforms in general, due to the relative weaknesses of frequent minority and coalition governments (Christensen and Laegreid, 2006: 9), and perhaps also due to their less confrontational political culture that requires reforms to be endorsed by wide support. As a matter of fact, just as one can distinguish between hard and soft NPM, it is also possible to distinguish between zealous promoters of marketization, well represented in the Anglophone world, and advocates of modernization in the direction of a 'neo-Weberian' state, well represented in continental Europe. The United Kingdom, Australia, New Zealand and – more superficially – the United States form the core NPM countries, with a strong market orientation in reforms. For example, the objectives of the 'Next Steps Initiative', implemented since the end of the 1980s in the United Kingdom without a legislative act, clearly mimicked corporate management; individual agencies were created and subject to performance requirements and targets, and these agencies were headed by CEOs whose salaries were performance-related (Lynn, 2006: 118). Continental states also favour an output orientation, but expect quality in service delivery to be better achieved through devices of public consultation, professionalism, and *ex post* controls promoting accountability, rather than through market-like mechanisms (Pollitt and Bouckaert, 2004: 99–100). All this makes generalizations about the impact of NPM difficult.

An additional problem lies in the fact that it is not always possible to distinguish genuine administrative reform from symbolic politics. For instance, reforms are often accompanied by rankings or accreditation processes, whose symbolic force should not be underestimated. Djelic and Sahlin-Andersson (2006: 25), who aptly describe such devices as 'ritualized performance displays', eloquently state, 'Virtue is the embodiment of goodness; virtuosity is the embodiment of excellence. Celebrations tend to be highly rationalized – with the assumption that virtue and virtuosity can be (scientifically) assessed, measured and compared'. But symbols not only accompany reform undertakings, there may also be a gap between rituals, the rhetoric of modernization, and administrative practice. In some cases administrative reforms were nothing more than window-dressing for 'swallowing the pill' of painful measures like budget cuts. Thus, they did not really aim to achieve gains in quality of delivery, but were rather intended to protect policy-makers from the risk of losing their popularity. In such cases, it hardly makes any sense to appraise reforms in terms of whether or not they attained proclaimed goals.

A crucial question is how much and in which direction administrative reform has affected the power balance between elected politicians and public managers, and to what extent it has altered the degree of political control over the bureaucracy. Given that national paths differ and unintended effects occurred, it is again difficult to draw any general conclusions. Christensen and Laegreid (2001a) concluded in a comparative study that reform under strong political control in Australia and New Zealand ended up, paradoxically, with more administrative autonomy, whereas the reform process in Norway and Sweden took place under greater administrative control, but political control was less weakened. What seems to have occurred generally is that those politicians who truly accepted the enhancement of the administration's operational autonomy realized that they ran the risk of committing *hara-kiri* with regard to their own role and prerogatives. They thus reasserted their power through a new wave of repoliticization of the civil service; in the end the 'partyness' of the government seems to have increased, paradoxically, during a period of dissolution of the 'partyness' of society, as suggested in Chapter 1 (Katz and Mair, 2009: 760).

Among elected officials, members of the executive appear to be the ultimate winners of this cyclical process: 'reforms meant to weaken the role of political leaders have resulted in greater political intervention in the day-to-day management of government' (Peters and Pierre, 2004: 284). The gains in government officials' influence were made possible by the deinstitutionalization of the bureaucracy that they initiated a couple of years or decades before. Members of executives exploit the new possibilities acquired through reforms to recruit 'adequate' people, and they no longer recruit pure 'managers' but, above all, people committed to their preferences. Such practices denote a non-negligible gap between initial intentions and actual reform, especially as politicians realized that reforms risked resulting in less power over more remote managers. Politicians now possess better instruments for control, such as the design of contracts setting goals that can be measured through performance indicators. Furthermore, performance evaluations of service provision or of administrative units can be instrumentalized by politicians. As they are not simply a reflexive mechanism designed to enhance disinterested learning, they are not necessarily commissioned to neutral persons, can be strategically manipulated, and give rise to controversial interpretations. Those politicians or bureaucrats with an interest in exhibiting their results will not hesitate to brandish them, whereas those whose results are negatively evaluated will seek to downplay the conclusions of evaluation reports, discredit their authors, or find excuses and shift blame.

The reasons for the rather unexpected consequences of reforms on the power of executive officials are not only political – in the narrow sense of an understandable deeply-entrenched obsession with control – but also functional. The fragmentation of the administration and the autonomization of its segments can cause coordination problems. More control from the top then becomes necessary, if we consider that coordination will not necessarily occur spontaneously among decentralized units (Bouckaert *et al.*, 2010). In a sense, the myth of NPM as an announced success story has been followed by a 'counter-narrative' of NPM failure, and probably by adherence to new myths on the virtues of integration as a goal and on the promises of coordination as a means. After all, it is easy to pronounce reform 'failure' because it is often unrealistic to try to conciliate all reform objectives, and because it may take time until the expected virtuous effects become visible (Pollitt and Bouckaert, 2004: 7). It is likely that the more firmly beliefs in the NPM myth are anchored, and the more drastic the NPM reforms, the more pronounced will be the disenchantment and the pendulum-like movement accompanying 'second', post-NPM reforms (Christensen and Laegreid, 2006 and 2006a). In the United Kingdom, for example, the need for integration among the various administrative units responsible for service delivery has given rise to a new wave of reforms favouring inter-sectoral initiatives, as most public problems require not only the joint intervention of several public agencies, but also, obviously, coordination between them. An approach based on the rhetoric of 'joined-up' government (Pollitt, 2003), also called a 'whole-of-government' approach in the Antipodes, has become more prevalent. As noted above, despite new labels, the quest for coordination is not a major novelty either, and, as with NPM, reforms in the direction of 'joined-up government' are also based on sometimes excessively optimistic and naïve beliefs.

The more recent process of re-aggregation should probably be seen simultaneously as a manifestation of the reassertion of the centre, and as an attempt to remedy some of the limits of first-generation reforms with regard to their problem-solving capacities. Second-generation reforms can be viewed as correctives intended to reaffirm political control over agencies and to address the lack of intersectoral coordination. It appears then that politicians are able to learn from the original reforms in two respects: strategically, reasserting their authority, and functionally, redrawing reforms in order to remedy coordination problems. However, one should not interpret the more recent reforms as a simple return to the *status quo ante*. Researchers often observe a 'layering' process (Streeck and Thelen, 2005) leading to a hybrid organizational mix: second-generation reforms did not replace but rather tend to supplement first-generation reforms, thus adding more complexity to the administrative system instead of simplifying it (Verhoest and Laegreid, 2010).

But did the centre really lose its power in a first phase? With more administrative autonomy, whether through NPM reforms or through the development of independent agencies (see Chapter 6), politicians can also more easily shift the blame to bureaucrats; sceptics thus suspect that politicians' loss of power was an excuse, rather than reality. With the separation of politics and administration advocated by NPM, ministers can evade parliamentary control by maintaining that the issue at stake lies under the responsibility of the administration, while in the context of increased mediatization (see Chapter 2), high-ranking civil servants no longer operate in the shadow of their ministers. Managers have lost anonymity (Aucoin, 2012: 189) and may be required to justify their actions to Parliament, even though they have no electoral mandate (Du Gay, 2000). NPM would in fact entail an attenuation of ministerial accountability, and consequently the real challenge for it would be reaching the appropriate balance between decentralization and control (Hammerschmid *et al.*, 2006: 1). This is not an easy task, considering the findings of Pollitt and Bouckaert (2004: 147) who observed that some managers believed that they had more freedom to act, but that they were also subject to increased surveillance. For example, managers may enjoy more autonomy *ex ante* in managing funds ('freeing managers to manage') – in other words, a larger scope of delegation of competences – but may then be subject to closer *ex post* scrutiny by the minister. More managerial authority does not necessarily contradict more political control. Executive politicians probably acquire better tools to make administrators accountable, while being able to disguise political clumsiness as managerial failure (Pollitt and Bouckaert, 2004: 156–7). And if managers fear that they might serve as scapegoats in case of failure, the Damoclean sword of increased accountability may be inimical to the proclaimed goals of creativity and innovation.

The upward accountability relations between members of the bureaucracy and their political superiors are thus evolving. NPM reforms implied that the administration would be awarded more autonomy, but the reforms also led to the reassertion of control of the bureaucracy by politicians, unlike collaborative governance, where bureaucracy seems to have acquired more leeway in the management of policy networks. However, it seems reasonable to think that directly elected citizens' representatives are not the major beneficiaries of this reassertion; for example, parliaments are not very active in using their monitoring tools, simply because MPs have other priorities and not much time to monitor the implementation of the laws that they pass, or scrutinize their outcomes. The downward accountability of the bureaucracy is now – in principle, at least – enhanced. But accountability to whom? Most notably, to narrow populations that become legitimate accountability-holders if, as in collaborative governance, they can make credible claims about their affectedness by state policies. Given the primacy conferred to accountability relations at the street-level, accountability through electoral mechanisms becomes less effective. Moreover, it is even argued that in many cases consumer empowerment has also been forgotten (Pollitt and Bouckaert, 2004: 166). Even when feedback by service users exists, its interpretation often lies in the hands of politicians and management who can use it as an instrument for their own strategic purposes.

It would be too bold to formulate general statements on the consequences of administrative reforms, which are highly context-sensitive; but it may well be that we are facing an executive drift in that case as well, as with the internationalization of politics. For executive politicians, administrative reform sometimes facilitated blame-shift; sometimes it resulted in unbearable administrative discretion, and in a backlash leading to the reassertion of control; and sometimes, it was just words, not policy. The political accountability of the administration may have increased, but this does not mean more democratic accountability of governments to parliaments or citizens. Accountability in one part of the delegation chain – between administrators and members of executives – may be strengthened, but, simultaneously, accountability may be weakened between administrators and the citizenry as a whole, while the street-level accountability of administrators to individual stakeholders or service users may be confined to the symbolic sphere of managerial discourse.

## The 'accountability agenda': failed promises, limited relevance?

Participatory experiments are so diverse that it is hard to draw generalizations about their implications. Evidence can be provided both in support of the argument that these experiments can truly influence decision-making, and against it. One assertion that can be made with certainty, however, is that only a few experiments explicitly target the democratization of decision-making, and even fewer lead to the formulation of policy options endorsed by public authorities.

These experiments are not designed as alternatives but rather as supplements to the traditional mechanisms of representative democracy, and we also observed that they may deploy subtle effects, for example pressing power-holders to stick to their commitments and justify their choices. One should consider, however, that the growth of participatory forms of policy-making takes place in a context of wider transformations in governance; arguably, most novel governance modes are not genuinely participatory, and some of them are not participatory at all. The diffusion of participatory experiments mostly takes place at a local level, and public authorities seldom consider themselves bound by their outcomes. Hence, it would be overoptimistic to think that the trend towards more participatory forms of governance can counterbalance the technocratic and elitist bias present in other emerging forms of governance. Participatory reforms do not represent the most important game in town as far as contemporary governance is concerned.

As to NPM reforms and their derivatives, there is an oft-recited mantra that they would not only be the most appropriate means for enhancing the efficiency of public administrations, but they would also induce a 'win–win' scenario. Administrators would be better able to exploit their creative potential, politicians would benefit from more time to strategic planning and more efficient control instruments, and in the end, users of public services would receive deliverables of higher quality. Unsurprisingly, as it is frequently the case with such ambitious undertakings, considerable disenchantment followed the implementation of reforms and concomitant organizational adjustment.

The impact on the quality of democracy of the administrative reforms discussed in this chapter is – to say the least – mixed. Did elected officials gain better control over the administration, due to the acquisition of more sophisticated instruments for performance measurement? Probably yes, but this applies more to members of the executive branch than to members of legislatures. Furthermore, when reforms led to organizational fragmentation, they triggered claims for more joined-up government, which usually means more intervention from the top. These may well be indicators of executive drift in our democracies, to be added to the presidentialization of politics (Chapter 1) and to the effects of policy internationalization (Chapter 3). At the same time, executive branch politicians are now probably better able to shift the blame for policy failures to unelected top managers, who are increasingly exposed to media criticism.

What has happened within the bureaucracy below this level? At present, street-level bureaucrats are operating more under the shadow of being evaluated by customers, but this mainly seems to serve to empower managers, to whom the frontline are accountable, rather than the citizens themselves. Finally, some categories of clients or stakeholders may indeed gain in influence, but this happens at the expense of alternative and more egalitarian channels of citizen influence, such as the vote in parliamentary elections. It is thus likely that administrative reforms reinforce the trend towards advocacy forms of democracy that has been discussed in previous chapters. Overall, the positive democratic impact of reforms associated with an accountability agenda is limited in the case of participatory devices, and ambiguous in the case of administrative reforms. By no means can it outweigh the negative impact of reforms in governance modes that are deprived of any such agenda.

# Chapter 6

# Limits To Majority Rule: Agencification and Judicialization

Representative democracy is, above all else, party democracy (see Chapter 1). More fundamentally, democracy is the exercise of power (*kratein*) by the *demos*. In representative democracies, this kind of power is exercised by the party, perhaps the coalition of parties, that has a majority in parliament or, perhaps more precisely, by the government enjoying support from one or several parties in the parliament. Although there is a philosophical debate as to whether unanimity would be a more robust basis of legitimacy for collectively binding decisions (Manin, 1997), in practice the majority principle has established itself as a sufficient basis for legitimacy for formal decision-making in democratic regimes, with the exception of specific requirements for qualified majorities, most notably for constitutional revisions. Competitive elections reduce the risk of abuse of power by the majority: The perspective of alternation of power allows not only for counting on a reversal of decisions with which the minority disagrees, but it also acts as a self-restraining mechanism for majorities, too. Knowing that they are not going to enjoy the benefits of power forever, majorities would not appreciate being exposed to retaliation by those they have oppressed. This mechanism does not protect, however, the so-called 'structural' minorities: The minorities that, because of their religion or their language, for instance, are in permanent numerical inferiority and cannot reasonably expect that they will become part of the majority in the future.

Hence, as suggested in the introduction to this book, in democracies the republican principle of popular sovereignty – exercised through representative or, much less frequently, through direct majoritarian mechanisms – is combined in varying degrees with a liberal (also called 'constitutionalist') principle emphasizing the need to constrain majority rule (Mény and Surel, 2002). According to this principle, 'public power is or should be limited and subject to some higher form of control by reference to law' (Scott, 2010: 1). An example of such a barrier to the exercise of power is the obligation to achieve concurrent majorities for decision-making in federal-type systems: the need to pass legislation through the Senate in the United States, where small and large states have equal representation; the need to obtain the consent of a majority of cantons for constitutional revisions in Switzerland; the need for a qualified majority (based on sophisticated calculations) in the European Union, (or sometimes – although it occurs less and less – a requirement of the unanimity of member-states). The existence of veto points in the decision-making process – a bicameral legislature or an independent constitutional court – is a typical embodiment of the idea that the more political power is fragmented between a number of institutions, each with different preferences, the more incentives there will be to come to decisions privileging the common good.

The classic Madisonian conception of a checks-and-balances system is emblematic of such a concern, and it remains its most sophisticated theoretical elaboration to this day. Among the American 'Founding Fathers', James Madison was particularly preoccupied with the negative consequences of 'factionalism', that is, of power captured by particular interests or, as phrased in *The Federalist Papers*, No. 10, by:

> a number of citizens, whether amounting to a majority or minority of the whole, who are united and actuated by some common impulse or passion, or interest, adverse to the rights of other citizens, or the permanent and aggregate interests of the community.

Madison did not put much faith in the civic virtue of individuals: he thought that they were inclined to privilege their selfish and partisan interests. They are, according to him, 'much more disposed to vex and oppress each other than to co-operate for their common good' (*The Federalist Papers*, No. 10). Logically, he was concerned about the risk of arbitrariness in the case of rule by the most powerful among factions; in other words, by majority tyranny. This risk should be countered, according to Madison, by the diffusion of power: checks and balances should protect the community from unreflective excesses of the majority's will, due to passion, interest, or manipulation, actions that the majority itself might later 'lament and condemn' (*The Federalist Papers*, No. 63). When political influence is fragmented across several bodies and deliberations become necessary among them, the decision-making process becomes lengthier, and this is deemed to favour reasonableness to the detriment of passion (Manin, 1994: 60–2). In fact, Madison did not consider that political leaders were necessarily endowed with a superior civic virtue, and he judged that the most appropriate way to exert control over them was to create a system of interdependence and mutual supervision: in contemporary terms, a system of horizontal accountability.

However, although power fragmentation among institutions operating along distinct logics may appear necessary, it is also controversial. As regards, for instance, the role of the judiciary, most judges run no risk of removal from office by the citizenry, even when they are (often indirectly) elected. Critics of the advent of judicial power are epitomized in catch phrases or words like 'government of judges' or 'juristocracy'; for some, a judicial review of political decisions leads to 'disenfranchisement' and is thus incompatible with freedom and democratic self-rule (Waldron, 2006). Even though one might not agree that there is an incompatibility by essence, there might be a problem of dosage. It seems that there is nowadays a trend towards an ever-increasing role for the judiciary in public matters, so that 'judicialization' (which will be scrutinized later in this chapter) tips the balance between populist and liberal principles in our democratic systems in the latter's direction and, by the same token, slightly away from democratic self-rule (Mény and Surel, 2002). This new imbalance is, according to Mény and Surel, one of the factors causing the success of anti-establishment ('populist') parties, which can more credibly claim that people are being dispossessed from their power by self-serving elites.

More recently, an additional limit has appeared by design to the rule of governmental majorities: 'agencification'. Both agencification and judicialization deliberately aim to check abuses of power, albeit with different rationales. While courts are expected to ensure minority protection and the safeguarding of individual rights, the rationale of regulation by independent agencies is not so much to protect rights, but to safeguard the public interest from the alleged self-interest of politicians, or from the risk of capture of decision-making by particular interests. Agencification is part of the trend of administrative reform described above. In the USA, the development of agencies operating at arm's length from government and electoral politics is not new, but independent agencies recently experienced considerable transnational diffusion. Unlike the judiciary, agencies are not counter-majoritarian institutions as their role is not to check the power of majorities. But they are *non*-majoritarian bodies of 'delegated governance'

(Flinders, 2004a), and this means that political majorities of the moment are not supposed to influence them:

> In just the same way that politicians usually understand that they should stand back from the processes of the law and distinguish the different realm of legal judgments from the realm of political judgments, so too procedural judgments suggest that politicians may have to learn to stand back from the unelected bodies and to distinguish their judgments from political judgments. (Vibert, 2007: 77)

In practice, agency autonomy is likely to vary along a number of dimensions: There is, for instance, no necessary coincidence between autonomy over financial matters, personnel appointments, or policy decisions (Bouckaert and Peters, 2004). However, with the creation of autonomous agencies, the legislator opts for self-restraint because it does not trust itself much: the metaphor of Ulysses who asked to be bound to the mast in order not to cede to the charm of the sirens' song is sometimes used to portray that particular preventive mechanism (Elster, 2000). Distinguishing between what happens in time one, and what might happen in time two is helpful here. In time one, the legislator decides to tie the hands of future legislators in the event they would wish to pass in time two measures that, inspired by a different political agenda, would be considered in time one to cause harm to the common good. Agency independence that immunizes agencies from political pressure is a guarantee against such a risk.

The recent combination of agencification with judicialization possibly leads, then, to further limits on the positive power of governmental majorities, that is, on their power to impose collectively binding decisions compatible with their preferences, thanks to their control over the democratically authorized institutions. However, the cumulative effect of the transformations scrutinized in this book is usually overlooked in the literature, with few exceptions, such as Hirschl, who notes in the concluding section of his critical book on the advent of 'juristocracy': 'In short, a large-scale transfer of crucial policy-making prerogatives from majoritarian decision-making arenas to relatively insulated domestic and transnational policy-making bodies has been established over the last thirty years' (Hirschl, 2004: 216). Although his treatment is cursory, Hirschl interestingly relates this transfer to a number of political developments described in this book, such as the increased versatility of the electorate, media commercialization, or centrifugal tendencies like regionalization.

The effects of the trends mentioned above require closer scrutiny. Interestingly, they can be considered to improve or decrease the quality of democracy, depending on one's trust in the virtues of politicians. We will start with the effects of agencification, since it can be considered as part of the wave of administrative reforms considered in the previous chapter.

## Agencification by contagion

As suggested earlier, the concentration of power in the core executive can, paradoxically, go hand in hand with restrictions in the scope of power. Power is more concentrated, but a large portion of it escapes the political authorities. No matter whether this outcome results from voluntary political choice or from inescapable functional imperatives, the traditional governmental-administrative state machine loses part of its steering role. Collaborative governance is an aspect of this process, related to the need to cope with various facets of social complexity (see Chapter 4). Another aspect is the delegation of competences to independent agencies – especially in the field of the regulation of market competition. Unlike deliberative procedures or even cooperative forms of governance, the rationale of this latter shift is more technocratic than participatory. While the inclusion of stakeholders is positively valued in deliberative experiments and in collaborative governance, and while proximity to them is valued in other reforms of NPM inspiration, the proximity to the regulated is viewed here as entailing the risk of capture. On the other hand, agencification at large – including, for example, the set-up of agencies for service delivery – is indeed inspired by NPM principles (Christensen and Laegreid, 2006). Although the 'NPM ideal-type agency' hardly exists, the NPM influence is discernible in quite a number of agency features. This is the structural disaggregation – or 'unbundling' (Pollitt and Talbot, 2004) – of the bureaucracy into smaller single-purpose units deemed to be more flexible and familiar with the sector of operations; more *ex ante* operational discretion for the administration ('letting managers manage') that is supposed to favour professionalism; and a preference for modes of *ex post* accountability based on results and no longer on the requirement of legalistic compliance with cumbersome rules (Verhoest *et al.*, 2010: 6–8). Yet one should not forget that NPM is an item from the neoliberal agenda, while in the case of delegation of regulatory prerogatives to agencies, things are more complex. Such delegation is a by-product of the liberalization, privatization, and deregulation movement, too, but rather in the sense of a counter-movement based on learning by policy-makers: it soon appeared that deregulation required public *re*-regulation, and for the latter to be credible, it needed to be delegated to bodies formally independent of the government.

With 'agencification', formal law-making remains within the realm of classic parliamentary and governmental bodies, but single-purpose independent agencies rather than the traditional state bureaucracy issue important individually binding decisions that clearly impact the market or a policy sector. This can be considered as a replication of the model of independent central banks, where this is expected to lead to more efficient inflation control, as regulatory functions are deliberately removed from the circuit of democratic politics. As noted above, agencies have a long-standing tradition in the United States: The first one, the Interstate Commerce Commission, was established in the 1880s, and agencies proliferated in the 1930s during the period of the New Deal (Scott, 2003; Talbot, 2004). But in other parts of the world, and most notably in the vast majority of European countries, agencification in the field of regulation is largely related to the much more recent diffusion of policies of deregulation, which result in turn from the joint dynamics of globalization and neoliberalism. This does not mean that economic globalization and neoliberal ideology are merely two sides of the same coin (or, to put it in Marxist terms, respectively, 'infrastructural' change mirrored in changes in the 'superstructure'). The circulation of policy ideas follows its own logic, and neoliberal recipes for economic policy, for instance, were largely a reaction to failures (such as stagflation) of the Keynesian state interventionist paradigm, largely acknowledged by social-democrats as well.

What happened was that deregulation generated claims for re-regulation: Although deregulation is deemed to favour competition, which is beneficial to the collective well-being, new regulatory authorities had to be designed to ensure that competition was not distorted. Mention is often made of the development of a 'regulatory capitalism', and two of the major specialists in the field observed an interesting paradox: 'In an era in which regulation has become synonymous with red tape, and deregulation has become a major electoral platform of the New Right, regulatory authorities have been created in unprecedented numbers, and with unprecedented autonomy' (Jordana and Levi-Faur, 2004: 1). Interestingly, Levi-Faur added elsewhere: 'Indeed, these regulatory institutions are even more popular than privatization. In telecommunications, for example, about 90 countries have made some significant moves toward privatization of their formally state-owned operator, but 120 countries have established regulatory author-ities' (Levi-Faur, 2006: 506).

The movement towards re-regulation concerned the whole area of market competition, but also specific policy sectors such as telecom-munications, electricity, energy, and financial markets. Gilardi (2005) notes that the percentage of European countries having a regulatory agency in the areas of electricity, telecoms, finance, and competition increased from roughly 20 per cent in the early 1980s to more than 90 per cent in the mid-1990s. Relying on a dataset covering 15 policy sectors in 48 OECD and Latin American countries, Jordana *et al.* (2011: 1344) confirm not only the diffusion of the agency model, but also the accelerating pace of this process: the number of agencies that were set up grew up from fewer than five per year until the 1980s to more than 15 per year from the 1990s to 2002. They conclude: 'What we found goes well beyond our initial expectations and what was known and appreciated in the established literature. The process of "regulatory agencification" has indeed exploded and in this process regulation has become a distinct and salient function in the institu-tions of policy making'.

In the United Kingdom, agencies employ three-quarters of the people who would traditionally be considered as civil servants. Although other countries displayed less enthusiasm for the creation of independent agencies (Bale, 2005: 65), the OECD estimated that arm's-length bodies account for between 50 and 75 per cent of public expenditure and employment in its member countries (Pollitt *et al.*, 2004: 7). Agencification extends beyond the OECD world, but in Europe it is closely related to European integration, and in the European Union itself there are now over 20 policy agencies. Giandomenico Majone – a leading specialist on regulation – portrays the EU as a regulatory state: rule making compensates at this level for the weak taxation capability and consequent low-spending capacity of the EU. He eloquently writes:

> The only way for the European Commission to increase its influence is to expand the scope of its regulatory activities: rule making puts a great deal of power in the hands of the Brussels authorities, in spite of the tight budgetary constraints imposed by the member states. In other words, since the EC lacks an independent power to tax and spend, it could increase its competencies only by developing as an almost pure type of regulatory state. (Majone, 1997: 150)

Major features of this type of state are the shift from centralized bureaucracies to single-purpose agencies, and from direct accountability to political superiors to more plural forms of accountability largely relying on results and performance indicators (Levi-Faur, 2007: 104). The EU has become a major promoter of this regulatory style (Kelemen, 2011): in many sectors EU legislation requires member states to create independent regulatory agencies and, as we shall see below, the EU seeks to propagate 'best practices' by encouraging the formation of multilevel networks involving regulatory bodies at European and nation level. Finally, agencification is also a consequence of 'risk' society: the domains of pharmaceuticals, food, or the environment also need to be regulated, and independent bodies whose task is to avoid accidents and enhance quality of life are entrusted with the implementation of regulations.

The scope of agencies is very broad: they 'carry out inspections, issue licences, pay benefits, run scientific research and development programmes, regulate public utilities, maintain the public infrastructure, develop and operate databases, adjudicate applications, administer museums, safeguard the environment, offer information services, run prisons, collect taxes and many other functions' (Pollitt *et al.*, 2004: 6). Vibert provides telling illustrations of how unelected expert bodies immediately and intimately affect various aspects and periods of our lives:

> First, their influence extends into most areas of daily life. The air we breathe, the water we drink, the food we eat, the electricity we use, the phone calls we make, the value of the coins and banknotes in our pockets, our access to media, the disputes we get involved in, are all influenced in basic ways by their activities. Secondly, unelected bodies have a crucial impact at key stages in a person's life-cycle. In the early stages of life they may influence the nutrition we receive, the quality of schools we attend and the value of the types of education diplomas we receive and our job prospects. At a later stage in life they may decide the information or financial structure that determines the benefits from a pension arrangement, and they may affect the choices we have of medicines or treatments to combat wear and tear in the final stage of our lives. Thirdly, the unelected affect the way we are able to deal with life's accidents and chances, fortunes and misfortunes. They may, for example have a decisive say over the risks we take in using different forms of transport, or eating different foodstuffs. (Vibert, 2007: 7)

Given the variety of their tasks, agencies are inevitably diverse in their architecture and, like other managerial reforms, agencification is subject to variation across nations and sectors. New organizational creations are 'tamed' by previously existing politico-administrative systems (Pollitt, 2004: 329), so that, despite the diffusion of agencification, one encounters multiple 'implementation habitats' (Verhoest *et al.*, 2010: 4). Nevertheless, there seems to be a global logic driving the agencification process in the field of regulation, through the search of an alternative mode of political control than public ownership: 'Regulation-*for*-competition created a "new state" that is more neomercantilist than neoliberal' (Levi-Faur, 2007: 110, emphasis in the original). In the field of market regulation, independent regulatory agencies (IRAs), also called non-majoritarian regulators (NMRs), receive competences for the issuing and enforcement of licences for operating in the market, the authorization of operations such as mergers or takeovers, the prevention of anticompetitive behaviour and the setting of price limits, the supervision of financial institutions, standard-setting, the elaboration of secondary legislation such as directives, the imposition of fines, and so on (Maggetti, 2009: 148; Norton, 2004: 786). An IRA or NMR can be defined

> as an unelected body that is organizationally separated from governments and has powers over regulation of markets through endorsement or formal delegation by public bodies. Formal delegation means the transfer of formal powers by governments and legislatures – notably through public law. Endorsement means 'de facto' or 'de jure' recognition. NMRs, thus, offer an example of the 'de facto' transfer of powers away from elected bodies to unelected ones. (Coen and Thatcher, 2005: 330)

This transfer of power is primarily justified by the fact that bodies that are independent from the government are more credible in their ability to make long-term consistent commitments that are immune to changes resulting from the frequently short-term horizon of politicians, mainly due to selfish electoral concerns. Independence should protect from political uncertainty, and mainly from policy shifts caused by alternations in governmental offices. Credible commitments and signals of policy stability aim at tranquillizing investors, whose privileged position is further enhanced by globalization thanks to increased 'exit' power, but also at broader and more diffuse groups such as consumers. The idea is that politicians are inevitably partial because the logic of the political game forces them to satisfy particular constituencies, lobbies, or groups in order to gain, retain, or increase power. Reflecting a rather grim image of democratic politics, delegation to independent bodies exemplifies a 'logic of discipline' (Roberts, 2010): Discipline is required to achieve impartiality that is threatened by the dysfunctions of party politics. By contrast, depoliticized bodies allegedly perform for the common good, including in its long-term dimension, and the objectivity of depoliticized bodies is considered as a constitutive element of their legitimacy (Rosanvallon, 2008: 22, 190, and 130). Much of the credibility of independent agencies is supposed to derive precisely from the fact that they are more convincing about their impartiality than other political or social actors. They 'are largely free from any suspected bias that manufacturers or service providers may have, for example to suppress risk information; they are free from the bias politicians may have either to downplay or exaggerate facts; and they offer an informed guide through the disputes about the evidence within the scientific community itself' (Vibert, 2007: 46).

Further, being staffed by experts, independent agencies are more credible in their ability to reach decisions that rely on correct causal assumptions. Their development relies on the belief of a functional differentiation between the political marketplace and the sphere of disinterested expert judgment: 'Politicians are out to sell their wares, and not to offer dispassionate advice' (Vibert, 2007: 89). As it is the rule in NPM-inspired reforms, it is believed that administration can be separated from politics. In this case, the manifestation of such a separation lies in the distinction between value judgments and goal orientations that are left to politicians, and the production of technically optimal decisions that should lie in the exclusive realm of problem solving oriented expert bodies. It suffices, nevertheless, to have a quick look at developments in market regulation to notice that independent regulators are not just producers of bare statements of facts, but active norm promoters and policy 'entrepreneurs'. They not only become crucial players in regulation, but they can also play a central law-making role in their area of competence: for example, competition authorities in reforms of competition legislation (Verschuere, 2009). This happens especially with a weak legislature, and when regulators enjoy strong discretion (Maggetti, 2009: 145–96).

Few would doubt that the straightforward distinction between political and non-political tasks that leads to a denial of the political role of technocratic bodies is controversial, and decisions by agencies often inevitably entail value judgments, for example, on the degree of competition that is appropriate in an economic sector, or the degree of protection from risks that it is suitable to achieve. Nevertheless, the myth of depoliticized policy-making remains attractive and powerful. This is due to the fact that partisan politics is regularly considered to lead – as a result of electoral competition – to problematic policy choices, so that the myth periodically re-emerges, espousing different forms. For example, Lehmbruch (1977) showed over three decades ago that 'corporatist' policy-making in the fields of economic, labour market, or social policy – through agreements between 'responsible' interest groups rather than through the parliamentary process – appeared as a solution leading to choices more suited to the collective well-being than those made by short-term oriented and electoralist politicians, tempted by 'overpromising'. Today, the myth of a normatively necessary, and in practical terms possible, depoliticization is related to the broader mistrust in politicians. Without adhering himself to it, a defender of the legitimacy of agency independence refers to the perception of 'venality, sleaziness and lack of moral fibre of elected politicians' (Vibert, 2007: 109).

Thus it is not surprising that delegation to agencies should, in principle, exceed the 'normal' extension of delegation. In classic relations of delegation between 'principals' and 'agents' – such as periodic delegation of our power to decide our fate to the representatives we elect, and in a next step of their own prerogatives to members of the bureaucracy – 'agents' remain under the (theoretical) control of 'principals', who have an interest in monitoring their behaviour in order to prevent the latter 'shirking' and privileging their own interests instead of loyally executing the tasks assigned to them. In the case of independent agencies by contrast, credibility and expertise are so prioritized (and politicians are considered to lack both of them) that larger agency autonomy becomes necessary, with agencies becoming 'trustees' enjoying 'fiduciary' competences rather than mere delegates (Majone, 2001).

However, an overly functionalist view on the diffusion of agencification would be naive. Agency autonomy is not privileged just because it is considered to be the most suitable option for better regulation. For example, comparative empirical research does not lend much support to the idea that agencies are set up by politicians because this enhances credible commitments (Verhoest *et al.*, 2010: 268). There may be less noble reasons for delegation, and politicians can reap benefits by restricting their authoritative power. They can shift the blame for policy failure to the newly empowered agency executives, and we know that this is a particularly useful strategy at a time when the level of public trust for them is low (Flinders, 2012: 100–102). In addition, even senior bureaucrats may find it attractive to outsource more routine operational work to have more freedom for more prestigious and strategic activities: this is part of their 'bureau-shaping' discretion (Dunleavy, 1991). Furthermore, it is not always easy to measure how much discretion agencies really enjoy in comparison to traditional bureaucracies. One should not take formal acts of delegation of competences to independent agencies at face value: it may be rational for politicians to content themselves with symbolic delegation, while retaining in reality control over the operation of agencies. Formal and *de facto* agency independence are not necessarily correlated (Maggetti, 2009; Yesilkagit and Van Thiel, 2008). This means that, in reality, politicians do not necessarily relinquish much of their power: for instance, recent research on 213 Dutch agencies concluded that they generally still perceive their parent minister as their primary principal (Yesilkagit and Van Thiel, 2012).

It can be objected that viewing the promoters of administrative reform in general, and of agencification in particular, as strongly strategically minded entails the risk of considering them overly rational. Not only is administrative reform the product of disparate developments, but politicians may delegate their authority just because this is a norm of conduct that is taken for granted around them, and not so much upon reflection. Subjective beliefs matter: as with the welfare state that was more strongly challenged in the Anglo-American world than in Scandinavian countries, where it was much more resource-consuming (but also deeply socially entrenched), delegation of authority to agencies reached its peak in the United Kingdom, although the UK government suffered less from credibility problems than did laggards in delegation, such as France or Italy (Maggetti, 2009: 39). Independent agencies have not necessarily been proliferating because they have proved their higher efficiency, but through a cross-national process of diffusion mainly based on sometimes uncritical mimetism: on the reputation of 'success stories' or, worse, on sheer geographical proximity (Gilardi, 2008). Wilks and Bartle (2002) refer to this as an 'orgy of borrowing', while Pollitt and colleagues talk about 'fashion' and a 'contagious agency fever', or at least an 'agency flu':

> (O)ne thing that certainly did converge was the hype itself – i.e. the general belief that something (not too well specified) called an *agency* (or equivalent) was a modern thing to have and would

symbolize a government's progressive attitude towards the state apparatus. An agency represented modernization that stopped short of privatization. It sounded modern and managerial, but not overtly ideological. Thus agencification infected the conference circuit and the international organizations like an epidemic. One might also say that agencies became a kind of administrative fashion accessory. (Pollitt *et al.*, 2001: 286)

It should also be noted that contagion does not run only through horizontal diffusion: we saw that the European Commission is an important driving force of agencification. In addition, conditionality matters, at least in developing countries. Many among the latter are in the delicate position of being badly in need of attracting foreign investment while being stigmatized as treating investors badly; hence, international lending institutions require that they establish independent authorities to reassure investors. In such cases, national governments do not tie their hands by themselves, but are forced to do so. Their sovereignty is reduced, but this is not the only development related to agencification that can be detrimental to democracy.

## More accountability, less democracy?

Embodying the 'logic of discipline', IRAs have been portrayed as 'guardian' institutions; yet the question 'Who Guards the Guardians?' (Shapiro, 1988) is crucial. In their report to the Council of Europe, Schmitter and Trechsel suggest that the tendency towards bureaucratization of politics is no longer confined to ministries and the traditional administrative agencies, but is 'increasingly to be found in the growing number of guardian institutions and the spread of networks of governance' (Schmitter and Trechsel, 2004: 70). An important issue is to what extent regulation by autonomous agencies really entails the (desired) technocratization of political decision-making. NPM also implies that administration should be awarded more autonomy, but the reform outcomes in that respect have been ambiguous. Agencification aims at the depoliticization of administrative functions. Does post-delegation behaviour fit this pattern? Again, evidence is mixed.

We noticed that the more agencies enjoy technocratic autonomy, the more they become key players. It may also be expected that the more agencies are autonomous, the more they will be in a position to substitute their own preferences to those of elected officials (Maggetti, 2009: 217–20). This seems to find confirmation in recent empirical work by Norwegian political scientists Egeberg and Trondal (2009): They demonstrated that agency officials pay less attention to signals from executive politicians than do administrative officials belonging to ministerial departments, although agency members assign more weight to political signals if ministerial departments display a strong organizational capacity. And it may happen that, once established, an agency gradually acquires more autonomy than anticipated and formally stipulated (Wilks and Bartle, 2002). All this may be problematic in terms of democratic accountability, and must be balanced against gains in terms of policy 'quality' and 'optimality' in resource allocation expected from agencification.

We know, however, that politicians have a number of tools in their hands to control *ex post* those to whom they have conceded more discretion *ex ante*. Do they make use of these tools? A comparative study in the UK, Germany, France, and Italy of independent authorities in charge of regulation of competition in general, as well as of the utilities and finance, showed that politicians generally did not make use of the control instruments they had in their hands, such as the appointment or dismissal of agency personnel, the reversal of agency decisions, or the reduction of agencies' budgets and competences (Thatcher 2005). The most interesting thing, however, is that the findings of this study lead to a sort of 'observational equivalence': not only can they be interpreted differently, but they can also generate contradictory interpretations. Thatcher (2005) mentioned two of them: control instruments have not been used because politicians had underestimated the costs (in terms of information gathering, for instance) incurred by their use, or control instruments have not been used because political control could be achieved through alternative methods (such as informal contacts) or indirectly through the mere threat of resorting to sanctions. If the first interpretation is correct, then agencies are strongly autonomous and indeed escape control; if the second interpretation is correct, agencies are autonomous in theory, but not in practice. There is some evidence that the shadow of sanctions matters even for autonomous agencies, so that an 'autonomization paradox' is detected: given that autonomy is accompanied by more stringent results-based controls, agencies perceive themselves as being more controlled than before (Verhoest *et al.*, 2010: 263) and, in line with the second interpretation, they operate under the 'Damoclean sword' of political oversight. Yet this is not a general rule: it seems that this form of control is more easily activated if the agency's tasks have high political salience or if control is facilitated by the visibility of agency operations and outcomes (Pollitt *et al.*, 2004: 21 and 25).

In such cases, one might argue that not only has deregulation been followed by re-regulation through agencies but also that agencification itself is followed by a reassertion of the centre. In addition, as with other NPM-inspired reforms (see Chapter 5), claims for more coordination appeared in response to the fragmentation of the administration caused by agencification, and more coordination usually implies more central political steering (Pollitt, 2004: 335–6). In some cases, this reassertion of the centre also manifested itself *ex ante*: the autonomization of some branches of the administration was offset by targeted appointments of board members. Those were not necessarily party sympathizers, but experts sharing the same 'orthodox' policy preferences – for example, a strong belief in the virtues of competition – with elected politicians (Christensen and Laegreid, 2006a). If agency board members have now more discretion than in the past, this would be then to give them more leeway to attain the political goals that they share with elected officials, both being part of the same policy community. However, once again we cannot consider this as a general rule. In his comparative study Thatcher (2005) did not find much evidence of politicians seizing this opportunity, and in reference to the United Kingdom, Flinders (2009a) speaks about 'shrinking reach and diluted permeation' of political patronage over agency boards, commissions, and quangos, which undermines the idea that clientelism in ministerial appointments is widespread. As with other (NPM and post-NPM) administrative reforms, the effect of agencification on the relations between politics and the bureaucracy is highly context-dependent. Convergence in agencification remained superficial, taking place largely at the level of discourse while remaining much more limited in practical matters such as status, appointment practice, and financial or managerial agency autonomy. Thus 'crucial relationships with ministers, ministries and legislatures are far from uniform' (Pollitt *et al.*, 2001: 287): the ministry may be too interventionist or it may be too passive, so that the overall picture is quite murky and mixed (Pollitt *et al.*, 2004: 22).

Some, like Majone (1997: 161), even consider that the accountability of the traditional civil service to ministers who are directly responsible to parliament is often a myth and provides an excuse for not imposing stringent requirements of transparency and reason-giving (although we have seen in Chapter 5 that administrative reform is changing that). The situation was particularly critical in systems where strong executives were supported by disciplined parliamentary majorities and enjoyed much greater expertise than legislatures (Thatcher, 2002: 142). Agencies, by contrast, tend to be more open to diverse interests than traditional 'iron triangles' of power entailing close connections between the political-administrative apparatus and privileged interests (Thatcher and Stone Sweet, 2002: 17 and 19). Agencies also have to convince various audiences about their positive policy role, so it would be an error to equate their independence to a lack of accountability. Reporting and auditing are important episodes in agencies' organizational life, and the 'giving reasons requirement', a 'mild self-enforcing mechanism for controlling discretion' (Shapiro, 2002: 230), particularly applies to them. In concrete cases in which an agency decision is contested, the agency 'may expect to be asked to provide reasons for the appropriateness of its decision in light of possible alternatives' (Gehring, 2004: 692). Agency leaderships may no longer be directly accountable to a ministerial superior, but they have account-giving obligations to other forums. They are subject to managerial surveillance by agency boards, to financial surveillance by auditing institutions, and to legal surveillance by courts.

One should add to agencies' formal accountabilities a practical obligation on them to justify their policy to other forums, such as stakeholders (firms from the regulated sector, consumer associations) or the media in the case of salient issues. Such forums have no direct sanctioning power, but their support is necessary for agency legitimacy, and they consequently exercise the soft power of naming and shaming. As agency legitimacy relies on both procedural and substantive bases, agencies must convince forums of the successful achievement of quite a number of requirements (Majone, 1997: 163; Sosay, 2006: 172). Procedural requirements concern a clear assignment of tasks that allows evaluation and assignment of responsibility, the giving of reasons and transparency constraints that facilitate judicial review and public participation, due process provisions, or refraining from applying discretion arbitrarily. Requirements on substantive performance concern policy consistency, expertise, fairness, protection of diffuse interests, and resistance to external interference in the production of regulatory decisions. All this is supposed to generate widespread belief that agencies are not only performing well but are also the most appropriate kind of institution to be in charge of regulatory tasks, thanks to their professionalism and to a *modus operandi* that closely resembles the (perhaps idealized) operation of the scientific system (Vibert, 2007).

Nevertheless, it should be asked whether, by democratic standards, accountability to actors other than the democratic principals of the delegation chain (citizens, members of parliament and executives) can adequately compensate for a possible lack of political control. Agencies have been designed as independent in order to be protected from political influence. Pleading for a return to more political control through the government might jeopardize the efficient achievement of agencies' functions, and probably there is no need for such a plea because, as noted above, the discretion of many agencies seems to be constrained in practice by the shadow of control and sanctions exerted by ministries. However, if parliaments (not governments) were to exert more efficient oversight over agencies' operations, this would shorten the traditional chain of accountability consisting of the administration being accountable to the minister who is, in turn, accountable to parliament (Menon, 2003: 423), and it would contribute to reversing the tendencies towards deparliamentarization. Some parliaments already perform this function through specialized committees: Chief executives of UK agencies are often directly accountable to parliamentary select committees (Pollitt *et al.*, 2001: 286). Moreover, in the UK a number of parliamentary scrutiny committees have introduced procedures for screening *ex ante* senior appointments to public bodies, which can be considered as a significant alteration of the executive–legislative relationship (Flinders and Matthews, 2010: 649). One may expect parliaments to be even more active in political systems where they are less subordinate to government. On the other hand, guardian institutions should be able to deter the members of democratic institutions from behaving in an irresponsible way. It would thus be suitable to promote 'a system of horizontal checks based on *reciprocal* vigilance between guardian and democratic institutions' (Schmitter and Trechsel, 2004: 59; emphasis added). The coupling between agencies and parliamentary bodies should be enhanced, and both should engage in deliberative processes that enhance mutual learning.

Nevertheless, the 'multilevel' character of contemporary governance is a factor that is likely to limit the impact of these kinds of remedies to deficits of democratic accountability, because it decouples agencies from their domestic environments. We have seen that there are transnational networks – sites where members of agencies share their experiences –operating as learning forums. Although their formal power is weak, some of them constitute genuine epistemic communities that improve the knowledge base of agencies and that contribute to the development of a common professional *esprit de corps*. This strengthens agencies' autonomy vis-à-vis domestic pressures, but it also ties them more tightly to their foreign counterparts: 'Participation in such networks is likely to shape one's world view, and successes and failures in the terms of the network members are liable to meet with approval and disapproval' (Scott, 2010: 14). Slaughter (2004: 55), for instance, indicates that European agencies such as the European Agency for the Evaluation of Medicinal Products closely cooperate with their national counterparts in networks, linking together national agencies that have an interest in maintaining their reputation in the network. Martens (2008) emphasizes the links between the European Commission and national agencies that are established within a networked transnational administrative space, where the EU Commission or an EU agency, such as the European Environmental Agency, is the core partner. The European Competition Network (ECN) is another case in point: A relatively informal network implicating the European Commission together with national regulatory authorities. Although this network has no legal status, does not issue binding decisions, and therefore is not (and does not have to be) formally accountable, it serves as an important instance for the socialization of national regulators to common norms. The problem is, however, that, if the necessity to uphold reputation in the face of peer pressure is deemed conducive to the diffusion of 'best practice', the preferences of peers (members of transnational networks) may differ from the preferences of agencies' domestic constituencies and their elected representatives. Therefore, the 'peer accountability' (Goodin, 2003) of agencies partaking in networks may collide with agencies' accountability to their democratic 'principals'.

A number of formal European regulatory networks have now been established (by official EU decisions). The two most influential and well-established networks are the Body of European Regulators for Electronic Communications (BEREC) and the Committee of European Securities Regulators (CESR), but one should also mention the European Regulators Group for Electricity and Gas (ERGEG), the Committee of European Insurance and Occupational Pensions' Supervisors (CEOPS), the Committee of European Banking Supervisors (CEBS), the European Platform of Regulatory Authorities in the field of broadcasting, or the Working party on the protection of individuals with regard to the Processing of Personal Data (Coen and Thatcher, 2008; Eberlein and Newman, 2008). Their establishment can be seen as the result of a dual delegation, one 'upwards' from national governments and newly created independent agencies, and one 'downwards' from the European Commission. In a typical multi-level fashion, these networks 'rely on authority granted to member agencies at the domestic level to implement and enforce agreements reached at the European level' (Eberlein and Newman, 2008: 32). Such developments are thus joint effects of the internationalization of policy problems, which puts pressure to coordinate action at the transnational level, and the autonomization of agencies at national levels that gives them more latitude to act.

It is now empirically established that the international networking activities of IRAs facilitate their 'emancipation from their regulatees' (Maggetti, 2009: 137), thus providing a safeguard against the risk of agency capture. This contributes to fairer outcomes for the general public, notably consumers. On the other hand, even though networks are formally confined to an advisory role and to the production of soft law, international networking tends to short-circuit national political authorities and thus generates a deficit of democratic control. Because they consider national agencies important for the implementation of EU policy, the European Commission and European agencies seek to exert influence by forging partnerships with them that bypass national ministries. Such transnational links strengthen the centrifugal trends within national executives, because not only do agencies operate at arm's length from governments, but they also tend to become 'double-hatted' and to develop loyalties to EU institutions (Curtin and Egeberg, 2008), themselves imperfectly democratically accountable. Hence, due to the compound and accumulated structure of EU multilevel governance, the accountability problem is not confined to EU institutions but affects national ones, too (see Chapter 3). Through their participation in European networks, national agencies become in a sense parts of two administrations, the national and the European, and it is precisely because they are decoupled from other governmental bodies at a national level that 'they are exposed to being re-coupled into administrative webs that span national borders and levels of governance' (Egeberg, 2008: 238). In that case the negative effects of agencification and Europeanization on democratic control mutually reinforce.

Giandomenico Majone, perhaps the most authoritative theorist of the 'regulatory state', acknowledges that independent agencies are constitutional anomalies that do not fit well in the traditional framework of democratic controls. Majone asserts:

> The growing importance of non majoritarian institutions in all democratic countries, in spite of persistent doubts about their

constitutional status and democratic legitimacy, shows that for many purposes reliance upon qualities such as expertise, professional discretion, policy consistency, fairness, or independence of judgment is considered to be more important than reliance upon direct democratic accountability. (Majone, 2005: 37)

Being typical examples of 'output-oriented' organizations, these bodies should construct their legitimacy on their 'ability to generate and maintain the belief of being, of all feasible institutional arrangements, the most appropriate one for solving a certain range of problems' (Majone, 2005: 38). International networking probably enhances the agencies' capital of credibility, but the participation of agency staff in hardly palpable networks exacerbates the deficits in democratic accountability. What matters more to the people? Romano Prodi said in his speech to the European Parliament of 21 July 1999 as President designate of the European Commission: 'At the end of the day, what interests them [the people] is not who solves these problems, but the fact that they are being tackled'. In such a view people are not interested in whether decisions are taken by democratically acceptable means or not. It is also possible that, in a world of widespread distrust of politicians, people would trust more technocratic bodies for decisions that affect their lives. Vibert (2007) is convinced about that, but this mirrors an idealized view both of the operation of expert bodies – thoroughly neutral and evidence-based – and of the degree of citizen information about the complexities of policy-making. Actually, there is no evidence that the circle of people who consider that independent bodies are the best option for regulation is very broad. This is not because people disagree with that (even though they came to know now that the performance of financial market authorities in their task of bank surveillance has not been outstanding), but simply because the set-up and role of independent agencies seldom stimulate a wider public debate.

How many indeed among the ordinary citizens (perhaps even among professional politicians) are aware of the actual operation of independent authorities? Paradoxically again, important issues of political design and policy-making are insulated from the public sphere in spite of increased 'mediatization'. Certainly this does not have to do with deliberate opaqueness, but rather with the increased complexity of the state machinery. Based on official sources, Vibert (2007: 18) estimated that there are 250 independent bodies with executive responsibilities in the United Kingdom, of which about 120 have regulatory functions, but no central list of all delegated public bodies exists, and even the government has problems identifying them, so that there is no 'whole of government' view of regulation (Flinders, 2004a: 782; Norton, 2004: 786 and 795). With centrifugal trends, it is less of an exaggeration to state this about the UK (but the statement would apply much beyond): 'Ministerial departments are bureaucratic icebergs, under which the greater part of the state structure operates in delegated organizational forms largely beyond public view or parliamentary oversight' (Flinders, 2004a: 772). As for participation of the stakeholder public in the scrutiny of agency activity, it runs the risk of being limited to those groups that enjoy concentrated benefits or suffer concentrated costs from agencies' decisions. In other words, as Sosay notes, this may be nothing else than 'more participation by an increasing number of minorities organized around their particularistic interests in regulated areas' (Sosay, 2006: 184). Hence agencification is probably yet another factor that contributes to the shift from partisan to 'advocacy' democracy.

## Judicialization: part of juridification, sustained through internationalization

Judicialization also contributes to the declining role of the representative circuit. It can be defined as the increased – albeit subject to cross-country variation – influence of courts on policy-making, and more broadly on the behaviour of political actors (Stone Sweet, 2010: 7). Instead of merely applying the law, courts become in reality, even though often indirectly through their influence, law-makers themselves. European countries did not experience a system of dispersed judicial control comparable to that of the United States, where any court can declare a governmental decision unconstitutional (Bale, 2005: 74), because this was suspected of leading to a 'government of judges'. However, in Europe, too, the role of the judiciary has expanded, and parliamentary sovereignty has weakened in the name of the rule of law, or more precisely, usually in the name of (sometimes admittedly vague) constitutional principles.

The judiciary branch is less likely than it was in the past to feel constrained by traditional doctrines of separation of powers and, since World War II, 'virtually all legal systems have developed in ways that increase the power of judges to control policy outcomes' (Cichowski and Stone Sweet, 2003: 197). Inspired by law philosopher Hans Kelsen, variations of the Austrian model of concentrated judicial control exerted only by the constitutional court (introduced in that country as early as 1920) expanded in successive ways, starting from the aftermath of World War II. Such a model contrasts with American-style judicial review, although debates in Europe have been influenced by the American experience, and in practice in the USA, too, important cases on the interpretation of the constitution will nearly always be referred to the Supreme Court (Koopmans, 2003: 35). There was a discernible US influence especially in the shaping of post-Nazi and post-fascist institutions in Germany and Italy, yet Kelsen's disciples were also influential in the drafting of the post-war constitutions in these countries. A 'new constitutionalism' arose, establishing that legal systems should include a bill of rights and a system of judicial review to defend them (Shapiro and Stone, 1994). The collapse of dictatorships in Southern Europe in the 1970s triggered another wave of 'new constitutionalism', followed by yet another wave after the demise of Communism. Almost all new democracies in Central and Eastern Europe have constitutional courts, as their communist past generated a culture of suspicion vis-à-vis the incumbents, so that today only 10 out of the 27 EU-member states lack this institution. And out of 72 countries that were considered as free or partly free in 2000, but not yet in 1986, 42 countries had introduced a constitutional court (Hönnige, 2011: 348).

The 'contagious' diffusion of the new constitutionalism is one dimension of judicialization: increased judicial activism is another one. In the past 30 years, French, Italian, and German courts have invalidated more pieces of legislation than over their whole previous history (Bellamy, 2007: 11). In France, a minority of 60 parliamentarians (but neither ordinary courts nor ordinary citizens) can, since 1974, request that the *Conseil Constitutionnel* exert control of the constitutionality of laws, leading after the reform to a multiplication by a factor of 10 of the frequency of appeals to that court (Rosanvallon, 2008: 230). Given the fact that the constitutionality of important bills is almost exclusively challenged by opposition parties defeated in parliament, the French Constitutional Council is now widely seen as a sort of third (unelected) chamber, whose role is specialized in the assessment of the constitutionality of legislation. Although the *Conseil* exerts only an *a priori* and abstract (p)review of legislation, and legislation is protected from review after its promulgation, there is a 'deterrent' effect in the fact that the *Conseil* can prevent laws passed by the two legislative chambers entering into force.

In France, Germany, and Spain, more than half of all legislation abstractly reviewed by courts has been, at least partially, invalidated by them (Stone Sweet, 2000: 74), but one should not underestimate the indirect court influence. Legislators have to anticipate possible court vetoes when drafting pieces of legislation, and are thus constrained to self-censorship. Such an indirect effect is similar to the effect exerted by other sources of veto (presidential or people's veto by referendum) on bills, when they are taken in their 'shadow'. In earlier chapters, we saw that governance networks, bureaucracies, or agencies operate more or less in the shadow of political hierarchy; with judicialization, it is the formal legislators themselves that operate in the shadow of the judiciary. Anticipated objections by a powerful judiciary are in a sense internalized by legislators: if courts can be used with reasonable chances of success to block undesirable reforms, then political majorities will be inclined to make compromises with opponents. According to the 'law of anticipated reactions' (Friedrich, 1946), decision-makers will adapt their behaviour *ex ante* in order to avoid running the risk of legislation being invalidated *ex post* by the judiciary. Operating under the shadow of judicial sanctions, decision-makers must restrain themselves and incorporate what they estimate to be the point of view of judges. It can even be argued that, in heavily judicialized settings, legislators can hardly avoid engaging in constitutional deliberations, behaving thus as judges of the constitution: 'Governing with judges also means governing like judges' (Stone Sweet, 2000: 204). Members of constitutional courts in turn behave as legislators able to determine legislative outcomes (Stone Sweet, 2000: 202). In Germany, the *Bundesverfassungsgericht* was granted wide-ranging jurisdiction, perhaps the most wide-ranging of any court anywhere. Hence, parliamentary committees regularly invite legal experts and former constitutional judges to advise them, and engage in 'Karlsruhe astrology' – attempts to predict the future position of the court, which is located in Karlsruhe (Stone Sweet, 2002).

Directly or indirectly, 'judge-made' policy-making is on the rise, and this now encompasses in several countries 'mega-politics' issues, too, such as electoral processes and outcomes, or questions having to do with nation-building and collective identities. Although later we will focus on the structural trends that have enabled judicialization (such as social differentiation, individualization, Europeanization, and more generally internationalization), judicialization should also be viewed in the framework of power struggles between competing elites. Courts themselves may stand behind this process, but it is also triggered by political actors motivated by strategic calculations. As a matter of fact, possible opposition by courts should be seen not only as a constraint for policy-making but also sometimes as a resource. Judicialization can advance the goals of some political actors, such as preserving their hegemony through the insulation of policy-making from the vicissitudes of democratic politics (Hirschl, 2004). In a sense, appeals to courts can be considered as a functional equivalent of lobbying: courts provide an additional access point to advocates of policy causes. Such an access point is particularly attractive: 'The judicial route to policy reform can be maximally efficacious, since judicial rulemaking grounded in an interpretation of a constitutional right is immune from legislative override; such rulings can be changed only through a subsequent judicial decision or by constitutional amendment' (Cichowski and Stone Sweet, 2003: 197). Policy advocates thus have an interest in appealing to the courts in order to achieve their aims, even if the implementation of court rulings may be hard. For example, the US Supreme Court faced long resistance by local and state governments to its school prayer and desegregation decisions (Shapiro, 2002a: 37). It should also be noted that parties in governments can use as an excuse the presence of activist courts to shift the blame to scapegoats when they decide to abandon measures initially promised to party activists (Stone Sweet, 2002: 188).

Courts can be used as resources not only in policy-making but also in electoral competition: for example, in order to weaken political opponents (Maravall, 2003) if they are suspected of being involved in corruption 'scandals', as in the case of Italy in the 1990s (*mani pulite*), or more recently in France in cases related to illegal party funding. In these situations, the judiciary clearly manifested a desire for empowerment vis-à-vis political authorities, but was also perceived having been politicized. It may well happen that judicial activism becomes then a weapon in party competition, interestingly in combination with media attention on scandals. It may even be that the judiciary becomes a participant in the political process *per se*, as is the case with judges in Italy under the last Berlusconi government, when the prime minister's conflict with them became part of everyday politics.

As an indirect effect of judicialization, non-judicial solutions develop, too, in case of complaints, instead of litigation before courts. Most notably, the institution of the ombudsman is 'a mechanism for citizens to voice complaints and concerns about government administration' (Ansell and Gingrich, 2003: 171) and thus to improve accountability in its 'mandated horizontal' version (O'Donnell, 2007: 87–8).

Ombudsmen have a mandate to check other state institutions on behalf of citizens, though they may also conduct their own enquiries without a prior grievance formulated by private or legal actors. The ombudsman institution is typical of new mechanisms of accountability related to administrative reform, which have increased the opportunities for citizens to oblige public organizations to justify their behaviour in decisions directly affecting themselves. In recent years, the ombudsman institution has proliferated in Europe, following a well established Nordic tradition, and growth in its use is also substantial. Usually ombudsmen are better established at the local or sectoral level, although the institution exists now at the EU level, too, under the initial joint impulse of the Danish and Spanish governments. Interestingly, that was a case of 'contradictory consensus' (Palier, 2003: 177): the two governments were motivated by potentially conflicting concerns – the Spanish one wanting to enhance citizenship at European level by providing an additional channel for citizens to express their concerns, and the more Eurosceptic Danes wanting to create an additional check over EU institutions, especially the Commission, but also the Council (Song and Della Sala, 2008).

Unlike the formally binding effect that characterizes the decisions of tribunals, ombudsmen operate in a 'soft' way, by trying to persuade public authorities through careful arguments about their recommendations, and by publicizing ('naming and shaming') cases of breach of the rule of law or of maladministration. Therefore, in spite of their nonbinding character that distinguishes them from court rulings, recommendations by ombudsmen cannot easily be ignored because they can damage the image of a governing body. One should consider the indirect effects of the institution, too: although its core function is the redress of grievance, its existence is a signal to citizens, stakeholder groups, and NGOs that the state acknowledges the need to have an accountable bureaucracy. However, there is a problem: those able to file complaints with reasonable chances of success are not necessarily representative of the general population, something that also occurs when people turn to courts to protect their rights. Further, the influence of ombudsmen's recommendations on state administrations is a function of the prevailing political culture.

Apart from cross-national differences, the judicialization of politics may depend on the political conjuncture and is also subject to variations in intensity across policy sectors. Overall, however, it can be considered as part of a broader process of juridification (or juridicalization) of society. If judicialization refers to courts being increasingly activist and influential, juridification means more broadly the increasingly popular framing of social issues in legal terms (Blichner and Molander, 2008). This translates on the demand side into more claims for the use of law in social life as a medium to solve disputes and, on the supply side, into the expansion of legal regulation. Juridification appears as a consequence of liberalism in its broad meaning, to the extent that the latter favours the development of a 'claim culture' that fosters legalization:

> Liberalism should be interpreted here in the classical sense, stressing individual rights and liberties; notably, freedom from oppressive economic, social, and political forces, such as limitations to free enterprise, political tyranny, restrictive social control, and intolerant religious dogmas. All of these forms of liberalism – social, political, and economic – imply greater freedom for the individual (or corporation). Being less bound by informal conventions or formal regulations, the individual lives under greater uncertainty and has a greater likelihood of getting involved in conflict – and given his or her freedoms can afford to do so, whether in interpersonal relations (e.g. divorce), in relations with political and governmental actors (e.g. appealing government decisions), or in transactions in the market place. There is also a greater chance that this conflict will be carried over into the courtroom. There he or she will defend his or her position by referring to formal rights, thus couching the conflict in legalistic terms, while seeking assistance from legal experts. The case law produced by the case will add to the body of regulations, thus increasing legalism. (Van Waarden and Hildebrand, 2009: 259–60)

This kind of self-reinforcing process also translates into the 'constitutionalization' of national legal orders: Fundamental rights and freedoms become constitutionally entrenched and judicially enforceable (Cichowski and Stone Sweet, 2003; Cichowski, 2006). The 'rights revolution' (Epp, 1998) liberates judges from the straitjacket of law by allowing them to appeal to higher normative principles that acquire precedence over ordinary legislation lying in the competence of the legislature. Trends towards more social differentiation play a role as well: The movement for rights is closely related to the socio-cultural fragmentation of societies, and to the existence of social groups – such as ethnic and lifestyle minorities, women, people with a handicap – able to claim convincingly that they have strong preferences or particular characteristics that should be recognized through the constitution-alization of rights. Being merely aggregative – what counts is the count-ing of votes – the principle of majoritarian democracy is judged insufficiently complex and imperfectly legitimate in differentiated soci-eties (Zolo, 1992; Papadopoulos, 2003; Rosanvallon, 2008). Why should a political order decided even by a large number of members of the community be accepted by all others? Especially in fragmented societies then, political majorities must prove to be other-regarding in order to retain their legitimacy.

Evidence is inconclusive as to whether institutional systems based on majority rule are more abusive than those that limit governments through checks and balances (Przeworski, 2010). Nevertheless, systematic research undertaken in Switzerland has demonstrated that the use of mechanisms of direct democracy without any sort of judicial check on their outcomes tends to affect negatively those minorities – like immigrant or religious groups – with whom the majority has the least in common (Vatter, 2011). In order to counteract the risk of majority tyranny, federalist or other devices of power-sharing (for instance, over-representing minorities) have been set up in heteroge-neous societies. The EU system is an exemplar case where debates on the range of unanimity rule are regularly on the agenda, and the same happens for more technical, although no less sensitive, debates on how to calculate qualified majorities without causing a member-state to feel discriminated against. The advent of systems of multilevel governance increases, in turn, the likelihood of conflict between decisional levels, and this is yet another triggering factor of judicial intervention. But more generally, it is believed that acting in the shadow of judicial over-sight offers an incentive structure conducive to other-regardingness. Interestingly, as suggested by Pierre Rosanvallon (2008: 14) in his book on democratic legitimacy, although being *in* minority is synonymous with a lack of legitimacy for conceptions of democracy based on majority rule, claiming to be *part of* a minority – at least of a minority that has succeeded in persuading governors that it deserves recognition – is considered legitimate.

The culmination of fragmentation lies in individualization, and part of this trend manifests itself in the constitutionalization of rights. Individuals now feel that they deserve to be well protected against violations of their rights by state authorities or other parties in various aspects of social life: access to information, privacy protection, consumers' and patients' rights, etc. They can appeal to the courts, as well as to non-judiciary bodies such as ombudsmen, by invoking these violations. Personal respect, equity, and non-discrimination become core elements of the social demand (Rosanvallon, 2008: 109). Individualization is so pervasive that it also manifests itself in the economy. For instance, Rosanvallon (2008: 104–11) pertinently shows that such an 'economy of singularity' now resembles more the artistic sphere, where creativity is an asset. On the demand side, individuals are increasingly keen on customizing the goods they purchase and, on the supply side, even low-qualified jobs, such as in supermarkets or call centres, are distinct from traditional blue-collar work on the assembly line in that they require employees not merely to follow routines but also to adapt to sometimes changing face-to-face interactions. The concept of 'employability' accurately depicts such requirements for flexibility in order to make individual labour supply fit demands in the labour market. The individualization of society is indeed a demand-side explanation of judicialization: Individualist persons resort more to litigation in order to protect their rights. There may, however, be supply-side explanations, too: research carried out in France by Roussel (2007) shows that judicial activism is related to a redefinition of the professional identities of judges and to the emergence of a new professional ethos, where judges consider themselves less close to notables than in the past, and feel more critical and distrustful of politicians.

Originating in a changing social-cultural context, judicialization also gained weight thanks to internationalization. As international exchanges become denser there will be more demands for their regulation and thus for litigation:

> Internationally, there are more and more judicial procedures designed to adjudicate in disputes over breaches of international law. The diplomatic dispute settlement procedures under GATT, for instance, have been replaced by a judicial dispute settlement mechanism under the WTO, which is authorized to convict, and if necessary punish, states that do not fulfil their commitments…. International environmental regimes such as the ozone and the climate regime have various built-in, quasi-judicial procedures designed to cope with non-compliance, and an International Tribunal for the Law of the Sea has also been established. (Zangl, 2005: 73–4)

Not only does internationalization contribute to judicialization, but the judicial component is today stronger in international regimes:

> In most issue areas of international relations, adjudication systems, if they existed at all, were dominated by panels, bodies, committees or commissions like the UNHRC, made up of politically dependent state representatives. Today, however, there are more than 40, mostly independent, international courts or court-like bodies, most of which were established during the 1990s. (Zangl, 2005: 77)

In relation to internationalization, an additional dimension of constitutionalization lies in the domestication of the European Convention on Human Rights (ECHR) (Cichowski and Stone Sweet, 2003). Rulings by the European Court of Human Rights, a judicial institution of the Council of Europe, aim to make a country that is found guilty of violating the ECHR comply with the latter. Although the European Court has no power to remedy the injury caused by the violation, the rights protected by the ECHR are considered as a body of higher-order norms, so that they are often incorporated into domestic constitutional or statutory law, and they have led to considerable constraints on what national legislators can do (Cichowski, 2006: 57). In the United Kingdom, for instance, the passing in 1998 of the Human Rights Act incorporated the provisions of the EHCR into the British legal system. This was the first rights legislation in this country for 300 years (Hirschl, 2004: 8), and under this act it became mandatory for all British courts to take into account any judgment of the European Court of Human Rights (Cichowski, 2006: 61). There is no doubt that such developing of international human rights regimes reduces the domestic authority of states over their subjects. Individuals acquire direct access to international courts and can challenge the conduct of their governments (Cutler, 2003: 245–6). This is considered by some as a major symbolic manifestation of the authority that citizens hold over their governors:

> There is extraordinary symbolic power to the idea that people can hold governments to account in court, just as they can each other. Even if they cannot themselves initiate legal proceedings the fact that prosecutors acting on their behalf are entitled to do so reminds people that legislators are subject to the same laws as those they govern, and are susceptible to judgements in the same courts of law, and according to the same legal procedures as everyone else. (Lever, 2009: 814)

Surveys indicate that individuals who seem to be better aware of courts are 'more likely to subscribe to the mythology of judicial neutrality and objectivity in decision-making'; to know courts 'is to be exposed to a series of legitimizing messages focused on symbols of justice, judicial objectivity, and impartiality' (Gibson *et al.*, 1998: 345). Among such legitimizing messages, one should count the fact that courts, in contrast to legislatures, are able to frame their decisions as being dictated by the constitution or laws, and can thus place them on a procedural rather than a substantive level.

As regards the ECHR, it has been signed by 46 countries, and the upward trajectory of applications submitted to the European Court of Human Rights and of decisions issued by the latter has been phenomenal over the last 50 years (Cichowski, 2006: 58). About 160,000 appeals are currently pending, more than 50,000 new appeals come in every year, out of which only 30,000 can be handled. Ninety per cent of appeals are considered invalid, but in nearly 80 per cent of the valid cases the plaintiff wins, and compliance is effective in most countries, thanks to an efficient monitoring system. Decisions based on the ECHR have led to payment of monetary damages, and administrative, legislative, judicial, and even constitutional reforms (Keohane *et al.*, 2009). Nearly three-quarters of all cases involve the right to a fair trial (Cichowski, 2006: 62–3). Even if a state does not comply, its domestic accountability is enhanced because claims for the respect of rights gain resonance: the plaintiffs can go public and make non-compliance an issue in political debates (Sperling, 2009: 228). With such a record, threats to appeal to the European Court of Human Rights, which has become the final court of appeal for these kinds of issues, have a disciplining effect on the practices of several states, and national judges have also used the external leeway to extend their powers. Even in cases like the British one considered as an example of weak judicial review, courts can issue a 'Declaration of Incompatibility' of legislative provisions with the ECHR, which can (but not must) be used by the minister to initiate a fast-track procedure in order to amend or abrogate the incriminated piece of legislation (Lever, 2009: 813–14).

There seems to be an increasingly global consensus on an international human rights regime, with courts seeking to promote goals that they consider conducive to an improvement of democratic quality. Networking between judges contributes to such a consensus: judges around the world are using the ECHR, even in states that have not adopted it (Bevir, 2010: 169). The IMF and the World Bank have promoted as principles of good governance for developing countries an impartial, competent, and non-corrupt judiciary, combined with facilitated access to the courts for individuals (Halliday and Osinsky, 2006: 464). Some multilateral institutions include the protection of diffuse interests and of individual or minority rights in their agenda (Keohane *et al.*, 2009). They explicitly refer to the constitutionalist principle as the legitimacy basis for such action. They recognize that improvements in the respect of this principle may come at the cost of political participation, but consider the latter just as one value among others to be respected, and they are not alarmed by the fact that internationalization tips the balance at the prejudice of the populist principle.

To the twofold (national and international) constitutionalization of rights should be added a third element, the constitutionalization of the European Union, as a factor promoting judicialization in member-states (Cichowski and Stone Sweet, 2003). The formation of a supra-national and integrated legal regime in the European Union has been driven jointly by the European Court of Justice (ECJ), which enjoys an atypical degree of discretion as a court, by private litigants concerned with the (non-) enforcement at a national level of EU legislation, and by national judges increasingly involved (like national regulators) in transnational networks promoting mutual information, legal harmonization, and enforcement:

> The possibility of direct relations between a supranational court and national courts, or between a supranational regulatory agency and its domestic equivalent, pierces the shell of state sovereignty and creates a channel whereby supranational officials can harness the coercive power of national officials.... The ECJ essentially built its own power base in the European Union by interacting directly with national courts, cultivating relationships with national judges in order to encourage them to send up cases involving European law directly to it. Lower national courts quickly saw the advantage in using this option as a means of bypassing higher national courts in cases in which the lower national court likely had a different view of the law than did the higher court. And when the ECJ handed down its decisions back to the referring national court, that court could enforce the decision through the coercive force of the national legal system. (Slaughter, 2004: 145–6; see also Harlow and Rawlings, 2006; Bevir, 2010: 169–70)

In such a context, the loss of (sometimes admittedly arbitrary!) authority of national political instances is on a par with judicialization. Considered as the 'big bang' of European legal integration (Stone

Sweet, 2010: 29), the doctrines of supremacy and direct effect pronounced by the ECJ in the 1960s, and applying to the effects of its rulings upon national legal orders, have been decisive in that respect. Supremacy means the primacy of European over national law: It prohibits national authorities from relying on domestic legislation to justify lack of compliance with European law, and it requires national courts to resolve conflicts between national and European law in favour of the latter. Direct effect means that European law gives rights to individuals and companies that they can invoke against their own state authorities in courts. They can sue national authorities for not complying with obligations derived from EU membership, or for not properly transposing EU legislation into national law (Stone Sweet, 2000: 163). Schmidt (2006) writes that the ECJ, together with the Commission, has been very entrepreneurial in the European system of governance:

> not only has the ECJ taken jurisdiction over the final interpretation and the enforcement – along with the Commission – of agreed rules and laws, it has also acted as a 'purposeful opportunist' by setting precedents that have expanded its own powers as well as those of the Commission in cases such as the mutual recognition of products, equal pay for women, and migrant workers' benefits. (Schmidt, 2006: 55)

In the United Kingdom, for instance, the doctrine of parliamentary sovereignty prohibits judicial review of statutory laws. Administrative acts can be reviewed, but this can be seen as a concern for the parliamentary will to be preserved from administrative subversion. However, the development of European law has undermined parliamentary sovereignty, conferring on UK judges the power to review the compatibility of parliamentary legislation with EU law (Cichowski and Stone Sweet, 2003: 195). The ECJ is therefore an actor with whom national authorities must definitely reckon. Litigation rates have been skyrocketing since the 1970s, and ECJ rulings provide litigants with new opportunities before national courts to achieve domestic policy change in order to secure compliance with EU legislation (Cichowski, 2006a: 28 and 248). The role of the ECJ not only puts national governments under constraint but also 'is so well established that national constitutional courts have seen the balance of proof shift against them, and they have been integrated in a multi-level constitutional court system' (Zürn and Leibfried, 2005: 21). Yet while European integration has resulted in national courts losing autonomy, at the same time it 'has increased their independence from national executives as well as from one another, with lower courts emancipated from their hierarchical superiors through their recourse to the ECJ' (Schmidt, 2006: 70–1). The advent of such a multilevel system of 'transjudicial dialogues' also produces more diffuse effects. Relying on data from England and Wales, Jupille and Caporaso (2009) conclude that domestic courts, litigants, and lawyers use their experience with European legal principles and concepts to domesticate and indigenize them into purely domestic areas of law: for example, members of the legal profession increasingly read ECJ judgments and draw inspiration from them.

## Judges as account-holders and as legislators: a controversial role

Judicialization is also nurtured by the agencification movement. One of the key mechanisms of control of independent bodies is the supervisory function of courts. Majone explains the reasons that make classic vertical administrative accountability ineffective, leading to the site of accountability of public service providers moving to the courts:

> When direct administration is replaced by contractual relationships with more or less independent suppliers of services, it is no longer possible to resolve disputes through hierarchical channels. What used to be internal bureaucratic conflicts are 'externalized', leading to litigation. But once judges accept the appropriateness of their courts as sites for the resolution of disputes between governmental rule makers and autonomous agents, they become significant, sometimes the most significant, actors in the administrative process. (Majone, 1997: 156)

The role of courts is part of a more general change in the prevailing forms of accountability: towards not-necessarily-elected sites and less directly to democratic 'principals' (Benz *et al.* 2007). Aiming 'to limit the space for arbitrary or biased administration by legally mandating that public officials give reasons for their decisions' (Bevir, 2010: 166–7), the 'giving reasons' requirement has expanded the scope of judicial oversight over administrative practice as a mild form of judicial intrusion (Lever, 2009: 811). As suggested in greater detail by Vibert:

the new bodies take decisions or arrive at conclusions that can have a major impact on citizens or businesses or on government. It is therefore important that they provide an opportunity for all the evidence to be presented and an opportunity for its rebuttal by those claiming to have counter-evidence. If such standards are not followed, or if the institution is wrong on the facts, then an avenue for challenge is open through judicial review. (Vibert, 2007: 172–3)

At first glance it is something of a paradox that judicialization is occurring at a time when 'hard' law is losing its grip as an instrument of political regulation. However, this paradox is only apparent, as soft law can be fuzzy law, and may thus require ample interpretation, often to be found in court rulings. More generally, constitutional but also statutory legislation can be vague: for strategic reasons, because competing interests can compromise more easily at a fairly abstract level, or because reality is complex and all possible real-world situations cannot be anticipated by formal rules. Whatever the reason for their vagueness, norms may require clarification via interpretation, which in reality is often tantamount to delegation of part of rulemaking to the judicial system (Shapiro, 2002a: 56 and 2002b: 164). Constitutional courts, in particular, are not only – in the words of Hans Kelsen – a 'negative legislator' (or in the contemporary political science jargon 'veto players'), capable of striking down legislation produced by elected bodies that are in a sense accountable to them. They also formulate affirmative statements as to how the incriminated defective laws should be repaired (Sadurski, 2002: 10). Governments have to rewrite these laws; in reality 'corrective revision processes' lead to court-written legislation, because governments often simply copy the terms of court decisions (Stone Sweet, 2002: 189).

Contrary to agencification or to soft law, which may appear as constitutional or legislative anomalies, the improvements in the quality of decision-making – such as more fairness – expected from judicialization can be justified by reference to the classic requirements of the rule of law. Judicialization is primarily a manifestation of the increasing prevalence of the liberal or constitutionalist, as opposed to the populist, conception of democracy. What distinguishes judicialization from agencification is that it results from an explicit wish to develop counter-powers to governmental discretion in order to protect the individual, and not from the sheer will to enhance the efficiency of decision-making. Courts are part of checks-and-balances systems in which guardian institutions should watch over the government or the administration, so that it does not exceed its power or fail to respect the law, and does not violate fundamental rights (Bale, 2005: 73). As suggested by Sperling:

> Even in democratic states, courts appear distinctly undemocratic. But such unelected courts are 'undemocratic' by design. Their occupants are protected from sanction by the public, and hence from democratic accountability, so that they will be able to protect the rights of the minority or to back individual claims against a government's abuse of power. (Sperling, 2009: 222–3)

In a context of judicialization, citizens increasingly appeal to constitutional or statutory law to protect themselves from majoritarian caprices, or to denounce practices of maladministration when regulations are implemented. The judiciary can dispute the constitutionality of legislation, decide about the lawfulness of administrative practice, and have a say on the power balance in multilevel systems. Judicialization embodies a will to create a depoliticized site of power limiting the latitude of politicians. The initial intention of the advocates of judicialization was to (deliberately) 'remove certain decisions, for example concerning fundamental rights, from the electoral process and thus to tie the hands of the current majority' (Majone, 2005: 196). Liberal philosopher Benjamin Constant pleaded as early as the first part of the nineteenth century (referring then to the power of the monarch) for a *'pouvoir neutre'*. The rhetoric justifying the role of courts fits this conception: 'The traditional paradigm of the judicial process is of a neutral umpire adjudicating between two parties and dispassionately dispensing justice' (Sadurski, 2002: 9). By providing a feeling of assurance to citizens, the existence of an independent judiciary composed of disinterested professionals is deemed to increase the trustworthiness, and thus the social legitimacy, of the political system (Follesdal, 2010: 87–8). As already mentioned, experiences with totalitarianism in the twentieth century had a strong influence on the desire to safeguard rights. A sort of precautionary principle is introduced in policy-making, with the shadow of court rulings expected to deter political majorities or bureaucracies from ignoring the general interest or the common good. According to Stone Sweet:

> The democratic legitimacy of constitutional review rests on the ideology of higher law constitutionalism, which subordinates the exercise of all governmental authority, even that which is made according to the general will, to the law of the constitution. The new

constitutionalism assumes that parliament can do wrong, and that some wrongs must be corrected. (Stone Sweet, 2000: 50)

Nowadays, the role of the judiciary is seen as a welcome addition of reflexivity in the policy process (Rosanvallon, 2008: 222 and 231–2), similar sometimes to the role of Second Chambers of parliamentary assemblies. The self-restraint of democratically elected authorities to the advantage of non- or counter-majoritarian institutions has come to touch on many more fields than the mere protection of fundamental rights and liberties. The superior quality of court deliberation is considered as a crucial justification for the binding effect of decisions made by instances that lack democratic credentials: 'Deliberation and reason-giving are, in this sense, ways in which non-democratic institutions can go about getting people to go along with their decisions' (Ferejohn and Pasquino, 2002: 27). It becomes thus legitimate that a more objective discourse based on legal reasoning eclipses political debates that are strongly suspected of being biased by ideological and electoral considerations. In sum, it is assumed that there is a sort of trade-off between democracy and the quality of deliberation (Fishkin, 1991).

However, as suggested by one of the most prominent constitutional law specialists, 'the paradox faced by the people is that, in order to employ judges to police those to whom the people have assigned the power to govern, the people must surrender some power to govern to the judges' (Shapiro, 2002b: 164). Therefore, legal doctrine and political theory are profoundly divided in their normative assessment of the new constitutionalism. According to Przeworski (2010: 7), 'while some people consider any restrictions on majority rule, say judicial review, as antidemocratic, others see them as an essential ingredient of democracy', an opposition that can be portrayed as a clash between 'liberal idealists' and 'sceptical democrats':

Liberal idealists have tended to celebrate the trend, while sceptical democrats have condemned it.... Either constitutionalism reflects a noble commitment to rights principals (the sunny liberal view). Or it is a crass power grab on the part of an elite minority (the sceptical democratic view). Either judges are heroic and principled, while legislators are venal and self-interested (the sunny liberal view), or judges are out-of-touch elites, while legislators are authentic representatives of the people (the sceptical democratic view).... To advance theoretical development, it is necessary to move beyond such binary thinking. (Hilbink, 2008: 239)

Issues such as 'how much self-rule we are willing to sacrifice in order to keep the Leviathan within tolerable limits' (Dorf, 2006: 302), or 'under what circumstances, if any, *should* courts substitute their own policy preferences for those of the majority' (Shapiro, 2002a: 59, emphasis in the original) are settled neither legally nor politically. In addition, the amplitude of judicialization varies across states:

> The role that judges play in contemporary constitutional democracies is unlikely to be either the romanticized, heroic role that some liberals hold out for them or the conniving, tyrannical one that democratic skeptics have sketched. Indeed, construction of the judicial role in new constitutionalist countries varies tremendously, and these institutional variations complicate the effort to paint judges as either saviors or villains. (Hilbink, 2008: 239)

Nevertheless, when courts become policy players, the formal separation of powers is *de facto* undermined, and judicialization causes its own accountability problems: Fears of a 'government of judges' are related to the remoteness of the judicial system from the system of representative democracy. With judicialization, it is the least representative branch of government that gains power (Cichowski and Stone Sweet, 2003: 216), and also the least accountable one. Therefore, the question can also be raised of why 'judges, who (typically) are unelected and (typically) are insulated from the bureaucratic control of those who are elected, should be permitted to impose their own views about liberty, equality, and the like, upon the public as a whole' (Dorf, 2006: 301). One could however argue that doctrinal controversies on the role of the judiciary do not matter much to people. Is government by judges a socially legitimate form of government?

Mény and Surel (2002) argue that the decline of the populist component in our democracies is behind the origin of popular disaffection with politics, and we can indeed consider judicialization as a manifestation of such a decline. However, are claims against judicialization indeed popular? Citizens may even perceive courts as welcome checks to the arbitrariness of power: Data from the 2005–2008 World Values Survey show that in the United States, Great Britain, France, and Germany confidence in courts is broader than confidence in the national legislature and the national government. More impressively, with the exception of France among these countries, those expressing 'a great deal of' or 'quite a lot of' confidence in courts are about twice as many as those expressing the same feelings about legislature or government (Dalton, 2008: 247). But probably most interviewees are not aware at all of anything like an increasing judicialization, just as they do not know much about agencification. What we do know is that courts are mostly likely to be affected by deficits in social legitimacy when their decisions are perceived to be politicized – in other words, when the promise of judicial impartiality is considered to be broken. According to survey data (see Rosanvallon, 2008: 255), in 2007 for instance, only 47 per cent of American citizens considered the Supreme Court to be impartial, and 31 per cent judged it to be too conservative. Although ideological bias may be tolerable from elected public authorities, the lack of electoral legitimacy of judges makes their partiality and lack of independence unacceptable. Nevertheless, the degree of politicization of judges varies across political systems, and therefore their propensity to enjoy social legitimacy as well. Few courts in democracies are considered as politicized as the Supreme Court in the United States, owing, in part, to differences in the way judges are appointed.

This is not to deny that judicialization has a serious impact on political life. An independent and powerful judicial system can compensate for power asymmetry between rulers and their subjects by reducing the discretion of the political–administrative machinery. However, we noticed that appealing to an ombudsman may require some degree of familiarity with procedures, and the problem is aggravated regarding appeals to courts, where more resources in terms of expertise are necessary, and quite often financial or organizational resources as well. For instance, the range of issues that can be debated in courts and the kind of arguments that can be employed are determined by procedural rules with which one has to be familiar. As a result, even though individuals who feel disadvantaged by decisions also use litigation, it is mainly used by organizations backed by legal experts. Even if disadvantaged segments of society or marginalized concerns can benefit from litigation, it nevertheless also strengthens advocacy democracy. Key players in litigation are public interest groups, such as in the case of the EU, organizations defending women's or environmental causes (Cichowski, 2006a). A vibrant 'support structure' in society is needed for legal mobilization, and this can exist only if rights-advocacy organizations, professional lawyers educated in appropriate schools eager to engage in 'cause lawyering', sympathetic state agencies, and legal aid schemes are part of the landscape: 'The judicial process is time-consuming, expensive, and arcane; ordinary individuals typically do not have the time, money, or expertise necessary to support a long-running lawsuit through several levels of the judicial system' (Epp, 1998: 18). Consequently, even if stigmatized and marginalized groups can benefit from judicialization, individuals who are weakly familiar with courts fare poorly in comparison with well-resourced organizations that are repeat players in this game. It should be noticed, however, that resources also count in representative democracy, and that difficulty of access to the courts varies from country to country (Hilbink, 2008: 235–8).

An even more radical critique is not that the judiciary can be politicized, or that access to courts is selective, but more fundamentally that the legitimate role of courts in the policy process relies on an idealized picture of the judiciary. As suggested by Sadurski (2002: 4–5), the narrative that legitimizes the role of courts 'is a story about impartiality against bias, selflessness versus self-interest'; judges 'will see to it that noble Constitutionalism will prevail over dirty politics'. Bellamy (2007) is deeply sceptical about such a narrative. A first argument is that counter-majoritarianism is subject to social bias. As access to courts is limited, they may be less open to minority interests than representative bodies. It has been argued, for instance, that judges are not more representative of social and ideological pluralism than elected members of the legislature (Waldron, 2006: 1405), that they are not value-free, and that they usually decide in accordance with dominant cultural beliefs (Hirschl, 2004). Sadurski (2002: 6) estimates that the judiciary is ill-equipped to evaluate options in social-economic policies with important financial implications. However, again because appointment rules significantly differ, not all judges are equally unrepresentative (Hilbink, 2008: 233). Bellamy also argues that judicial decisions may appear arbitrary, simply because:

> despite widespread support for both constitutional rights and rights-based judicial review, theorists, politicians, lawyers and ordinary citizens frequently disagree over which rights merit or require such entrenchment, the legal form they should take, the best way of implementing them, their relationship to each other, and the manner in which courts should understand and uphold them. (Bellamy, 2007: 16)

The long history of the US Supreme Court shows indeed that its judgments on issues such as affirmative action or abortion unleashed acute political controversies (Koopmans, 2003: 44–62). The lack of a collective agreement on such issues has much more to do with conflicting deep social values than with the narrow self-interest of individuals. As noticed by Waldron:

> Defenders of abortion rights think the pro-life position would be tyrannical to women; but the pro-life people think the pro-choice position is tyrannical to another class of persons (foetuses are persons, on their account). Some think that affirmative action is tyrannical; others think the failure to implement affirmative action programs is tyrannical. And so on. (Waldron, 2006: 1396)

Bellamy further argues that it is questionable whether the judicial process is more foolproof, more sensitive to the protection of liberties, or more prone to consider scrupulously and open-mindedly all the dimensions of rights-related questions than the democratic process, where, after all, the various constituencies are represented: 'The need to represent broad constituencies enlarges the range of experiences with which law-makers must acquaint themselves and seek to address' (Bellamy, 2007: 34). However, despite the importance of the question, there is no systematic research that assesses whether judges protect rights better than parliamentarians do (Stone Sweet, 2002: 206). After all, court decisions are also frequently taken on the basis of the majority principle, and conflicts between judges often mirror conflicting views in the society at large. Courts do not escape pressure by public opinion; neither are they insensitive to its fluctuations. Probably, Bellamy falls into the idealization trap himself, by failing to acknowledge the amplitude of imperfections of the representative process. He fails to consider, for instance, that participation in democratic elections is often socially stratified, with turnout rates being as a rule lower among the least-educated segments of society, or that MPs do not necessarily fulfil the pledges made to their constituencies, and the latter may not be well-informed enough to sanction them for that. As with the democratic defects of other forms of governance considered in this book, such as cooperative policy-making, one should not use as a benchmarking tool an idealized image of the mechanisms of representative democracy.

## Gains or losses for the quality of democracy?

Through partly distinct avenues, agencification and judicialization both signal the 'rise of the unelected', although the profile of these unelected differs. Figure 6.1 summarizes the major factors in the origin of agencification and judicialization (in capitals).

The particularity of the rise of these kinds of unelected actors is that, depending on one's perspective, it can be considered to improve or decrease the quality of democracy. It would be hard to argue convincingly that the consequences of internationalization, as they were described in Chapter 3, are beneficial to democracy, with the exception of initiatives for external democracy promotion, such as those of the European Union (Lavenex and Schimmelfennig, 2012). By contrast, one's assessment of the consequences of agencification and judicialization closely depends on one's trust in the civic virtue of democratically elected rulers. If the independence of agencies is valued, this is related to the fact that politicians are considered to lack the expertise to deal

**Figure 6.1.** *The processes of agencification and judicialialization*

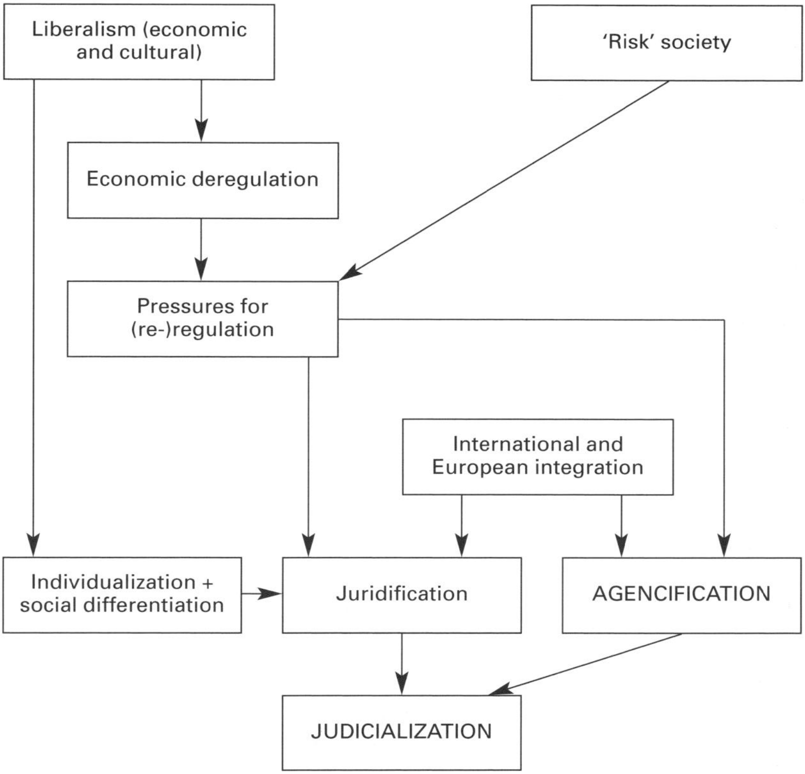

with complex regulatory matters; but more fundamentally, this is linked to a suspicion that they face strong incentives to prioritize particular interests – either their own, or those of constituencies that are close to them – over the satisfaction of the common good. In a similar vein, if courts are empowered, this is to a large extent because it is feared that the decisions of elected majorities might cause strong prejudice to minorities or violate individual and group rights.

Nevertheless, normative justifications of agencification and judicialization should not be taken for granted. Rosanvallon (2008: 26–30) claims that nowadays the 'subjective' sphere of electoral/partisan/representative politics is coupled with an 'objective' sphere of institutions of indirect democracy, notably courts and independent agencies. Yet, it is not so simple. The legitimizing principles are not the same for both types of bodies, which – as Rosanvallon himself (2008: 156) concedes – do not have the same functions in a framework of separation of powers. The depth of their entrenchment in the political order varies: The formal legitimacy of courts is more firmly rooted, sustained by core principles of power separation and the rule of law, while institutional designers establish independent agencies on a more *ad hoc* basis, because they believe in the benefits of impartiality and expertise for the achievement of regulatory functions. This is also why no one would consider the independence of the judiciary as a problem, while the independence of agencies is more controversial. Notwithstanding these differences, if one does not think that partisan politics leads to arbitrariness or undermines the collective wellbeing, then one might have good reasons to be concerned by evolutions that restrain the power of elected officials. For instance, critics of judicialization deplore its elitist bias, which is visible not only in the fact that the opinions of judges may not reflect adequately the pluralism of social values, but also in the fact that access to courts may require resources that are unevenly distributed.

On the other hand, perhaps the self-restraint imposed by agencification and judicialization to the representative circuit should not be overestimated. Even if agencies enjoy discretion by design, their practical autonomy varies, and the threat of *ex post* controls can operate as a disciplining device. Independence does not necessarily imply a lack of accountability, although it may well be that accountability to peers or stakeholders is privileged over democratic accountability. It has also been noticed that agencies can be politicized via their staffing, and courts can, in practice, be politicized as well. This means that some governments try to exert control over institutions that are *de jure* independent from them. Those who fear the power of the unelected would then be relieved to hear that the domestic power of this category of actors does not go as far as at the transnational level, whereas those who dislike the politicization of bodies that should be neutral by design would have good reasons to be concerned. But we should keep in mind that, no matter if we welcome it or not, governmental control over agencies or courts is yet another element of the executive drift. One should also keep in mind the mutually reinforcing effects between the above trends: agencification, for instance, contributes to judicialization. Perhaps more importantly, multilevel governance through networks seems to strengthen the domestic autonomy of agencies, as the advent of an international human rights regime domestically empowers the courts.

The picture is complex indeed; yet, whatever one's beliefs, there is a missing link in the legitimization of agencies and courts as effective actors in policy-making. Based on Rosanvallon's concepts, one would be inclined to think that their role as policy actors is better justified by the objectivity they are supposed to add into the policy process than by their legitimization as, albeit only indirectly, democratic bodies – simply because, in their case, the chain of delegation is very lengthy and fragile. Now the objectivity of such bodies would be normatively sustainable only if it would be broadly validated through enlightened consent. There is not much research on that subject, but this seems to be only partly the case. For instance, it has been shown through comparative research that the more people know about national high courts, the more they tend to be supportive of them (Gibson *et al.*, 1998). Yet, this conclusion is based on self-declarations of awareness whose reliability could be questioned: How many people really do know about the real scope of agencification and judicialization processes, and what concrete opportunities are they offered to critically assess them? How many people are offered the opportunity to express an informed judgment on the conditions under which these processes entail gains or losses for the quality of democratic life? Probably very few, not only in the citizenry at large, but among the circles of policy-makers as well.

## Chapter 7

# The Winter of Democracy?

In this final chapter, I first return to the major issues and trends discussed and try to connect them meaningfully. I then outline the major consequences for our political systems generated by these trends by identifying four major challenges that affect representative democracy. The final section is devoted to a (hopefully) balanced reply to the question of whether democracy is in a crisis or not.

## Challenges to democracy: their logics and implications

As the reader must have noticed, this book not only lists a number of things that have modified the operation of democratic political systems. It emphasizes parallels and interrelationships, as well as paradoxes and contradictions. As a matter of fact, it would be wrong to think that the changes adhere to a common 'grand' logic.

One could surely argue that liberalism is a major driving force of political changes and adjustments in modes of governance, and that the globalization of communication facilitates the diffusion of these changes and adjustments (something that is now empirically established for the diffusion of the 'agencification' process, studied in Chapter 6, at least). Yet such an explanation would be extremely reductionist, because it is situated at an overly abstract level and passes silently over contradictory movements. Economic competition, for instance, leads to media commercialization, with which political actors must cope, but it is contrary pressures for more regulation of economic activity that are the motive for rule-making by independent agencies or even of many transnational governance regimes. Liberalism has a social-cultural dimension as well, embodied in the individualization of society. This leads to the erosion of the role of parties as agents for the aggregation of social preferences, triggers pressures for more cooperative forms of governance, and generates a 'claims' culture that fosters judicialization. However, it is often very different forces that stand

214

between economic and cultural liberalism (Hooghe *et al.*, 2002). Although the neoliberal Right usually combines both, this is not true for other segments of the Right, which can be economically protectionist or culturally traditionalist, whereas an increasing part of the Left continues to firmly oppose economic liberalism while being at the forefront of claims for the cultural liberalization of our societies, by advocating, for instance, 'multiculturalism' as a core organise principle of social life.

This first section provides, then, a synthetic view of the changes that have come to affect the fate of democracy. In the introduction, it was assumed that the standard description of established democracies emphasizes the role of political representation. Either citizens believe they are represented by politicians, and support them, or large numbers no longer believe so, and become distrustful of them. The second option is often portrayed as a crisis of representation. In representative democracies, political parties traditionally form the crucial link between citizens and decision-makers. They are the major input vectors of citizens' preferences into the political system and, by means of their members' occupation of governmental and parliamentary positions, they are also the major output producers of decisions that are collectively binding for the citizenry. This circular model of democracy is no longer an adequate description of our political systems.

The first change discussed in the book is a new relationship between parties, society, and the state, the consequence of which is a shrinking legitimacy basis of representative democracy with political parties as its core actors. It comes as no surprise that changes affecting democratic systems produce winners and losers. More than seventy years ago, Schattschneider (1942: 1) asserted that 'modern democracy is unthinkable save in terms of political parties'. Schattschneider's assertion remains correct today regarding the formal description of democracies, but it should be largely qualified regarding the actual operation of democratic systems. As emphasized in Chapter 1, not only do citizens feel less loyal to parties, but they trust politicians less as well, and, without necessarily disliking the democratic form of the regime, they become disenchanted democrats. As a result, but also because our societies are highly heterogeneous, the partisan arena loses its aggregative function to the benefit of arenas of advocacy democracy, in which cause groups are the key players.

With the erosion of partisan loyalties, elections are becoming more competitive. Party identification has declined and citizens feel more at ease in sanctioning incumbent parties. In a context where differences between most party platforms, save those of fringe parties, are not easily discernible, and where it is increasingly difficult to attract voters, credible leadership becomes a competitive advantage, and personal attributes become focal points for voting choices. This is the electoral face of a personalization of politics that induces parties to become presidentialized. This is driven by strategic calculations, most notably by the desire to attract, through adequate campaigning emphasise leadership and governmental capabilities, an increasing number of floating, swing voters – those who are decisive for an electoral victory and who are the most volatile and least attached to a particular party doctrine. In addition, to attract a large segment of such voters, party leaders need to be able to be more flexible, less constrained in adjusting the party platform.

Hence, political parties are not losers as a whole. They tend to concentrate on their electoral role, and this generates winners and losers, too – this time within partisan organizations. The internal power balance within parties shifts in favour of leadership and to the detriment of the rank and file, and when parties are in government this is mirrored in a power shift in favour of the executive and to the detriment of the legislature. Thus, the presidentialization of politics has an executive side, too. Parliamentary assemblies as institutions become less effective in producing legislation and in holding the executive accountable. The parliamentary mark on representative democracy is less apparent. For distinct reasons, mediatization and internationalization reinforce different facets of the centralise trend within parties and cabinets:

- As suggested in Chapter 2, the mediatization of politics is sustained by parties' attempts to receive favourable media treatment, in a period when voters are weakly loyal to parties. Because the media follow a predominantly commercial logic, they need, in turn, to personalize and dramatize politics, and parties must adapt to that. Consequently, campaign management relies less on the mobilization of party machines than on the advice of communication specialists. For the moment, it is uncertain whether the new information technologies are going to change this trend.
- European integration has been a deliberate elitist undertaking since the end of World War II, and this has contributed domestically to the decline of parliamentary scrutiny over governmental and administrative action. But the effectiveness of legislatures is more seriously undermined by internationalization (Chapter 3). The

influence of democratic decision-making falls off as the nation-state encounters greater difficulty in achieving its functions efficiently in a sovereign way. The increasing role of supra- and transnational governance systems reduces the scope of democratic national politics, but it also offers a window of opportunity to national executives to emancipate themselves from domestic constraints. Thus, internationalization weakens domestic governmental accountability, and this amplifies the centralise effect of party presidentialization.

In such a context, the party becomes an extension of government, or even simply of the chief executive, who plays a crucial role in decision-making at the expense not only of parliaments but of the government at large as well. With presidentialization, political power appears concentrated in the hands of party leaders and of a narrow group of people around them – for instance, communication specialists for electoral campaigning, together with members of the core executive as regards policy-making ('court' government):

> There is general agreement that over the last thirty to forty years there has been a steady movement towards the reinforcement of the political core executive in most advanced industrial countries and that, within the core executive, there has been an increasing centralization of authority around the person of the chief executive – president, prime minister, or both. (Peters *et al.*, 2000: 7)

In a presidentialized government, political leaders do not govern through, but rather past, their parties. In nearly permanent campaigning, they seek to establish direct links to a heterogeneous and volatile electorate. The prevailing model of democracy is increasingly one with plebiscitary traits. However, this narrative does not allow the capture of all the complexities of policy-making.

Paradoxically, power concentration may be coupled with power fragmentation. Power may be concentrated within a narrow group of national executive members, but the scope of power of such a group is narrowed. The complexity of problems calls for problem-solving mechanisms that are multilevel and transcend national boundaries. Social fragmentation and the capacity of social segments to resist state authority call for compromise between institutions or between collective organizations, and this happens more easily within amorphous networks of actors of different nature. While politics is strongly

dominated by a competitive logic because parties seek to offer meaningful choices between rival governmental teams, policy-making
becomes cooperative because of problem, social, and institutional
complexity (Dryzek, 1990: 57–76). It is bureaucracies, then, that
become the 'orchestrators' of cooperative practice, regardless of the
rhetoric of civil society participation (Chapter 4).

This is but one manifestation of the shift of a substantial proportion
of political power, defined as the capacity to issue collectively binding
decisions, to spheres (sometimes far) beyond elected officials. This
happens even in systems of government where the locus of power is
deemed to lie in the hands of the prime minister. Not only are citizens
more remote from parties, but the same is true for political power. A
significant portion of this power no longer lies in the hands of elected
political representatives. With what Vibert (2007) aptly called 'the rise
of the unelected', the distance between those affected by political decisions and those at the origin of their production has grown.

Nevertheless, partisan competition continues, to a large extent, like
'business as usual', as if the rise of the unelected had not taken place.
For example, elections are more competitive, but one might ask oneself
for what kind of 'misconduct' the incumbents are sanctioned, given
that elections only partly affect policy substance. Instead, there is a
broadening gap between media-focused 'front-stage' politics and
'back-stage' policy-making. In electoral competition, parties act as if
such a disjunction did not exist, and this renders democratic accountability to a large extent fictitious because it leads to errors in the attribution of political responsibilities. Several factors lead to a shift of
power from elected actors, who have to cooperate with unelected
actors and even delegate or cede a good part of their policy-making
power to them.

The internationalization of policy-making (Chapter 3) is probably
the factor with the more straightforward impact upon the loss of
democratic control. Its intergovernmental component – governance
between governments in a great number of organizations – disempow-
ers parliaments and relies on a strong bureaucratic input. In addition,
internationalization empowers weakly accountable supranational
institutions and, much more alarming, various hybrid bodies and
private actors who become influential in global governance. More
specifically, European integration has led to the creation in several
fields of structures of multilevel governance where public actors
belonging to distinct decisional levels cooperate with non-public actors
of different nature. Both public–private partnerships in their narrow

sense and modes of collaborative governance between public and non-public actors at large prosper in domestic settings as well, because the official political authorities do not possess enough expertise on their own to take adequate political measures, or do not enjoy enough legitimacy to impose these measures on their addressees (Chapter 4). The assessment of the impact of these cooperative forms of governance on democracy is ambivalent.

These forms can be considered an improvement in the sense of pluralist, negotiated, and horizontal forms of policy-making. However, pluralism may be quite limited and biased in favour of the best-organized interests. In addition, collaborative governance often implies informal and non-transparent negotiations that are not the object of media interest and public scrutiny. Thus they lack visibility, and this impedes accountability. Finally, unelected members of bureaucracies and (sometimes self-proclaimed) representatives of particular interests are influential in such governance settings. The mass public sometimes blames 'Eurocrats' for a 'democratic deficit', but Chapters 3 and 4 show that such a deficit is more acute at the transnational level of governance and is not absent at the domestic level either.

Of course, there are also more participatory experiments, which are driven by a concern to involve ordinary citizens more closely in decision-making (Chapter 5). However, precisely because of their proliferation, the question of the effective policy impact of participatory experiments is key: only few of them lead to the formulation of policy options subsequently endorsed by public authorities. Besides, the growth of participatory forms of policy-making is accompanied by the development of other governance modes that are not really participatory (sometimes even of clearly technocratic nature), and that probably concern more important political issues. Transnational governance is a case in point, but even at the domestic level, administrative reforms did not seem to perform particularly well as regards their 'accountability agenda'.

These reforms took place in a context of suspicion towards traditional bureaucracies and under the illusion that the borrowing of recipes from the private sector necessarily leads to better performance. Although they were wrapped in rhetorics of consumer involvement, this often remained quite symbolic. One can also think of the diffusion across nations of agencies with strong administrative discretion (Chapter 6) in a *Zeitgeist* again marked by profound mistrust, but this time towards the positive contribution of politicians to the common good. One should not forget, however, that administrative reforms were initiated by politicians themselves, which makes some commentators argue that they facilitate blame-shifting strategies and allow politicians to evade accountability, especially in a situation of intense media interest for policy failure.

Under the banner of new public management, agencification, joined-up government, and the like, bureaucracies are nowadays continuously reformed; but what are the impacts of such reforms on the power of the various actors participating in the policy process and, most notably, on the political control over the bureaucracy? It is hard to answer this question, especially as the reform spirit is not devoid of ambiguities and the international diffusion of the reform movement is characterized by considerable divergence in implementation. It may well be that collaborative governance and administrative reform yielded contradictory effects with regard to the balance between executive office holders and administrators. Unlike collaborative governance, where bureaucracy seems to have the upper hand, it seems that in the end, administrative reforms led to a form of reassertion of the power of politicians over the bureaucracy. Reforms initially implied that the administration would be awarded more autonomy, but in a second phase, this probably scared politicians. Their power over the bureaucracy was reaffirmed through a new wave of repoliticization of the civil service.

One could welcome the gains obtained thereby in terms of political accountability of the bureaucracy, but in reality, things are more complicated. It is members of executives rather than members of elected assemblies who seem to be the ultimate winners of this cyclical process, so that we are facing an executive drift in that case, as with party presidentialization and the internationalization of policy-making. Moreover, the role of elections as the core accountability mechanism of representative democracy is further weakened, not only because the control of the bureaucracy by directly elected members of parliaments is insufficient, but also because the legitimate accountability forums now tend to be those populations at 'street-level', which, as in collaborative governance, can make credible claims about their affectedness by state policies. Accountability is less exercised through the individual vote than through the organized voice of narrow populations, or more commonly of advocacy groups deemed to represent the latter.

This is a limit to the effective impact of majority rule on service delivery, but majority rule is challenged more deeply. Democracy relies formally on majority rule, but minorities may suffer; to be legitimate majority rule requires justification (Chambers, 1996), which can be deficient. In the situations of strong differentiation that characterize our societies, sheer majoritarian power often proves not to be sufficiently legitimized, even though elected authorities are *de jure* authorized to act by virtue of the popular legitimacy that they enjoy. Cooperative forms of governance are set up precisely to remedy the insufficiencies of formal majority rule in a context of strong social fragmentation. Judicialization (Chapter 6) is related to a quest for additional formal sources of legitimacy for binding decisions. Driven by internationalization, too, judicialization is a manifestation of increasing concern about respect for minority and individual rights and for the rule of law.

The increased influence of courts on policy-making further contributes to the declining role of the partisan representative circuit. With judicialization, courts become policy actors, and this directly or indirectly leads to self-limitation of political officials. However, when judges are empowered, it is not only members of legislatures that operate under their shadow, but also the government and the administration. This is why governments may feel tempted to put independent judiciaries under political control, and sometimes they succeed. Governmental intrusion into the activities of the judiciary undermines its independence and endangers the division of powers. On the other hand, there is no agreement on the positive consequences of judicialization: it is the least representative branch of government that gains power, and access to courts may be subject to limits owing to an uneven distribution of resources similar to that impeding access to networks of collaborative governance. Not only is the normative justification of judicialization ambivalent, but its practical legitimacy is uncertain, too. This is so because, in spite of its pervasiveness, judicialization is not the object of political debates or media coverage (perhaps with the exception of the USA).

This is a more general problem, because the same could be said about other changes, like the role of weakly visible governance arrangements, expert bodies and collaborative networks, all lacking formal authorization but exerting (to varying degrees) political power – that is, the power to produce decisions that *in fine* have binding effects and are conducive to resource (re-)allocation. This role is more important than assumed at the national level and has considerably gained in prominence with the internationalization of policy-making. Such almost unnoticed changes have significant consequences for the quality of democracy. The question is, what would happen if the public came to perceive these trends as an attack on their capacity for self-determination, which is a constitutive feature of a democratic regime and whose respect is a necessary condition for democratic legitimacy. In a positive feedback loop, this would probably lead to even more cynicism about politics.

In the next sections, I suggest that the changes identified in this book generate four major challenges to democratic representative government:

- a decline in the role of representative institutions at the input and output side of politics;
- the creeping or deliberate technocratization of policy-making;
- the advent of 'advocacy' democracy;
- the divorce between the logic of front-stage and back-stage politics.

## The marginalization of parliamentary institutions

Recent literature on political parties has emphasized their weakness in aggregation of social preferences at the input side of politics. There is today less 'party on the ground' (Katz and Mair, 1994) and more 'advocacy democracy' (Dalton *et al.*, 2003) where cause groups are key vehicles for voice and the formulation of inputs to policy-making. Deparliamentarization (von Beyme, 2000) implies that parties (and especially their parliamentary component) are equally weakened in their functions related to the output side of the production of collectively binding decisions. The presidentialization of parties includes this dimension as well. Not only have parties partly lost their function of expression, they are also tending to lose their function of government. Parties are both challenged as vectors of preference aggregation and as agents of collectively binding decisions. It has even been argued by the late Peter Mair that it is because parties are challenged on the input side that they lack legitimacy to be core actors on the output side: 'If parties lack representative legitimacy, then it is difficult to justify their acquisition of a governing role or to argue against passing the whole business of governing directly to the judges, regulatory agencies, and the like' (Mair, 2009: 11).

Hence, not only are party militants marginalized, but also MPs, because parliaments lose influence in the policy process. In parliamentary systems, the exercise of initiative rights has to a large extent been delegated to government. Disciplined parliamentary majorities are not willing to scrutinize efficiently the executive's legislative proposals, while the opposition remains toothless, and parliaments seldom have sufficient resources to monitor systematically the way that their decisions are implemented by the administration. One should, of course, consider that there is significant international variation in the powers that parliaments dispose of, and factors like the degree of professionalization of parliamentary work are important. A combined index of *de jure* and *de facto* legislative power of parliaments in 23 established democracies ranges from 8.5 in France to 14.5 in the United States and in New Zealand (Sebaldt, 2009: 105). This variation may not seem very large; however, one should consider that parliaments are usually strong in one power dimension (for example, their role in selecting various types of office-holders) but weaker in another (for example, the *ex post* control of governmental activity) (Sieberer, 2011).

It is also claimed that the extent of the power shift to the benefit of the executive seems to have been overestimated, and that those supporting such a 'lazy' narrative confining to a 'caricature' overlook more subtle and informal intra-party and intra-parliamentary channels of legislative influence and control (Flinders and Kelso, 2011: 248). Parliaments are usually divided between governmental and opposition parties, but governments are not homogeneous either; hence, in Germany, for example, MPs belonging to majority parties bring in legislative amendments that fit the preferences of a particular ministry, but which have been disregarded by the Cabinet (Kropp, 2006: 291). In Chapter 3, informal channels of influence were identified affecting the relationships between national legislatures and governments in the European integration process; note, however, that opposition parties do not easily have access to them and that their informality and lack of visibility are inimical to public accountability.

One should also note that the theme of the 'decline of legislatures' is not new (Bryce, 1921), and the view of the existence of a Golden Age of parliamentary dominance in the past is incorrect (Flinders and Kelso, 2011: 255). Almost half a century ago, critics of technocracy pointed out that owing to the increasing complexity of political problems, bureaucracies and experts were tending to gain political influence (Meynaud, 1969). However, there is little empirical evidence of parliaments having been particularly powerful in the past. True, there were some notable exceptions such as the – disastrous in terms of governmental stability – *régime d'assemblée* of the French 4th Republic, but even in the UK – formally the stronghold of parliamentary sovereignty –historical research shows that majoritarian politics and the complexity of the state apparatus long prevented parliament from playing a surveillance role. The doctrine of ministerial responsibility proved to be largely fictitious in practice. Located at the interface between parliament and the administration, ministers acted as gatekeepers and accountability shields for the public bureaucracy rather than as swords against it, and select parliamentary committees formally in charge of inquiry functions were controlled by the governmental party and thus rendered inefficient (Flinders, 2004a).

Concentration of formal power in the hands of the top executive is a core feature of prime ministerial governments in majoritarian polities such as the UK. Yet even in the USA, where 'divided government' – frequently the House of Representatives or the Senate is not controlled by the presidential majority – may limit presidential power, concentration of power in the presidency was also observed in recent decades. Beginning with the Reagan administration in the 1980s and continuing today, regardless of the political party controlling the executive branch, a transformation occurred in the relationship between the president and Congress at the expense of the latter's political influence. According to Sassen (2006: 172), issue complexity and (subsequently) deregulation combined their effects to lead to an erosion of congressional autonomy. Interestingly, the shift of power to the presidency led, in turn, to a growing role for the Supreme Court, 'which emerged as one of the sites for scrutiny in cases where previously Congress might have been the critical actor' (Sassen, 2006: 175).

Today, presidentialization affects multiparty systems where coalition politics prevail. It is highlighted by:

> attempts to reorganize government so as to enhance the resources or strategic coordinating capacity available to the leader; signs of reduced opportunities for collective decision-making within the executive (for instance, reduced frequency or length of Cabinet meetings); the growth of bilateral decision-making processes involving the chief executive and individual ministers to the exclusion of the Cabinet collectively; and a tendency to promote non-party technocrats or politicians lack distinctive party power bases. (Webb *et al.*, 2011: 20)

Furthermore, even in systems where parties are supposed to be major players (such as 'partitocratic' systems like Belgium with multiparty coalitions and a high degree of partyness), or where the parliament could be a powerful veto point, interpartisan negotiations at summit level enable the circumvention of objections expressed by party organizations and the bypassing of formal veto points.

Several of the evolutions observed in the previous chapters negatively affect the role of parliaments on policy-making. Internationalization and European integration are deemed to tip the domestic balance between legislatures and executives in favour of the latter. In addition, one should consider the weakness or even absence of parliamentary control beyond the nation-state. This is a governance level where the chain of delegation is extremely lengthy; it may even be broken sometimes – for instance, in the case of influential expert groups or private governance arrangements lacking formal authorization to become policy-making actors. Even in domestic governance networks, MPs are seldom the key players and it is even doubtful if they can exert effective oversight over policies formulated or implemented by them. Administrative reform was intended to give more leeway to old and new bureaucracies, and even if politicians sought to regain control over the bureaucracy, thanks to better resources, members of executives proved more able to achieve that goal than members of legislatures. Finally, judicialization empowers the courts, including in an indirect manner, and casts their shadow over legislative processes.

Decision-making power is thus increasingly externalized in spheres that escape, partially at least, parliamentary control. This may be portrayed as a shift towards the 'self-restraining' state – a concept used by Schedler (1999) in the different context of new democracies, the meaning of which can be extended to describe this dynamic of externalization. One can ask if the power concentration that is induced by presidentialization contradicts such a dynamic. Yet the proponents of the presidentialization thesis write:

> Paradoxically, these processes may well go hand in hand with other initiatives designed to restructure the state by divesting the executive of power, for instance, through privatizing or hiving-off responsibilities to agencies. Thus, strategies conducive to the presidentialization of politics may be compatible with the sort of 'hollowing-out' strategies sometimes pursued by governments in order to overcome problems of 'ungovernability'. Where this happens, the core executive attempts to reduce the scope of its direct responsibility for government, while enhancing its coordinating power in the domain which it continues to regard as strategically critical. (Poguntke and Webb, 2005a: 32)

226 Democracy in Crisis?

Overall, parliaments lose influence because of a multifaceted depoliti-cization process characterized by power redistribution through 'arena-shifting' (Flinders and Buller, 2006). Political power at large is transferred to sites that are relatively free from political interference and control.

Recent research shows, nevertheless, that parliaments have started reacting to the loss of their power. Interestingly, the democratic consti-tutions of Central and Eastern European EU-member-states confer a greater role to legislatures than the older constitutions of West European democracies (Malovà and Haughton, 2002). This is proba-bly guided by the same suspicion over executive dominance that presided over the diffusion of judicial control in these countries (see Chapter 6). More generally, nowadays, MPs scrutinize more closely the behaviour of Cabinet members (Bergman and Strom, 2004: 90). Yet another typical reaction on behalf of parliaments is the strength-ening of the committee system, which provides legislative bodies with additional resources for policy-making (time for reflection, better staffing and logistics). It also enables MPs to specialize in frequently highly technical matters and to work in a problem-solving atmos-phere, even in adversarial political systems. In the United Kingdom, even though parliamentary reforms between 2001 and 2005 did not alter the power balance that is traditionally biased in favour of the executive, they enhanced the scrutiny capacity of the House of Commons, with select committees launching inquiries about hot policy issues (Flinders, 2007).

Other elements related to the modernization of parliaments are the increasingly common practice of committee-level hearings of minis-ters, experts, and administrative officials, and scrutiny and evalua-tion of policy implementation, all of which may be a harbinger of a new equilibrium in parliament–government relations. It may be objected that there is more parliamentary control over less (Christensen *et al.*, 2002), but even beyond the nation-state, we observed some emerging attempts to promote transnational networking between members of national parliaments in order to reduce informational asymmetries at their disadvantage (Chapter 3). The crucial problem is different: even though reparliamentarization may counteract the executive drift, it is challenged by other evolu-tions weakening representative democracy.

## The technocratization of policy-making

Deparliamentarization does not necessarily mean technocratization. For instance, concentration of power within presidentialized parties and governments may not be accompanied by a rise in bureaucratic power, but rather by a rise in the influence of communication specialists in a context of strongly competitive elections, a volatile electorate, and ruthless media scrutiny. Yet, trends towards a creeping technocratization of political power were clearly discernible in several chapters of this book. These trends are caused by internationalization that not only generates institution-building but brings with it thousands of experts (including private ones) who are more or less visible and who participate in more or less formal policy processes (Chapter 3). Similar trends seem to be the outcome of collaborative governance, with the administration playing a leadership role in the steering of the policy process – what specialists call the task of metagovernance (Chapter 4). It is not clear if administrative reform benefits managers or politicians in the end, but in situations in which it is profitable to the latter, the fewer members of the executive institutions benefit more than the more numerous, and directly elected, members of legislative institutions (Chapters 5 and 6). Finally, judicialization empowers the courts as institutions and judges as actors, and it indirectly increases the influence of other legal experts as well (Chapter 6).

Of course, one can contrast trends like the elongation of the delegation chain through the transfer of power to guardian institutions which are deliberately insulated (at least formally) from the democratic circuit, with other trends towards more 'short distance' democracy, like the proliferation throughout the world of participatory experiments involving ordinary citizens. However, this reverse trend is too limited to offset trends moving in the direction of elitism. Elitist tendencies are more discernible in high politics, whereas participatory experiments tend to be confined to low politics. They are often limited to the local level, to particular sectors (such as environmental policy), or to particular issues, such as the spatial allocation of public bads. They often result from top-down initiatives, yet even if they are set in place by public authorities, their influence on policy outputs is questionable. Furthermore, their democratic quality varies, but the proportion of the population that participates in these experiments does not exceed one or two per cent, a similar proportion to that of citizen *representatives* in parliamentary assemblies of different decisional levels, as acknowledged even by a sympathetic author (Rosanvallon,

2008: 326)! And we have seen that devices such as NPM-inspired reforms or cooperative forms of governance, which are supposed, in one way or another, to provide more direct access to policy-making for stakeholders as well, are prone to technocratic capture or to capture by organized interests.

In his essay *Post-Democracy*, Colin Crouch reaches a diagnosis that is partly similar, although we would not fully concur on the aetiology of the problem. Crouch asks: Are the voices of ordinary people now 'being squeezed out again, as the economically powerful continue to use their instruments of the influence while those of the *demos* become weakened?' (Crouch, 2004: 5). In post-democracy, 'virtually all the components of democracy survive' (p. 22), yet 'many citizens have been reduced to the role of manipulated, passive, rare participants' (p. 21), and 'politics and government are increasingly slipping back into the control of privileged elites in the manner characteristic of pre-democratic times' (p. 6). Crouch is indeed correct to say that political parties privatize or delegate substantial activities of service provision to non-elected bodies and concentrate on their image in the political marketplace (pp. 101–3). Partisan competition loses, thereby, much of its substance. This is, according to Crouch, clearly visible in the United Kingdom where 'the shift from Labour to New Labour can be read as the shift from a party suited to democratic politics to one prepared for post-democracy' (p. 64). Crouch points out a paradox between the politicians' obsession with opinion poll ratings and the increasing disempowerment of citizens. Relations with citizens are important as a source of legitimacy for the elites, but in reality, citizens do not count much, as what is encouraged is 'the maximum level of minimal participation' (p. 112). According to Crouch, the management of public opinion through the media-based public relations machine renders the disempowerment of the citizenry compatible with government dependence on public approval.

Crouch is also right, of course, that citizens are not always assiduous political participants, but he tends to attribute their marginalization to deliberate efforts by elites, whose common objective would be to stay in power while keeping citizens at a distance. However, lack of political participation also results from citizens' own decisions, for a variety of reasons – from a feeling of powerlessness with regard to their possibility to influence things, to exasperation with political conflict and compromise, or a rational preference for investing time and energy in other kinds of social and personal activities. Post-democracy is not necessarily dictated by the privileged role of global corporations and business lobbies, neither is it – as suggested by Crouch – a straightforward consequence of sociological changes, such as the decline of the working class and the correlated rise of non-manual work and service employment in post-industrial societies. Rather, evolutions in the political sphere lead to some sort of hollowing out of democratic politics – the internationalization of policy-making that enhances technocratic traits as well as the privatization of governance modes, the stronger policy role for unelected actors and institutions even within the nation-state, and concentration of remaining power in the hands of executives (or just in the hands of a subgroup within the executive).

The previous section concluded with the not-too-pessimistic argument that deparliamentarization might have reached a tipping point, with members of representative assemblies increasingly aware of their loss of political significance. It is hard to predict if a similar pendulum movement will take place with respect to technocratization. What should be emphasized is that not all processes that are potential candidates for technocratic policy-making, such as internationalization, collaborative governance, or administrative reform, are equally prone to it. For example, technocratization is more clearly discernible in collaborative governance than in administrative reform, and even more so in transnational policy-making. Domestically, some governance arrangements are more coupled to the representative circuit than others, while some are more open and some are more subject to public scrutiny. The extent to which these diverse governance arrangements are problematic as regards their legitimacy with respect to democratic normative requirements depends on their specific configuration, and this would require a detailed scrutiny of each of them. There are many questions to which scholars should be sensitive if they intend to assess how transformations in modes of governance affect the quality of democracy:

- What is the structure and what is the degree of formalization of the governance arrangements considered? Do representative institutions or elected officials play a crucial role in them? If not, does a mandate exist from them, and if so, how long is the chain of delegation? If a mandate exists, what is the role of democratically authorized bodies in the monitoring of the activity of such governance modes and in the critical control and endorsement of their outputs?
- How are the individual members of the various policy-making bodies designated, and to whom are they accountable? Whom do

they consider as the primary target of their accountability discourse? Does real-world accountability operate as prescribed on paper by formal accountability regimes (regarding justification, debate, and sanctions), if any? And, if not, why not?

- How influential are the policy-making arrangements? How soft or hard – that is, formalized and enforceable – are the norms they produce? Are these norms (formally or *de facto*) binding, and, if *de facto*, to what extent? What kind of motives drive actors to treat formally non-binding rules as binding?
- Are we just in the presence of 'self' regulation by a community, or of regulation of others, too? In both cases, what kind of spillover effects does regulation have *on* others? How extended is the circle of affected third parties, and how intensely are they affected?
- To what extent do those affected have a voice in the activity of norms production? How much, and through which mechanisms, is the 'congruence' principle between policy-makers and 'policy-takers' respected? Is some form of consent by the affected required? Or are at least governance outputs public, and thus subject to contestation?

All these questions require careful empirical scrutiny and precise responses, which is why this book must conclude with a plea for more research.

## The advent of advocacy democracy

If the decline of the representative circuit can be reversed, if the degree of technocratization varies across decision-making levels and policy sectors, there might not be too strong reasons to be concerned. The advent of so-called advocacy democracy (Dalton *et al.*, 2003) may yet be another reason why gloomy conclusions on democracy being in crisis could be disputed.

Advocacy democracy is one form of 'democracy with adjectives' (Collier and Levitsky, 1997) among others. 'With adjectives' is a term mainly used to characterize democratise countries that lack all the features of consolidated democracies and political systems whose democratic quality can be judged as limited. However, adjectives increasingly apply to the changing world of established democracies, too. In the advocacy form of democracy with adjectives, the key players are cause groups; in plebiscitary democracy, the key players are political leaders emancipated from partisan organizations (presidentialization); in audience democracy, the key players are the media; and in a monitory democracy, the key players are the media again, but also guardian institutions like courts, ombudsmen, auditing bodies, and the like. Each of these forms of democracy with adjectives captures part of the changes described in this book. At first glance, advocacy democracy seems the most promising among them, because plebiscitary democracy entails the concentration and personalization of power, audience democracy is bounded by media commercialization, and in monitory democracy, the monitors may themselves not be democratically accountable.

In advocacy democracy, cause groups challenge political parties' claims to express the interests and values of segments of the population, as well as their roles as guardians of the respect of such interests and values by state action. Beyond the national level, where partisan organizations are weaker (as at EU-level) or completely absent, cause groups take over these functions, usually under the banner of the 'global civil society'. This is often cited in support of the proposition that advocacy forms of democracy compensate for the atrophy of traditional representative channels at the domestic level, or for their absence in transnational governance. There are signs that the decisional impact of advocacy groups is increasing through the resonance of transnational social movements or with the participation of nonpublic actors in collaborative governance networks.

Some idealize the role of cause groups as the empowerment of civil society, uncorrupted by the sins of party politics. Advocacy democracy is put forward as superior, because it would be a more participatory form of democracy compared to traditional representative democracy. Cause groups are considered to be closer to people's preoccupations than the bureaucratic machines of established parties. Hence, so the argument goes, advocacy democracy provides more effective channels for political participation, a gain for democracy. Such a perspective is also typical of normative models of 'associative' democracy (Hirst, 1994). I am less optimistic; in addition, I cannot share the view of those – not necessarily the same – who believe that the accountability of rulers has never been as strong as in the current conditions of audience or monitory democracy (other democracies with adjectives).

Let me first clarify that if I am sceptical about the virtues of advocacy democracy, this has nothing to do with a principled position against participatory forms of democracy, and I do not intend to idealize traditional representative democracy. After all, representative democracy is not without flaws. It is no less a democracy with adjectives, and it has even been substantiated that initially the principle of representation was alien to democracy (Manin, 1997). It was consideration of modern political parties that, as early as in 1911, led Roberto Michels (1962) to formulate his 'iron law of oligarchy'. More recently, Italian political philosopher Norberto Bobbio (1987) listed a number of 'broken promises' of (representative) democracies, among them, most importantly, the persistence of oligarchic power. Social and cultural inequalities affect political participation, and it is unrealistic to believe that decision-making in representative polities adequately mirrors the plurality of social values and interests (Schattschneider, 1960).

Party government is affected by problems regarding delegation *ex ante* and accountability *ex post*. *Ex ante* authorization to rule on behalf of voters is not always 'enlightened', because voters are seldom well informed about the policy programmes of the parties or the profiles of the candidates, and given this deficit, there is suspicion that they can be manipulated by politicians or the media. Even in direct democracy campaigns, the prime movers are the elites, not the ordinary people (Kriesi, 2005). *Ex post* monitoring of the activities of governors is also negatively affected by informational asymmetries. Delegation theories draw attention to the danger that agents to whom principals delegate tasks shirk and pursue their own profit (Lupia, 2003). Politicians, in particular, have sufficient discretion not to fulfil some of their pledges and to do things that have not been mandated, without seriously fearing that their voters will become aware of their conduct and will sanction them. Jean-Jacques Rousseau's statement of 1762 in *The Social Contract* is famous in that respect: 'The people of England regards itself as free; but it is grossly mistaken; it is free only during the election of members of parliament. As soon as they are elected, slavery overtakes it, and it is nothing' (Rousseau, 1973, ch.15: 240).

Does this pessimistic diagnosis hold 250 years later, under conditions of permanent campaigning in the context of audience or monitory democracy? There is no straightforward answer. Citizens are increasingly emancipated from parties; some are more actively critical, while others feel dispossessed from their political influence and distrust politicians, and the latter are no longer the sole depositories of political power. In such a context, there is no doubt that more participatory forms of democracy would be desirable, although they should not be idealized. For instance, decisions made in Switzerland through direct democratic procedures (referenda) are more inimical to minorities, most notably to minorities such as immigrants with whom the native population cannot easily identify and considers as the outgroup, than decisions made in the parliamentary circuit (Vatter, 2011). Notwithstanding such reservations, if the major challenge to representative democracy came from more direct forms of participation, there would probably be no reason to write this book. The major threat is rather of a technocratic-elitist nature, whereas more participatory procedures either have a limited effect in terms of policy influence (deliberative experiments) or suffer from authorization and accountability deficits (advocacy democracy) that are not less serious than those of conventional representative democracy.

What is wrong then with advocacy democracy? The problem is that it conveys its own 'broken' promises. Are its sins worse than the sins of representative democracy? Not necessarily, but they are not less preoccupying, and this suffices to plead for a less enchanted view of this alleged supplement or, depending on situations, alternative to representative democracy. In addition, notwithstanding the weaknesses of representative democracy, one should not throw out the baby with the bath water. Unlike advocacy democracy, it provides institutionalized mechanisms conditionally authorise some actors to take collectively binding decisions, and it does this under conditions of formal political equality.

About fifty years ago, a famous specialist in comparative politics, Stein Rokkan (1966: 105), wrote that 'votes count, but resources decide'. Put in admittedly rather abrupt terms, in advocacy democracy, votes do not count much any longer, and resources decide more than in a representative democracy. Advocacy democracy lacks the (at least formal) egalitarian dimension of the 'one person, one vote' principle, as the kind of activities it implies often require skills (like organizational capacity) that are even less equally distributed than those necessary to decide in a competent manner between parties running in elections. It is an arena where cause groups organize minorities who have intense preferences, or who feel intensely affected by political decisions. As suggested by Burns (1999: 174), 'This system of "governance" is largely one of organizations, by organizations and for organizations.' This is not illegitimate as such; however, the social bias in mobilization by cause groups may be stronger than for political parties, and we know that these kinds of groups often make unreliable self-claims about their representativeness and are not always accountable to their alleged groups of reference. One may wonder, then, to what extent advocacy democracy is indeed *demo*cracy, in the classic sense of power by the people. Representative democracy may not be too much of a *demo*cracy either, but it provides more reliable (because institutionalized) opportunities to remedy the disease if people find it too painful.

## The divorce between front- and back-stage: a reinforcement loop

The previous sections have suggested that the evolution of established democracies can be dialectic, with trends possibly generating counter-trends. To mention but one example, the policy input by cause groups aims at mitigating the impact of technocratization, and these groups seek to critically scrutinize policy outputs emanating from technocratic circles. In addition, due to their contradictory nature, some evolutions may be considered paradoxical. For example, the parties' role as governor is challenged by the technocratization of policy-making, but this does not prevent party leaderships from presenting themselves to the public primarily as teams, or sometimes plainly as persons, who should be entrusted with the solution of policy problems. There is a paradox in that parties are increasingly seen as governors whilst they govern less. Party competition is highly mediatized and is characterized as a result by strong personalization and simplification of issues, especially as ideological and programmatic differences between competitors become less acute and the range of feasible policy options narrower. Yet, as formulated by Mair (2008: 227):

> To be sure, there is a choice between the competing teams of leaders and, given the growing evidence of bipolarity, that particular choice is becoming more sharply defined. But there is less and less choice in policy terms, suggesting that political competition is drifting towards an opposition of form rather than of content.

Competition is much less about political goals – a 'choice of society', as François Mitterrand claimed a bit dramatically in the campaign for the French presidential election of 1981 – and is perhaps also less about policy means to achieve the same goals. It has become much more a competition about who is better able to implement policies that no longer significantly differ between candidates. In a period in which their latitude for policy pursuit is diminished, mainstream parties have become primarily office-seekers. The electoral game has become more intense, but the stakes are much lower, so that there is, in a sense, an inverse relationship between the intensity with which the game is played and the importance of its outcome (Katz and Mair, 1996: 530).

Nowadays, the outcome of national elections is more uncertain, and governing parties are increasingly 'punished' by voters, as their electoral losses are higher than in the past (Strom *et al.*, 2003). The greater frequency of non-reelection can be related to the fact that voters become more ruthless with the incumbents because they trust them less, they are less loyal to them, and parties have fewer channels to influence them (Mair, 2009: 15). It also has to do with the prevalent negative campaigning, in which the defects of opponents are emphasized rather than one's own merits (Rosanvallon, 2006: 178–81). Negative campaigning, in turn, is a corollary of mediatization. We know now that more strongly commercialized media are in search of signs of failure and weak points of office holders, which produce news value. Although the policy choices of parties are largely convergent and policy-making escapes their influence to a significant extent, the citizenry is more critical towards what it considers to be weak performance of the incumbent party or parties.

This paradox is a symptom of the divorce between the sphere of politics and the sphere of policy-making. Not only is partisan politics in representative institutions losing its substance and technocratic policy-making gains, but the gap between the logic of the sphere of politics and the logic of the sphere of policy-making is widening. Such a divorce impedes effective accountability: those who are formally accountable to the citizenry delegate (more or less willingly) a non-negligible share of their power to actors whose activities are not mediatized and who are neither publicly visible nor democratically accountable; and sometimes they simply realize *ex post* the power shift. As a result, there are discrepancies or even contradictions between responsibility and effective power, and public expectations about responsibility are misplaced; inevitably, this is the source of frustration and disillusionment (Burns, 1999: 177).

Democracies are thus converging in the divorce between politics, characterized by bipolar competition, and policy-making, characterized by technocratic or at best collaborative styles. On the one hand, even fragmented multiparty systems with a coalition government are today often characterized by a bipolar logic of competition between party coalitions (Mair, 2009: 8–9). On the other hand, a cooperative logic tends to develop in policy-making even in Westminster systems of prime ministerial government (Bevir and Rhodes, 2006). European integration contributes to the divorce. The gap between '*politique d'opinion*' and '*politique des problèmes*' (Leca, 1996: 345–6) observed in national politics is accentuated at the EU level because the sphere of *politique d'opinion* is practically absent, with the exception of the situations where some sectoral and well-organized interests can mobilize their constituencies on specific issues (Eriksen *et al.*, 2007). There is little public space for debate on the pros and cons of European integration, perhaps with the exception of referendums on treaty ratification. Vivien Schmidt (2006), for instance, refers to the process of European integration as 'policies without politics' (p. 268), and she also finds problematic the lack of 'communicative discourse' (pp. 39–43) at the EU level. Beyond the European level, visible events like WTO conferences or G-8 and G-20 meetings are highly mediatized and have generated public contestation by transnational social movements. The same cannot be said about less visible policy-making processes that bear the marks of experts and private actors.

To some extent, we can speak of more democracy than in the past in the national sphere of political competition. Not only are elections more competitive, but party members or even party sympathizers have more influence (for example, via primaries) over candidate nominations, and electoral systems increasingly allow for candidate preference votes (Bergman and Strom, 2004: 90). Referendum consultations are becoming more frequent too; for example, newly democratized Central and East European countries have introduced in their constitutions the possibility of popular consultations initiated not only from above, that is by the head of the state, the government, or a majority of parliament, but also from below, that is by citizens. This is not just a formal option, but an opportunity that is effectively used by the citizenry. Since 1990, the proportion of referendum consultations held as a result of popular initiatives has been nearly twice as high in Eastern as in Western Europe, and citizens of East European countries have voted against the preference expressed by their governments about twice as frequently as in Western Europe (Schmitter and Trechsel, 2004: 83–6).

More generally, it is argued that positive power (the capacity to make collectively binding decisions) is now strongly counterbalanced by negative power (the capacity to check, and even to block, decisions). In a recent *magnum opus,* John Keane (2009: 688–91) cited the advent of several, quite heterogeneous, expressions of 'monitory' democracy:

A new historical form of democracy, a variety of 'post-parliamentary politics' defined by the rapid growth of many different kinds of extra-parliamentary, power scrutinising mechanisms.... Within and outside states, independent monitors of power begin to have tangible effects. By putting politicians, parties and elected governments permanently on their toes, they complicate their lives, question their authority and force them to change their agendas – and sometimes

smother them in disgrace…. Elections, political parties and legislatures neither disappear, nor necessarily decline in importance; but
they most definitely lose their pivotal position in politics…. Some
monitors, activist courts, electoral commissions and consumer
protection agencies, for instance, use their claimed 'neutrality' to
protect the rules of the democratic game from predators and
enemies. Other monitors publicise long-term issues that are
neglected, or dealt with badly, by the short term mentality encouraged by election cycles…. The central grip of elections, political
parties and parliaments on citizens' lives is weakening. Monitory
democracy is the age of surveys, focus groups, deliberative polling,
online polling, and audience and customer voting.

Keane is right that elections, political parties and legislatures lose their
pivotal role. However, the main reason is not more stringent control
over the activities of elected actors, but a degradation of democratic
quality that takes place back-stage, hardly visible to the mass public.
As asserted by a major specialist of democratic theory, all sorts of organizations are producing today a 'ubiquitous jargon of transparency,
capacity building, empowerment, stakeholders, good governance and
the like' (Pateman, 2012: 13). Although not by intent, this kind of
discourse obscures the degradation of democracy back-stage.
Academic discourse on the advent of 'audience' or 'monitory' democracy is also to some extent misleading, because it captures only part of
the reality: the developments that take place front-stage.

In audience democracy, the life and acts of politicians are placed
under close media surveillance, and one may even say that part of public
action is largely conditioned by media coverage. Take, for example, the
case of security policy, where the effect of media narratives on criminal-
ity and on 'dangerosity' is strong. Simply because the public mood
seems to be influenced by media dramaturgy, politicians cannot afford
the cost of ignoring it. It is also true that several institutions and devices,
such as laws on freedom of information, now exist to enable better
monitoring of rulers' activity. All this seems to increase the role of
publicity, yet significant parts of policy-making escape visibility and
public scrutiny. Consequently, genuine democratic accountability is
eroded: under the impact of mediatization, 'image and style increasingly
(push) policies and substance aside', write Farrell and Webb (2002:
122). Mediatization mainly affects the symbolic politics of the political
spectacle; the media concentrate much of their attention on checking
the public action (and increasingly the private life) of politicians, who

are the most visible targets, whether or not they play the most decisive roles in policy-making.

As suggested by Christensen and Laegreid (2006: 12), 'being criticized and embarrassed politically while at the same time being deprived of influence and information is a bad combination'. It is, then, no surprise that politicians seek to escape this uncomfortable situation by shifting the blame to actors who cannot be sanctioned by the electorate, such as agencies at the domestic level or other national governments and supranational authorities at the international level. This prejudices effective political accountability, and the same can be said about the fact that media coverage misses a significant part of public activity, because media outlets are not interested in it – they cannot produce meaningful and sellable 'news' out of it – or because journalists lack expertise to deal with its complexities and technicalities. Even a sympathetic observer of recent developments begins his account with the following note: 'Politicians compete for sound-bites but the real work of running democracies is now carried out by the unelected' (Vibert, 2007: 1). He concludes eloquently with the following assertion: 'The same forces that enable an unelected central bank governor to speak with authority, so that markets listen, also devalue the words of an elected finance minister whose words might be regarded as spin and that can be discounted by markets' (Vibert, 2007: 165). One can indeed conclude from such developments that 'power and accountability have been divorced, if not *de jure* so *de facto*, and we now need to assess what this means for democratic governance' (Pierre, 2009: 592). The sphere of representative politics tends to be democratized, but effective accountability is being hollowed out. Both retrospective evaluations of office-holders by the citizenry, based on appraisals of their policy achievements, and prospective mandates based on anticipations of their capacity or willingness to fulfil their promises become difficult, if not meaningless.

This is not tantamount to a conspiratorial view of politics, if we define the latter as the belief that a sort of secret government leads the world without citizens being aware of that, and that democratic life is only superficial, a sort of camouflage whose only function would be to conceal how things really happen in politics (Rosanvallon, 2008: 289). Leaving aside the blame-shifting strategies of some actors, democratic accountability is undermined for structural reasons and not because decision-making actors are malevolent. Speaking of an uncoupling or a divorce between spheres basically means that the *modus operandi* differs between the realm of policy-making and the realm of electoral politics. This leads to a different game in each of them, with different rules and different players as well. It suffices to think that policy-making is partly denationalized, whereas electoral politics basically remain national (or subnational). The divorce is also visible in the fact that, while in the sphere of politics there seems to be more democracy but less effective accountability the opposite seems to be the case in the sphere of policy-making – more, but less democratic, accountability (Papadopoulos, 2010).

What we observe today is a proliferation of accountability mechanisms more closely related to the concrete activities of decision-making bodies, including accountability to ombudsmen and courts, to auditing institutions, to management boards and stakeholder panels, and to 'peers' participating in the same policy networks or expert groups. These mechanisms may be welcome but they do not offset the deficit engendered by the growth of democratically unaccountable policy-making, illustrated most notably by the rise of private governance bodies; neither do they offset the loss of significance of the individual vote as the classic accountability mechanism of representative democracy. Moreover, there are problems with such accountability mechanisms. Mutual accountability may be high between the actors involved, but the democratic credentials of several of them are disputable. There are also inequalities in actors' capacities to effectively hold decision-makers to account. In addition, 'account-holders' may be self-selected, or even selected by those supposed to provide accounts to them.

Finally, the uncoupling between spheres can produce a spiral of mutually reinforcing effects (positive feedback loops). The depoliticization of policy-making hollows out party competition, for example, horizontally by delegation to domestic 'non-majoritarian' institutions, or vertically by delegation to supranational bodies. This decline in substance of political competition provides additional grounds for further depoliticise the policy-making process (Mair, 2005: 32), resulting into a broader gap between the competitive logic of audience democracy and the technocratic or cooperative logic of back-stage governance. The broader this gap, the more likely there will be dissatisfaction with the policy performance of incumbent parties. The competitive logic of electoral politics leads to an inflation of policy pledges, whereas the depoliticized logic of policy-making forces decision-makers to cope with structural constraints and compromise. Dissatisfaction with the 'reality principle' may generate new demands for alternatives of plebiscitary nature, especially under the influence of the mass media, which seeks to dramatize and personalize politics for its own commercial reasons. Yet more disappointment may arise in a next phase if initially charismatic leaders cannot fulfil their (inflationary) promises. As Klijn (2008: 23) eloquently suggests, 'We tire quickly of our heroes in a drama-democracy'.

The ultimate result may well be a vicious circle of political distrust, in which an inflation of promises in the field of competitive politics leads to an expectations gap; this gap leads to disenchantment among the public with political performance and to low trust for politicians. In a next step, the distrustful public is more likely to succumb to a perception gap: even if political performance is satisfactory, this is no longer acknowledged due to a negativity bias (Flinders and Kelso, 2011: 251–4) that is also cultivated by commercialized media. For the moment, this kind of spiral effect mainly eroded respect for politics and politicians, and democracy as a value seems to remain immune to criticism. However, one cannot exclude that spillover effects affect more generally and more deeply the foundations of democratic legitimacy. This may happen if the current economic crisis, which produces severe social hardship in a number of countries, persists. In Greece, for instance, the overtly racist party 'Golden Dawn' polled nearly 7 per cent of the vote in two consecutive elections in 2012; at the start of 2013 it is credited with nearly twice as much of the vote, according to polls. This is a remarkable score for a party that advocates violence and is much more radically anti-system and extremist than the other anti-establishment nationalist parties with which our democracies are now familiar. In Greece, 'Golden Dawn' capitalizes not only on hardship caused by the crisis and by austerity policies, but also on a widespread diffusion of the feeling that insecurity is fuelled by immigration, on the discredit of this country's political class, and on the fact that violence has become 'an acceptable way to settle public disputes' (Andronikidou and Kovras 2012: 716). The last factor may be idiosyncratic in the universe of established democracies, but will Greece remain an isolated case?

## After the winter?

Figure 7.1 summarizes the different paths leading to the four challenges (in capitals) to representative democracy described in the previous sections. This is a stylized view: it does not present all the intricacies of the processes analysed in this book.

241

Figure 7.1.   *The four challenges to representative government*

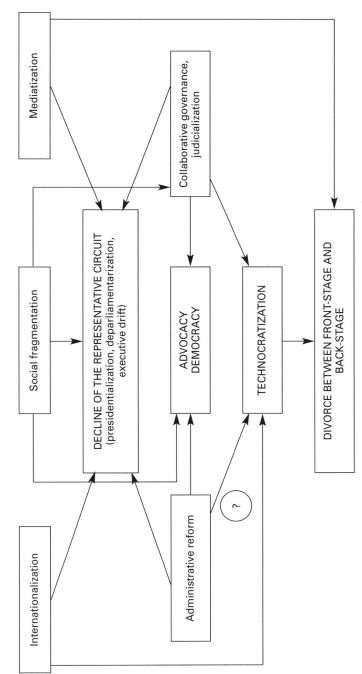

Would it be excessive to say that the challenges depicted above denote a crisis of democracy, as the title of this book suggests? 'Crisis' is a diagnosis that should be used with caution – hence, the question mark in the book title. In my view, these challenges have a negative impact on various important facets of the quality of democracy: representation, participation, and accountability. But whether one should speak of a crisis or not depends very much on one's views of what democracy should be, as well as on one's assessment of discernible opportunities for improvement.

This book suggests that we are witnessing a shift of decision-making functions to bodies remote from the representative process, collaborative governance frequently characterized by limited pluralism, transnational governance with weak democratic accountability and increased privatization, and mostly local participatory experiments with a limited impact. To use an image, there may be more school boards today populated by people having abandoned the search for influence through partisan electoral channels (advocacy democracy), but the other side of the coin is monetary policy delegated to increasingly independent central banks (including the European one) that are composed of usually narrow-minded technocrats from the financial sector, or norm-setting being delegated to private bodies at a remote transnational level. The declining role of parliamentary institutions, the uncoupling of the sphere of the political dramaturgy and the sphere of decision-making that operates under the influence of technocrats or of particular interests – all of this makes prospects for the quality of democracy none too optimistic none too bright.

To be sure, such a judgment cannot be straightforward, as wisely asserted by Yves Mény (2010: 264): 'In many cases, the frontier between the "democratically imperfect" and the "unacceptably undemocratic" is thin and calls for debate and dialogue rather than proclamation of absolute truth and excommunications'. However, if we consider the practical, and not just the abstractly normative side of democratic legitimacy, we have to consider that when people become aware of democratic deficits, their disenchantment as democrats may become stronger.

For example, we know that what had once been called a 'permissive consensus' on the elitist character of the European integration has eroded in the last decades. But if European integration triggers feelings of distrust and alienation among the mass public, this may not be the case for various manifestations of technocratic policy-making, simply because they still remain to a large extent unknown to the wider public. Many of the governance processes discussed in this book are often hardly visible to the 'lay' citizen, and are sometimes ignored by professional politicians as well. They deviate from common knowledge of how our political systems work, and even from textbook accounts on this subject. Were citizens to become more familiar with all the aspects of extensive delegation and externalization of power outside the democratic circuit, this would probably amplify distrust. That would, no doubt, be the case if citizens were better acquainted with the privatization of governance, or more generally, with various forms of governance where democratic control is hardly effective. Were they to become better known, changes on the output side of democracies might contribute to further citizens' disaffection from democracies on the input side. There are possible positive feedback loops between trends towards a further oligarchization of policy-making (output) and trends towards citizens' disaffection (input) from politics. Such loops can be reinforced if people become more fully aware of the amplitude of oligarchization. Does this mean that we have entered the era of 'post-democracy', as asserted by Colin Crouch?

This book began with a quote from Guy Hermet's work on the winter of democracy. Hermet (2007: 12) further suggests metaphorically that 'democracy has reached winter age without having to fear an immediate heart attack'. He believes that we are now in the same situation as that described by Alexis de Tocqueville in his *L'Ancien Régime et la Révolution*, where less than a decade before the French Revolution, people were not aware that 'revolution had taken place unnoticed before the Revolution' through a number of incremental changes. Unlike in France of the 1780s, and contrary to Hermet's claims, it seems exaggerated to believe that we shall soon witness the advent of a new regime, or that we have already experienced the rise of 'post-parliamentary governance' (Andersen and Burns, 1996), and this notwithstanding the multiple signs of erosion of the quality of democracy. This does not mean, of course, that what has happened to democracies is insignificant, even though, as in the France of a bit more than two centuries ago, the changes continue to remain unnoticed by many people.

Surprisingly, it is mainly populist demagogues who have noticed the degradation of democratic quality. They exploit it and capitalize on it. There is, however, no reason to leave the monopoly of critique to them, especially as this kind of critique is not disinterested and is often extremely reductionist. For example, established parties are regularly demonized for their selfishness, while the degradation of democracy does not necessarily profit them and there is no mono-causal explanation for it. At the end of the introduction, I under-scored that political science should provide people with the tools that are necessary to evaluate critically evolutions that concern them. Such a critical evaluation should be fact-regarding and rely on realis-tic perceptions; it cannot be derived from a simplistic and idealized image of what democratic processes should look like.

An important word of caution is that the loss of substance of democratic policy-making does not result from deliberate action. The agencification and judicialization processes analysed in Chapter 6 are exceptions, but in such cases, the democratic loss is considered an acceptable trade-off with regard to the benefits of impartiality (not to mention that, for better or worse, agencies and courts may in reality be subject to the influence of elected officials). If the loss of substance happens by stealth, this is because policy and institutional designers (correctly) put high on their agenda the achievement of policy goals (efficiency, effectiveness, impartiality), but their 'framing' is hardly sensible to the issue of democratic control over policy-making. Considering the great variety of governance arrangements, there is a large number of elected and unelected designers of policy and institu-tions who should be sensitized to the importance of such a control.

With the transformation of governance emerge various kinds of *de facto* rulers whose democratic authorization and accountability are deficient. In a recent book, Pepper Culpepper (2010) portrayed as 'quiet politics' the kind of informal, discreet, and sometimes collusive relations that exist between business and political actors. With phenomena such as collaborative and privatized governance, 'quiet' activities, which are inherently political because they affect a broad range of non-consulted interests, are expanding. We should definitely be worried by the fact that the scope of decision-making that escapes visibility in the public sphere, a condition for contestability and democratic control, is widened. The advent of new forms of *arcana imperii*, where secrecy and informality prevent the public opinion 'tribunal' (Bentham, 1990: 27) from playing its role, is perhaps no longer a deliberate art of government, but is not considered a prob-lem either.

This should precisely be problematized, because we learn from history that 'the most untroubled decision-makers were those who escaped democratic politics altogether' (Hobsbawm, 1994: 580).

Not only elites, but also ordinary citizens should become familiar with the causes, nature, and consequences of recent developments. Raising collective awareness is an important (and difficult enough!) task, since it makes monitorial activities more evidence-based. For instance, problematise the trade-offs between possible gains in terms of policy quality and possible losses in terms of democratic quality associated with a specific mode of governance enables citizens to decide to what extent such a trade-off is acceptable. Were people to become more familiar with a series of developments presented in this book, they might, for instance, ground their assessments of network forms of governance on their degree of pluralism or on their openness to the influence of elected actors, while they might feel ambivalent about judicialization that may contribute to impartiality and provide venues for contestation (however, mostly to well-organized segments) but confers at the same time a policy-making role to the least representative branch of government. They might also find that administrative reforms, or even participatory experiments, are not sufficient to compensate for the decreasing influence of the democratic circuit, especially as reforms are themselves subject to limits and bias.

The diffusion of a more evidence-based view of changes may, however, not suffice, because in itself, it does not alleviate the democratic deficit that they induce. Discussing in detail possible avenues for democratic renewal would go beyond the (primarily analytical and explanatory) goal of this book. However, some 'design thinking' (Stoker, 2010: 80) is also needed if we think that the prescription of remedies likely to counteract the degradation of democratic quality should follow from the evaluation of the current state of things. Disaffection and cynicism are not fatal, but they can only be combated if possible solutions to the problem of disempowerment are submitted to the people. Advocacy forms of democracy are often cited as one of them, especially beyond the national level where the role of democratically elected bodies is weaker, or even non-existent. Although current proposals on how to democratize decision-making largely focus on such forms of democracy because they are deemed to bring civil society back in, we know that they may not be exempt from flaws like elitism and lack of equality. Other alternatives should be considered, and I would like to conclude the book by sketching two of them, which are more complementary than exclusive.

Without idealise representative democracy, there is still much potential for an empowerment of representative institutions as collective bodies or of their individual members. As a matter of fact, a source of hope lies in the learning capacity of the disempowered, such as members of parliaments. Reference was made in Chapter 3 to networks of national parliamentarians that have emerged with the aim of checking the activity of international organizations, or to similar developments within the European Union. This principle could be extended. Closer scrutiny of the activities of decisional arenas situated too far from the national-territorial realm of democratic politics or staffed with unelected people (such as governance networks, agencies, private or informal rulemaking bodies) is required.

It is probably unrealistic to expect that the effective locus of power will shift again to traditional representative institutions. But if their members, mainly through networking and specialise, could enhance and extend their supervisory function to bodies that currently do not consider themselves threatened by the shadow of their accountability to the citizenry or to its elected representatives, this would indeed improve the quality of democratic governance. Further, supervision by elected bodies should not only be exerted on the content of decisions, but also on processes, thus combining the output and throughput functions. Typically, elected bodies should care that whenever pluralism is praised as a virtue of a policy-making body, it does not remain a dead letter, that resource inequalities among the participants are not too high, and that the publicity of decisions – which allows effective accountability, consent, and contestation from outside – is secured. Such a supervisory activity does not necessarily present the characteristics of a zero-sum game. A closer interface between various policy-making bodies and elected officials should also give to the former the opportunity to convince the latter through 'reason giving', so that accountability mechanisms serve for mutual learning (Bovens, 2007).

This step is probably not sufficient, however, because it would be unwise to ignore that elected officials now suffer from lack of public trust. Therefore, governance arenas should be more closely coupled not only with representative institutions, but also with more participatory bodies involving lay citizens. As pointed out in Chapter 5, such bodies are proliferating, but their potential remains largely unexploited. A crucial issue is that of their impact on decision-making – 'where the rubber hits the road' (Culpepper *et al.* n.d.: 5). Here, too, it is unrealistic to think that to '"get a grip" and connect up to the "main game"' (Goodin 2012: 806) is easy; participatory bodies do not have many chances to take over decisional functions strongly entrenched in other bodies. However, it is conceivable that they could acquire more soft power. For that purpose, they should formulate policy recommendations and thus contribute to the input process. But they should also make sure that these recommendations are widely publicized, monitor how decision-making bodies take them into account, and report on that. If their composition and design make them credible with regard to their representativeness and their competence, then it would be more difficult for decision-makers to ignore their recommendations.

Deliberative techniques have now made possible representative participatory experiments on a large scale, such as the European one, in which deliberative opinion polls were organized recently, albeit without any expectation that they would influence (elite) decisions on the future of European integration. There is no reason why such experiments could not be implemented even beyond the EU level, but it is only if they are not purely symbolic exercises as regards their contribution to decision-making that they will avoid the stigma of 'political curiosities' (Culpepper *et al.*, n.d.: 33), and will inspire more confidence from citizens instead of being ignored or, worse, mocked.

These developments are mutually compatible and can produce cumulative effects. Reforms along these lines would have a potential to empower *both* ordinary citizens and professional politicians and would affect all (input, throughput, output) dimensions of the policy process. There is no inevitability in vicious circles leading to a degradation of the quality of democracy and then possibly to a spiral of ever-broader political distrust and cynicism. If democracy is in crisis, this may be a provisional state. However, if the degradation happened by stealth, a renewal can only take place if it is acknowledged in the first place – and then, through a conscious effort to counteract it. It is not certain that this will happen. Taking seriously, for example, considerations of democratic authorization and accountability in the multitude of emerging governance forms requires that a radical learning process takes place, upsetting the dominant frames of those who establish them about what matters most in modes of governance. Moreover, a rehabilitation of the parliamentary circuit requires an effort from elected politicians, and the imposition of serious political influence by participatory devices requires an effort from ordinary citizens.

Yet neither can it be asserted that the crisis of democracy is here to stay. There is no teleology in politics. Think about the recent financial crisis, which seriously undermined the credibility of technocrats as regulators. Those mostly affected in their credibility were the ones supposed to be the most credible. History teaches us that the course of politics is reversible, and today's winners may well be tomorrow's losers. After all, in nearly all parts of our world, there is nothing like a permanent winter.

# Bibliography

All quotations from books in French are translated by Yannis Papadopoulos.

Aarsether, Nils *et al.* (2009). 'Evaluating the Democratic Accountability of Governance Networks: Analysing Two Nordic Megaprojects', *Local Government Studies* 35(5): 577–594.

Abers, Rebecca (2000). *Inventing Local Democracy. Grassroots Politics in Brazil*. Boulder, CO: Lynne Rienner.

Adam, Silke and Michaela Maier (2010). 'Personalisation of Politics – A Critical Review and Agenda for Research', *Communication Yearbook* 34: 214–57.

Akkerman, Tjitske (2005). 'Challengers and Cartels. Conceptualising the Representative Role of Parties'. Paper for presentation to the workshop 'Political Parties and Democracy', ECPR Joint Sessions, Granada, 14–19 April 2005.

Allern, Elin H. and Karina Pedersen (2007). 'The Impact of Organisational Changes on Democracy', *West European Politics* 30(1): 68–92.

Alonso, Sonia et al. (eds.) (2011). *The Future of Representative Democracy*. Cambridge: Cambridge University Press.

Andersen, Svein S. and Tom R. Burns (1996). 'The European Union and the Erosion of Parliamentary Democracy: A Study of Post-parliamentary Governance', in Svein S. Andersen and Kjell A. Eliassen (eds.) *The European Union: How Democratic Is It?* (pp. 226–51). London: Sage.

Andronikidou, Aikaterini and Iosif Kovras (2012). 'Cultures of Rioting and Anti-Systemic Politics in Southern Europe', *West European Politics* 35(4): 707–725.

Ansell, Chris and Alison Gash (2007). 'Collaborative Governance in Theory and Practice', *Journal of Public Administration Research and Theory* 18: 543–71.

Ansell, Christopher and Jane Gingrich (2003). 'Reforming the Administrative State', in Bruce E. Cain, Russell J. Dalton and Susan E. Scarrow (eds.) *Democracy Transformed? Expanding Political Opportunities in Advanced Industrial Democracies* (pp. 164–91). Oxford: Oxford University Press.

Athens News (2012) 'Papademos welcomes Europe's vote of confidence', http://www.athensnews.gr/portal/8/53756, accessed 3 February 2012.

Aucoin, Peter (2012). 'New Political Governance in Westminster Systems: Impartial Public Administration and Management Performance at Risk', *Governance* 25(2): 177–199.

Auel, Katrin (2007). 'Democratic Accountability and National Parliaments –

Redefining the Impact of Parliamentary Scrutiny', *European Law Journal* 13(4): 487–504.

Auel, Katrin and Arthur Benz (2005). 'The Politics of Adaptation: The Europeanisation of National Parliamentary Systems', *The Journal of Legislative Studies* 11(3–4): 372–93.

Avant, Deborah D. *et al.* (2010). 'Who Governs the globe ?', in Deborah D. Avant, Martha Finnemore and Susan K. Sell (eds.) *Who Governs the Globe?* (pp.1–31). Cambridge: Cambridge University Press.

Avery, James M. (2009). 'Videomalaise or Virtuous Circle ?', *The International Journal of Press/Politics* 14(4): 410–33.

Avritzer, Leonardo (2002). *Democracy and the Public Space in Latin America.* Princeton: Princeton University Press.

Bache, Ian (2008). 'Europeanization and Multi-level Governance: Empirical Findings and Conceptual Challenges'. ARENA working paper 16.

Bache, Ian (2010). 'Partnership as an EU Policy Instrument: A Political History', *West European Politics* 33(1): 58–74.

Bache, Ian and Jan Olsson (2001). 'Legitimacy through Partnership? EU Policy Diffusion in Britain and Sweden', *Scandinavian Political Studies* 24(3): 215–237.

Baiocchi, Gianpaolo (2005). *Militants and Citizens: Local Democracy on a Global Stage in Porto Alegre.* Stanford, CA: Stanford University Press.

Bale, Tim (2005). *European Politics. A Comparative Introduction.* Basingstoke: Palgrave Macmillan.

Barber, Benjamin R. (1996). *Jihad vs. McWorld: Terrorism's Challenge to Democracy.* New York : Ballantine Books.

Barnett, Michael and Martha Finnemore (2004). *Rules for the World: International Organizations in Global Politics.* Ithaca, NY: Cornell University Press.

Bartolini, Stefano (2005). *Restructuring Europe. Centre Formation, System Building, and Political Structuring between the Nation State and the European Union.* Oxford: Oxford University Press.

Beisheim, Marianne *et al.* (2010). 'Global governance through public-private partnerships', in Henrik Enderlein, Sonja Wälti and Michael Zürn (eds.) *Handbook on Multi-level Governance* (pp. 370–382). Cheltenham: Edward Elgar.

Bell, Daniel (1960). *The End of Ideology: On the Exhaustion of Political Ideas in the Fifties.* Glencoe, NY: Free Press.

Bellamy, Richard (2007). *Political Constitutionalism. A Republican Defence of the Constitutionality of Democracy.* Cambridge: Cambridge University Press.

Bengtson, Christina (2007). 'Interparliamentary cooperation within Europe', in John O'Brennan and Tapio Raunio (eds.) *National Parliaments within the European Union. From 'victims' of integration to competitive actors?* (pp. 46–65). London: Routledge.

Bentham, Jeremy (1990). *Securities against Misrule and other Constitutional Writings for Tripoli and Greece* (ed. Philip Schofield), Oxford: Clarendon Press.

Benz, Arthur and Yannis Papadopoulos (2006). *Governance and Democracy. Comparing National, European, and International Experiences.* London: Routledge.

Benz, Arthur, Carol Harlow and Yannis Papadopoulos (eds.) (2007). 'Accountability in EU multi-level governance', special issue of the *European Law Journal*, July 2007, 13(4).

Bergman, Torbjörn and Kaare Strom (2004). 'Shifting Dimensions of Citizen Control', *Scandinavian Political Studies* 27(2): 89–113.

Bernstein, Steven and Benjamin Cashore (2007). 'Can Non-state Global Governance be Legitimate? An Analytical Framework', *Regulation and Governance* 1(4): 347–71.

Beus, Jos de (2006). 'Truth about Audience Democracy and in it – Manin's Model of Political Communication in Mature Democracies', manuscript.

Bevir, Mark (2010). *Democratic Governance.* Princeton: Princeton University Press.

Bevir, Mark and R.A.W. Rhodes (2006). 'Prime Ministers, Presidentialism and Westminster Smokescreens', *Political Studies* 54: 671–90.

Bevir, Mark and R.A.W. Rhodes (2007). 'Decentred Theory, Change and Network Governance', in Eva Sörensen and Jacob Torfing (eds.) *Theories of Democratic Network Governance* (pp. 77–91). Basingstoke: Palgrave Macmillan.

Bevir, Mark and R.A.W. Rhodes (2008). 'The Differentiated Polity as Narrative', *British Journal of Politics and International Relations* 10: 729–34.

Bexell, Magdalena *et al.* (2010). 'Democracy in Global Governance: The Promises and Pitfalls of Transnational Actors', *Global Governance* 16: 81–101.

Blagescu, Monica and Robert Lloyd (2009). 'Accountability of transnational actors: is there scope for cross-sector principles?', in Anne Peters, Lucy Koechlin, Till Förster and Gretta Fenner Zinkernagel (eds.) *Non-State actors as Standard Setters* (pp. 270–303). Cambridge: Cambridge University Press.

Blichner, Lars C. and Anders Molander (2008). 'Mapping Juridification', *European Law Journal* 14(1): 36–54.

Blondiaux, Loïc (2008). *Le nouvel esprit de la démocratie. Actualité de la démocratie participative.* Paris: Le Seuil.

Blondiaux, Loïc and Yves Sintomer (2002). 'L'impératif délibératif', *Politix* 15(57): 17–35.

Blumler, Jay G. and Dennis Kavanagh (1999). 'The Third Age of Political Communication: Influences and Features', *Political Communication* 16(3): 209–30.

Blumler, Jay G. and Michael Gurevitch (2001). '"Americanization" Reconsidered: UK–US Campaign Communication Comparisons Across Time', in W. Lance Bennett and Robert M. Entman (eds.) *Mediated Politics. Communication in the Future of Democracy* (pp. 380–403). Cambridge: Cambridge University Press.

Bobbio, Norberto (1987). *The Future of Democracy: A Defence of the Rules of the Game*. Cambridge: Polity Press.

Boli, John (2006). 'The Rationalization of Virtue and Virtuosity in World Society', in Marie-Laure Djelic and Kerstin Sahlin-Andersson (eds.) *Transnational Governance. Institutional Dynamics of Regulation* (pp. 95–118). Cambridge: Cambridge University Press.

Borgonovi, Francesca (2008). 'The Relationship between Education and Civic and Social Engagement'. Paper presented at the Social Outcomes of Learning Project Experts Group Meeting, Paris, 19 June.

Bornschier, Simon (2005). 'Unis contre la mondialisation? Une analyse de la convergence programmatique des partis populistes de droite européens', *Revue internationale de politique comparée* 12(4): 415–32.

Borras, Susanna and B. Guy Peters (2011). 'The Lisbon Strategy's Empowerment of Core Executives: Centralizing and Politicizing EU National Co-Ordination', *Journal of European Public Policy* 18(4): 525–45.

Börzel, Tanja A. and Carina Sprungk (2009). 'The Goodness of Fit and the Democratic Deficit in Europe', *Comparative European Politics* 7(3): 364–73.

Börzel, Tanja A. and Thomas Risse (2005). 'Public–Private Partnerships: Effective and Legitimate Tools of Transnational Governance?', in Edgar Grande and Louis W. Pauly (eds.) *Complex Sovereignty: Reconstituting Political Authority in the Twenty-first Century* (pp. 195–216). Toronto: University of Toronto Press.

Bouckaert, Geert and B. Guy Peters (2004). 'What is Available and What is Missing in the Study of Quangos?', in Christopher Pollitt and Colin Talbot (eds.) *Unbundled Government. A critical analysis of the global trend to agencies, quangos and contractualisation* (pp. 22–49). London: Routledge.

Bouckaert, Geert *et al.* (2010). *The Coordination of Public Sector Organizations: Shifting Patterns of Public Management*. Basingstoke: Palgrave Macmillan.

Bovens, Mark (2007). 'Analysing and Assessing Accountability. A Conceptual Framework', *European Law Journal* 13(4): 447–68.

Bovens, Mark *et al.* (eds.) (2010). *The Real World of EU Accountability. What Deficit?* Oxford: Oxford University Press.

Braithwaite, John and Peter Drahos (2000). *Global Business Regulation*. Cambridge: Cambridge University Press.

Brandsma, Gijs Jan (2010). *Backstage Europe. Comitology, Accountability and Democracy in the European Union*. Ph.D. dissertation: University of Utrecht.

Brandsma, Gijs Jan *et al.* (2008). 'How Transparent are EU "Comitology" Committees in Practice?', *European Law Journal* 14(6): 819–38.

Brants, Kees (1998). 'Who's Afraid of Infotainment?', *European Journal of Communication* 13(3): 315–35.

Brants, Kees *et al.* (2010). 'The Real Spiral of Cynicism? Symbiosis and Mistrust between Politicians and Journalists', *The International Journal of Press/Politics* 15(1): 25–40.

Bryce, James (1921). *Modern Democracies*. London: Macmillan.

Burns, Tom R. (1999). 'The Evolution of Parliaments and Societies in Europe. Challenges and Prospects', *European Journal of Social Theory*, 2(2): 167–94.

Büthe, Tim (2010). 'Private Regulation in the Global Economy: A (P)review', *Business and Politics* 12(3): Article 2.

Büthe, Tim and Walter Mattli (2010). 'Standards for Global Markets: Domestic and International Institutions', in Henrik Enderlein, Sonja Wälti and Michael Zürn (eds.) *Handbook on Multi-level Governance* (pp. 455–76). Cheltenham: Edward Elgar.

Cabannes, Yves (2006). 'Les budgets participatifs en Amérique Latine', *Mouvements* 47–48: 128–38.

Cain, Bruce E., Russell J. Dalton and Susan E. Scarrow (eds.) (2003). *Democracy Transformed? Expanding Political Opportunities in Advanced Industrial Democracies*. Oxford: Oxford University Press.

Callon, Michel *et al.* (eds.) (2001). *Agir dans un mode incertain. Essai sur la démocratie technique*. Paris: Editions du Seuil.

Cartier, Marie *et al.* (2008). *La France des petits-moyens*. Paris: La Découverte.

Cashore, Benjamin (2002). 'Legitimacy and the Privatization of Environmental Governance: How Non State Market-Driven (NSMD) Governance Systems Gain Rule Making Authority', *Governance* 15(4 (October): 503–529.

CEPEL (1996). *La négociation des politiques contractuelles*. Paris: L'Harmattan.

Chadwick, Andrew (2006). *Internet Politics*. Oxford: Oxford University Press.

Chambers, Simone (1996). *Reasonable Democracy*. Ithaca, NY: Cornell University Press.

Chevallier, Jacques (2004). *L'Etat post-moderne*. Paris: Librairie générale de droit et de jurisprudence.

Christensen, Tom and Laegreid, Per (eds.) (2001). *New Public Management. The Transformation of Ideas and Practice*. Aldershot: Ashgate.

Christensen, Tom and Per Laegreid (2001a). 'A Transformative Perspective on Administrative Reforms', in Tom Christensen and Per Laegreid (eds.) *New Public Management. The Transformation of Ideas and Practice* (pp. 13–39). Aldershot: Ashgate.

Christensen, Tom and Per Laegreid (2006). 'Introduction – Theoretical approach and research questions', in Tom Christensen and Per Laegreid (eds.) *Transcending New Public Management. The Transformation of Public Sector Reforms* (pp. 1–16). Aldershot: Ashgate.

Christensen, Tom and Per Laegreid (eds.) (2006a). 'Rebalancing the State: Reregulation and the Reassertion of the Centre', in Tom Christensen and Per Laegreid (eds.) *Autonomy and Regulation: Coping with Agencies in the Modern State* (pp. 359–79). Cheltenham: Edward Elgar.

Christensen, Tom *et al.* (2002). 'Increasing Parliamentary Control of the Executive? New Instruments and Emerging Effects', *The Journal of Legislative Studies* 8(1): 37–62.

Christmann, Anna *et al.* (2012). 'The Communicational Dimension of Democratic Accountability in Metropolitan Governance. Media Reporting and Legitimacy in Four European Mega- and Metacities'. Paper prepared for presentation at the IPSA World Congress of Political Science, Madrid, July 8–12 2012.

Cichowski, Rachel A. (2006). 'Courts, Rights, and Democratic Participation', *Comparative Political Studies* 39(1): 50–75.

Cichowski, Rachel A. (2006a). *The European Court and Civil Society. Litigation, Mobilization and Governance.* Cambridge: Cambridge University Press.

Cichowski, Rachel A. and Alec Stone Sweet (2003). 'Participation, Representative Democracy, and the Courts', in Bruce E. Cain, Russell J. Dalton and Susan E. Scarrow (eds.) *Democracy Transformed? Expanding Political Opportunities in Advanced Industrial Democracies* (pp. 192–220). Oxford: Oxford University Press.

Cleuren, Herwig (2008). 'Administrating Participatory Budgeting in Porto Alegre: Street-level Officials and Organisational Preconditions', *Revista Chilena de Administracion Publica* 12: 19–41.

Coen, David and Mark Thatcher (2005). 'The New Governance of Markets and Non-Majoritarian Regulators', *Governance* 18(3): 329–46.

Coen, David and Mark Thatcher (2008). 'Network Governance and Multi-level Delegation: European Networks of Regulatory Agencies', *Journal of Public Policy* 28(1): 49–71.

Coleman, Stephen and Jay G. Blumler (2009). *The Internet and Democratic Citizenship. Theory, Practice and Policy.* Cambridge: Cambridge University Press.

Collier, David and Steven Levitsky (1997). 'Research Note: Democracy with Adjectives: Conceptual Innovation in Comparative Research', *World Politics* 49(3): 430–51.

Considine, Mark and Kamaran A. Afzal (2011). 'Legitimacy', in Mark Bevir (ed.) *The SAGE Handbook of Governance* (pp. 369–85). London: Sage.

Conzelmann, Thomas and Klaus-Dieter Wolf (2008). 'The Potential and Limits of Governance by Private Codes of Conduct', in Jean-Christophe Graz and Andreas Nölke (eds.) *Transnational Private Governance and its Limits* (pp. 98–114). London: Routledge.

Crouch, Colin (2004). *Post-Democracy.* Cambridge: Polity Press.

Crozier, Michel and Erhard Friedberg (1977). *L'acteur et le système*. Paris: Editions du Seuil.

Crozier, Michel *et al.* (1975). *The Crisis of Democracy. Report on the Governability of Democracies to the Trilateral Commission*. New York: New York University Press.

Culpepper, Pepper D. (2010). *Quiet Politics and Business Power*. Ithaca, NY: Cornell University Press.

Culpepper, Pepper D. *et al.* (n.d.). 'Beyond Elections? Deliberation and Democracy in the European Union', unpublished manuscript.

Curtin, Deirdre and Morten Egeberg (2008). 'Tradition and Innovation: Europe's Accumulated Executive Order', *West European Politics* 31(4): 639–61.

Cutler, A. Claire (2002). 'Private International Regimes and Interfirm Cooperation', in Rodney B. Hall and Thomas J. Biersteker (eds.) *The Emergence of Private Authority in Global Governance* (pp. 23–40). Cambridge: Cambridge University Press.

Cutler, A. Claire (2003). *Private Power and Global Authority*. Cambridge: Cambridge University Press.

Dahlgren, Peter (2007). 'The Internet, Public Spheres and Political Communication: Dispersion and Deliberation', *Political Communication* 22: 147–62.

Dalton, Russell J. *et al.* (2002). 'The Consequences of Partisan Dealignment', in Russell J. Dalton and Martin P. Wattenberg (eds.) *Parties without Partisans. Political Change in Advanced Industrial Democracies* (pp. 37–63). Oxford: Oxford University Press.

Dalton, Russell J. (2004). *Democratic Challenges, Democratic Choices: The Erosion of Political Support in Advanced Industrial Democracies*. Oxford: Oxford University Press.

Dalton, Russell J. (2008). *Citizen Politics. Public Opinion and Political Parties in Advanced Industrial Democracies*. Washington, DC: CQ Press.

Dalton, Russell J. and Mark Gray (2003). 'Expanding the Electoral Marketplace', in Bruce E. Cain, Russell J. Dalton and Susan E. Scarrow (eds.) *Democracy Transformed? Expanding Political Opportunities in Advanced Industrial Democracies* (pp. 23–43). Oxford: Oxford University Press.

Dalton, Russell J. and Martin P. Wattenberg (2002). 'Unthinkable Democracy: Political Change in Advanced Industrial Democracies', in Russel J. Dalton and Martin P. Wattenberg (eds.) *Parties without Partisans. Political Change in Advanced Industrial Democracies* (pp. 1–36). Oxford: Oxford University Press.

Dalton, Russell J. and Martin P. Wattenberg (2002a). 'Partisan Change and the Democratic Process', in Russel J. Dalton and Martin P. Wattenberg (eds.) *Parties without Partisans. Political Change in Advanced Industrial Democracies* (pp. 261–85). Oxford: Oxford University Press.

Dalton, Russell J. *et al.* (2003). 'Democratic Publics and Democratic Institutions', in Bruce E. Cain *et al.* (eds.) *Democracy Transformed? Expanding Political Opportunities in Advanced Industrial Democracies* (pp. 250–75). Oxford: Oxford University Press.

Della Porta, Donatella and Tarrow, Sidney (2004). *Transnational Protest and Global Activism*. Lanham, MD: Rowman and Littlefield.

Della Porta, Donatella *et al.* (2006). *Globalization from Below: Transnational Activists And Protest Networks*. Minneapolis: University of Minnesota Press.

Delli Carpini, Michael X. and Bruce A. Williams (2001). 'Let Us Infotain You: Politics in the New Media Environment', in W. Lance Bennett and Robert M. Entman (eds.) *Mediated Politics. Communication in the Future of Democracy* (pp. 160–81). Cambridge: Cambridge University Press.

Dezalay, Yves and Bryant G. Garth (1996). *Dealing in Virtue: International Commercial Arbitration and the Construction of a Transnational Legal Order*. Chicago: University of Chicago Press.

Diamond, Larry and Marc Plattner (eds.) (1993). *The Global Resurgence of Democracy*. Baltimore: The Johns Hopkins University Press.

Dijkstra, Geske (2007). 'Supranational Governance and the Challenge of Democracy: The IMF and the World Bank', in Victor Bekkers *et al.* (eds.) *Governance and the Democratic Deficit* (pp. 269–92). Aldershot: Ashgate.

Djelic, Marie-Laure and Sigrid Quack (2003). *Globalization and Institutions*. Cheltenham: Edward Elgar.

Djelic, Marie-Laure and Kestin Sahlin-Andersson (2006). 'Introduction: A world of governance: The rise of transnational regulation', in Marie-Laure Djelic and Kerstin Sahlin-Andersson (eds.) *Transnational Governance. Institutional Dynamics of Regulation* (pp. 1–28). Cambridge: Cambridge University Press.

Donaghy, Maureen M. (2011). 'Do Participatory Governance Institutions Matter? Municipal Councils and Social Housing Programs in Brazil', *Comparative Politics* 44 (1): 83–102.

Dorf, Michael C. (2006). 'Problem-solving Courts and the Judicial Accountability Deficit', in Michael W. Dowdle (ed.) *Public Accountability. Designs, Dilemmas and Experiences* (pp. 301–28). Cambridge: Cambridge University Press.

Dorf, Michael C. and Charles F. Sabel (1998). 'A Constitution of Democratic Experimentalism', *Columbia Law Review* 98(2): 267–473.

Dowding, Keith *et al.* (eds.) (2001). *Challenges to Democracy*. Basingstoke: Palgrave Macmillan.

Downs, Anthony (1957). *An Economic Theory of Democracy*. New York: Harper and Row.

Dryzek, John S. (1990). *Discursive Democracy*. Cambridge: Cambridge University Press.

Dryzek, John S. (2000). *Deliberative Democracy and Beyond*. Oxford: Oxford University Press.

Dryzek, John S. (2010). *Foundations and Frontiers of Deliberative Governance*. Oxford: Oxford University Press.

Dryzek, John S. and Aviezer Tucker (2008). 'Deliberative Innovation to Different Effect: Consensus Conferences in Denmark, France, and the United States', *Public Administration Review* 68: 864–76.

Du Gay, Paul (2000). *In Praise of Bureaucracy*. London: Sage.

Dunleavy, Patrick (1991). *Democracy, Bureaucracy and Public Choice: Economic Explanations in Political Science*. Hemel Hempstead: Harvester Wheatsheaf.

Duran, Patrice (1999). *Penser l'action publique*. Paris: Librairie générale de droit et de jurisprudence.

Easton, David (1965). *A Systems Analysis of Political Life*. New York: John Wiley.

Eberlein, Burkard and Dieter Kerwer (2004). 'New Governance in the European Union: A Theoretical Perspective', *Journal of Common Market Studies* 42(1): 121–42.

Eberlein, Burkard and Edgar Grande (2005). 'Beyond Delegation: Transnational Regulatory Regimes and the EU Regulatory State', *Journal of European Public Policy* 12(1): 89–112.

Eberlein, Burkard and Abraham L. Newman (2008). 'Escaping the International Governance Dilemma? Incorporated Transgovernmental Networks in the European Union', *Governance: An International Journal of Policy, Administration, and Institutions* 21(1): 25–53.

Egeberg, Morten (2008). 'European Government(s): Executive Politics in Transition?', *West European Politics* 31(1): 235–57.

Egeberg, Morten and Jarle Trondal (2009). 'Political Leadership and Bureaucratic Autonomy: Effects of Agencification', *Governance* 22(4): 673–88.

Elias, Norbert (1991). *La société des individus*. Paris: Fayard.

Elster, Jon (1998). 'Introduction', in Jon Elster (ed.) *Deliberative Democracy* (pp. 1–18). Cambridge: Cambridge University Press.

Elster, Jon (2000). *Ulysses Unbound: Studies in Rationality, Precommitment, and Constraints*. Cambridge: Cambridge University Press.

Epp, Charles R. (1998). *The Rights Revolution: Lawyers, Activists, and Supreme Courts in Comparative Perspective*. Chicago: The University of Chicago Press.

Eriksen, Erik O. *et al.* (eds.) (2007). *The European Union and the Public Sphere: A Communicative Space in the Making?* London: Routledge.

Erman, Eva and Anders Uhlin (eds.) (2010). *Legitimacy Beyond the State? Re-Examining the Democratic Credentials of Transnational Actors*. Basingstoke: Palgrave Macmillan.

Esser, Frank and Barbara Pfetsch (2004). 'Meeting the Challenges of Global Communication and Political Integration', in Frank Esser and Barbara Pfetsch (eds.) *Comparing Political Communication* (pp. 384–410). Cambridge: Cambridge University Press.

Eymeri-Douzans, Jean-Michel (2008). 'Les réformes administratives en Europe: logiques managérialistes globales, acclimatations locales', *Pyramides* 15: 71–93.

Falkner, Gerda *et al.* (2005). *Complying with Europe: EU Harmonisation and Soft Law in the Member States.* Cambridge: Cambridge University Press.

Farrell, David M. and Paul Webb (2002). 'Political Parties as Campaign Organizations', in R.J. Dalton and M. P. Wattenberg (eds.) *Parties without Partisans. Political Change in Advanced Industrial Democracies* (pp. 102–28). Oxford: Oxford University Press.

Ferejohn, John and Pasquale Pasquino (2002). 'Constitutional Courts as Deliberative Institutions: Towards an Institutional Theory of Constitutional Justice', in Wojciech Sadurski (ed.) *Constitutional Justice, East and West. Democratic Legitimacy and Constitutional Courts in Post-Communist Europe in a Comparative Perspective* (pp. 21–36). The Hague: Kluwer Law International.

Ferlie, Ewan and Keith J. Geraghty (2005). 'Professionals in Public Services Organizations. Implications for Public Sector Reforming', in Ewan Ferlie, Laurence E. Lynn Jr. and Christopher Pollitt (eds.) *The Oxford Handbook of Public Management* (pp. 422–45). Oxford: Oxford University Press.

Fishkin, James S. (1991). *Democracy and Deliberation. New Directions for Democratic Reform.* New Haven: Yale University Press.

Fishkin, James S. (2009). *When the People Speak. Deliberative Democracy and Public Consultation.* Oxford: Oxford University Press.

Flinders, Matthew (2004). 'Distributed Public Governance in the EU', *Journal of European Public Policy* 11(3): 520–44.

Flinders, Matthew (2004a). 'MPs and Icebergs: Parliament and Delegated Governance', *Parliamentary Affairs* 57(4): 767–84.

Flinders, Matthew (2007). 'Analysing Reform: The House of Commons, 2001–5', *Political Studies* 55: 174–200.

Flinders, Matthew (2009). *Democratic Drift. Majoritarian Modification and Democratic Anomie in the United Kingdom.* Oxford: Oxford University Press.

Flinders, Matthew (2009a). 'The Politics of Patronage in the United Kingdom: Shrinking Reach and Diluted Permeation', *Governance* 22(4): 547–70.

Flinders, Matthew (2012). *Defending Politics. Why Democracy Matters in the Twenty-First Century.* Oxford: Oxford University Press.

Flinders, Matthew and Jim Buller (2006). 'Depoliticization, Democracy and Arena Shifting', in Tom Christensen and Per Laegreid (eds.) *Autonomy and Regulation: Coping with Agencies in the Modern State* (pp. 53–79). Cheltenham: Edward Elgar.

Flinders, Matthew and Alexandra Kelso (2011). 'Mind the Gap: Political Analysis, Public Expectations and the Parliamentary Decline Thesis', *British Journal of Politics and International Relations* 13: 249–68.

Flinders, Matthew and Felicity Matthews (2010). 'Think again: patronage, governance and the smarter state', *Policy and Politics* 38(4): 639–56.

Follesdal, Andreas (2010). 'The Legitimacy Challenges for New Modes of Governance: Trustworthy Responsiveness', *Government and Opposition* 46(1): 81–100.

Friedrich, Carl J. (1946). *Constitutional Government and Democracy. Theory and Practice in Europe and America*. Boston: Ginn and Co.

Fung, Archon (2006). 'Varieties of Participation in Complex Governance', *Public Administration Review* 66: 66–75.

Gastil, John and Levine, Peter (eds.) (2005). *The Deliberative Democracy Handbook*. San Francisco: Jossey-Bass.

Gaudin, Jean-Pierre (1995). 'Politiques urbaines et négociations territoriales. Quelle légitimité pour les réseaux de politiques publiques?', *Revue française de science politique* 45(1): 31–55.

Gaudin, Jean-Pierre (1999). *Gouverner par contrat*. Paris: Presses de Sciences Po.

Gaxie, Daniel (1978). *Le cens caché*. Paris: Editions du Seuil.

Gbikpi, Bernard and Jürgen R. Grote (2002). 'From Democratic Government to Participatory Governance', in Jürgen R. Grote and Bernard Gbikpi (eds.) *Participatory Governance. Political and Societal Implications* (pp. 17–34). Opladen: Leske+Budrich.

Gehring, Thomas (2004). 'The Consequences of Delegation to Independent Agencies: Separation of Powers, Discursive Governance and the Regulation of Telecommunications in Germany', *European Journal of Political Research* 43(4): 677–98.

Gibson, James L. *et al.* (1998). 'On the Legitimacy of National High Courts', *American Political Science Review* 92(2): 343–58.

Gilardi, Fabrizio (2005). 'The Institutional Foundations of Regulatory Capitalism: The Diffusion of Independent Regulatory Agencies in Western Europe', *Annals of the American Academy of Political and Social Science* 598: 84–101.

Gilardi, Fabrizio (2008). *Delegation in the Regulatory State: Independent Regulatory Agencies in Western Europe*. Cheltenham: Edward Elgar.

Gilliam Jr., Frank D. and Shanto Iyengar (2007). 'News Coverage Effects on Public Opinion about Crime', in Doris A. Graber (ed.) *Media Power in Politics* (pp. 127–37). Washington, DC: CQ Press.

Goetz, Klaus H. (2003). 'Executives in Comparative Context', in Jack Hayward and Anan Menon (eds.) *Governing Europe* (pp. 74–91). Oxford: Oxford University Press.

Goldstein, Judith *et al.* (eds.) (2001). *Legalization and World Politics*. Cambridge, MA: MIT Press.

Goodin, Robert E. (2003). 'Democratic Accountability: the Distinctiveness of the Third Sector', *European Journal of Sociology* 44(3): 359–393.

Goodin, Robert E. (2012). 'How Can Deliberative Democracy Get a Grip?', *The Political Quarterly* 83(4): 806–811.

Goodin, Robert E. and John S. Dryzek (2006). 'Deliberative Impacts: The

Macro-Political Uptake of Mini-publics', *Politics and Society*,34(2): 219–44.

Grande, Edgar (1996). 'The State and Interest Groups in a Framework of Multi-Level Decision-Making: The Case of the European Union', *Journal of European Public Policy* 3(3): 318–38.

Grande, Edgar (2000). 'Charisma und Komplexität: Verhandlungsdemokratie, Mediendemokratie und der Funktionswandel politischer Eliten', in Raymund Werle and Uwe Schimank (eds.) *Gesellschaftliche Komplexität und Kollektive Handlungsfähigkeit* (pp. 297–319). Frankfurt am Main: Campus Verlag.

Grande, Edgar and Louis W. Pauly (2005). 'Complex Sovereignty and The Emergence of Transnational Authority', in Edgar Grande and Louis W. Pauly (eds.) *Complex Sovereignty: Reconstituting Political Authority in the Twenty-first Century* (pp. 285–99). Toronto: University of Toronto Press.

Graz, Jean-Christophe and Andreas Nölke (2008). 'Beyond the Fragmented Debate on Transnational Private Governance', in Jean-Christophe Graz and Andreas Nölke (eds.) *Transnational Private Governance and its Limits* (pp. 1–26). London: Routledge.

Haas, Peter M. (1992). 'Introduction: Epistemic Communities and International Policy Coordination', *International Organization* 46: 1–35.

Hajer, Maarten A. (2009). *Authoritative Governance. Policy-making in the Age of Mediatization*. Oxford: Oxford University Press.

Hall, Peter and David Soskice (2001). *Varieties of Capitalism: the institutional foundations of comparative advantage*. Oxford: Oxford University Press.

Hall, Rodney Bruce and Thomas J. Biersteker (2002). 'The Emergence of Private Authority in the International System', in Rodney Bruce Hall and Thomas J. Biersteker (eds.) *The Emergence of Private Authority in Global Governance* (pp. 3–22). Cambridge: Cambridge University Press.

Halliday, Terence C. and Pavel Osinsky (2006). 'Globalization of Law', *Annual Review of Sociology* 32: 447–70.

Hallin, Daniel C. and Paolo Mancini (2004). 'Americanization, Globalization, and Secularization', in Frank Esser and Barbara Pfetsch (eds.) *Comparing Political Communication* (pp. 25–44). Cambridge: Cambridge University Press.

Hallin, Daniel C. and Paolo Mancini (2004a). *Comparing Media Systems. Three Models of Media and Politics*. Cambridge: Cambridge University Press.

Hammerschmid, Gerhard *et al.* (2006). 'Balancing Decentralisation and Accountability – Different Paths and National Understandings in EU Countries'. Paper prepared for the IPMN Conference, St Gallen, June 2006.

Harlow, Carol and Richard Rawlings (2006). 'Promoting Accountability in Multi-Level Governance: A Network Approach'. EUROGOV paper C-06-02.

Hay, Colin (2007). *Why We Hate Politics*. Cambridge: Polity Press.

He, Baogang and Mark E. Warren (2011). 'Authoritarian Deliberation: The Deliberative Turn in Chinese Political Development', *Perspectives on Politics* 9(2): 269–89.

Held, David (1996). *Democracy and the Global Order.* Cambridge: Polity Press.

Hendriks, Carolyn M. (2005). 'Consensus Conferences and Planning Cells: Lay Citizen Deliberations', in John Gastil and Peter Levine (eds.) *The Deliberative Democracy Handbook* (pp. 80–110). San Francisco: Jossey-Bass.

Hendriks, Carolyn M. (2006). 'When the Forum Meets Interest Politics: Strategic Uses of Public Deliberation', *Politics and Society* 14(4): 571–602.

Hendriks, Carolyn M. *et al.* (2007). 'Turning Up the Heat: Partisanship in Deliberative Innovation', *Political Studies* 55(2): 362–83.

Hermet, Guy (2007). *L'hiver de la démocratie ou le nouveau régime.* Paris: Armand Colin.

Hibbing, John R. and Elizabeth Theiss-Morse (2005). *Stealth Democracy: Americans' Beliefs About How Government Should Work.* Cambridge: Cambridge University Press (1st edn. 2002).

Hilbink, Lisa (2008). 'Assessing the New Constitutionalism', *Comparative Politics* 40(2): 227–45.

Hill, Carolyn and Laurence Lynn (2005). 'Is Hierarchical Governance in Decline? Evidence from Empirical Research', *Journal of Public Administration Research and Theory* 15(2): 173–95.

Hindman, Matthew (2009). *The Myth of Digital Democracy.* Princeton: Princeton University Press.

Hirschl, Ran (2004). *Towards Juristocracy. The Origins and Consequences of the New Constitutionalism.* Cambridge, MA: Harvard University Press.

Hirschland, Matthew J. (2006). *Corporate Social Responsibility and the Shaping of Global Public Policy.* Basingstoke: Palgrave Macmillan.

Hirst, Paul (1994). *Associative Democracy. New Forms of Economic and Social Governance.* Cambridge: Polity press.

Hobsbawm, Eric (1994). *Age of Extremes: The Short Twentieth Century, 1914–1991.* London: Michael Joseph.

Holzinger, Katarina (2001). 'Negotiations in Public Policy Making: Exogenous Barriers to Successful Dispute Resolution', *Journal of Public Policy* 21(1): 71–96.

Homburg, Vincent *et al.* (2007). 'Introduction', in Christopher Pollitt, Sandra van Thiel and Vincent Homburg (eds.) *New Public Management in Europe. Adaptation and Alternatives* (pp. 1–9). Basingstoke: Palgrave Macmillan.

Hönnige, Christoph (2011). 'Beyond Judicialization: Why We Need More Comparative Research About Constitutional Courts', *European Political Science* 10(3): 346–58.

Hood, Christopher (1983). *The Tools of Government.* London: Macmillan.

Hood, Christopher (2011). *The Blame Game. Spin, Bureaucracy, and Self-Presentation in Government.* Princeton: Princeton University Press.

Hood, Christopher and B. Guy Peters (1994). 'Understanding RHPOs', in Christopher Hood and B. Guy Peters (eds.) *Rewards at the Top* (pp. 1–24). London: Sage.

Hooghe, Liesbet and Gary Marks (2008). 'European Union?', *West European Politics* 31(1): 108–29.

Hooghe, Liesbet and Gary Marks (2009). 'A Postfunctionalist Theory of European Integration: From Permissive Consensus to Constraining Dissensus', *British Journal of Political Science* 39(1): 1–23.

Hooghe, Liesbet *et al.* (2002). 'Does Left/Right Structure Party Positions on European Integration?', *Comparative Political Studies* 35(8): 965–89.

Hupe, Peter and Arthur Edwards (2012). 'The Accountability of Power: Democracy and Governance in Modern Times', *European Political Science Review* 4(2): 177–94.

Hurrell, Andrew and Anand Menon (2003). 'International Relations, International Institutions, and the European State', in Jack Hayward and Anan Menon (eds.) *Governing Europe* (pp. 395–412). Oxford: Oxford University Press.

Hurrelmann, Achim *et al.* (2005). 'Is There a Legitimation Crisis of the Nation-State?', in Stephan Leibfried and Michael Zürn (eds.) *Transformations of the State?* (pp. 119–37). Cambridge: Cambridge University Press.

Inglehart, Ronald (1999). 'Postmodernization Erodes Respect for Authority, but Increases Support for Democracy', in Pippa Norris (ed.) *Critical Citizens* (pp. 236–56). Oxford: Oxford University Press.

Jenson, Jane and Susan D. Phillips (2001). 'Redesigning the Canadian Citizenship Regime: Remaking the Institutions of Representation', in Colin Crouch, Klaus Eder and Damian Tambini (eds) *Citizenship, Markets, and the State* (pp. 69–89). Oxford: Oxford University Press.

Jönsson, Christer and Jonas Tallberg (eds.) (2010). *Transnational Actors in Global Governance. Patterns, Explanations and Implications.* Basingstoke: Palgrave Macmillan.

Jordan, Liza (2007). 'A Rights-Based Approach to Accountability', in Alnoor Ebrahim and Edward Weisband (eds.) *Global Accountabilities. Participation, Pluralism, and Public Ethics* (pp. 151–67). Cambridge: Cambridge University Press.

Jordana, Jacint and David Levi-Faur (2004). 'The Politics of Regulation in the Age of Governance', in Jacint Jordana and David Levi-Faur (eds.) *The Politics of Regulation. Institutions and Regulatory Reforms for the Age of Governance* (pp. 1–28). Cheltenham/Northampton: Edward Elgar.

Jordana, Jacint *et al.* (2011). 'The Global Diffusion of Regulatory Agencies: Channels of Transfer and Stages of Diffusion', *Comparative Political Studies* 44(10): 1343–1369.

Jupille, Joseph and James A. Caporaso (2009). 'Domesticating Discourses: European Law, English Judges, and Political Institutions', *European Political Science Review* 1(2): 205–28.

Justice, Jonathan B. and Chris Skelcher (2009). 'Analyzing Democracy in

Third-Party government: Business Improvement Districts in the US and UK', *International Journal of Urban and Regional Research* 33(3): 738–753.

Katz, Richard S. and Peter Mair (1994). *How Parties Organize: Change and Adaptation in Party Organizations in Western Democracies.* London: Sage.

Katz, Richard S. and Peter Mair (1995). 'Changing Models of Party Organization and Party Democracy', *Party Politics* 1(1): 5–28.

Katz, Richard S. and Peter Mair (1996). 'Cadre, Catch-all or Cartel? A Rejoinder', *Party Politics* 2(4): 525–34.

Katz, Richard S. and Mair, Peter (2009). 'The Cartel Party Thesis: a Restatement', *Perspectives on Politics* 7(4): 753–56.

Keane, John (2009). *The Life and Death of Democracy.* New York: W.W. Norton and Co.

Keane, John (2012). 'Silence and Catastrophe: New Reasons Why Politics Matters in the Early Years of the Twenty-first Century', *The Political Quarterly* 83(4): 660–668.

Keck, Margaret and Kathryn Sikkink (1998). *Activists Beyond Borders: Advocacy Networks in International Politics.* Ithaca, NY: Cornell University Press.

Kelemen, R. Daniel (2011). *The Transformation of Law and Regulation in the European Union.* Cambridge, MA: Harvard University Press.

Keohane, Robert O. *et al.* (2009). 'Democracy-Enhancing Multilateralism', *International Organization* 63: 1–31.

Khagram, Sanjeev *et al.* (eds.) (2002). *Restructuring World Politics: Transnational Social Movements, Networks, and Norms.* Minneapolis: University of Minnesota Press.

Kies, Raphaël (2010). *Promises and Limits of Web-deliberation.* Basingstoke: Palgrave Macmillan.

Kirchheimer, Otto (1966). 'The Transformation of Western European Party Systems', in Joseph La Palombara and Myron Weiner (eds.) *Political Parties and Political Development* (pp. 177–200). Princeton: Princeton University Press.

Kitschelt, Herbert (2000). 'Clients, Politicians, and Party Cartellization: Political Representation and State Failure in Post-Industrial Democracies', *European Journal of Political Research* 37(1): 149–79.

Kittilson, Mike C. and Susan E. Scarrow (2003). 'Political Parties and the Rhetoric and Realities of Democratization', in Bruce E. Cain, Russell J. Dalton and Susan E. Scarrow (eds.) *Democracy Transformed? Expanding Political Opportunities in Advanced Industrial Democracies* (pp. 59–80). Oxford: Oxford University Press.

Klijn, Erik-Hans (2008). *'It's the Management, Stupid'. On the Importance of Management in Complex Policy Issues.* The Hague: Lemma.

Klotz, Robert (2004). *The Politics of Internet Communication.* Oxford: Rowman and Littlefield.

Kohler-Koch, Beate (2003). 'Interdependent European Governance', in Beate Kohler-Koch (ed.) *Linking EU and National Governance* (pp. 10–23). Oxford: Oxford University Press.

Kohler-Koch, Beate (2008). 'Civil society in EU governance – a remedy to the democratic deficit account?' *Newsletter of the IPSA Committee on Concepts and Methods* 4(1): 3–6.

Koole, Ruud (1996). 'Cadre, Catch-all or Cartel? A Comment on the Notion of the Cartel Party', *Party Politics* 2(4): 507–23.

Koopmans, Tim (2003). *Courts and Political Institutions*. Cambridge: Cambridge University Press.

Koppell, Jonathan G.S. (2010). *World Rule. Accountability, Legitimacy, and the Design of Global Governance*. Chicago: The University of Chicago Press.

Kriesi, Hanspeter (2005). *Direct Democratic Choice. The Swiss Experience*. Lanham, MD: Lexington Books.

Kriesi, Hanspeter (2012). 'Personalization of national election campaigns', *Party Politics* 18(6): 825–844.

Kriesi, Hanspeter *et al.* (2006). 'Globalization and the transformation of the national political space: six European countries compared', *European Journal of Political Research* 45(6): 921–56.

Kriesi, Hanspeter *et al.* (2006a). 'Comparative analysis of policy networks in Western Europe', *Journal of European Public Policy* 13(3): 341–61.

Kropp, Sabine (2006). 'Ausbruch aus "executiver Führerschaft"? Ressourcen- und Machtverschiebungen im Dreieck von Regierung, Verwaltung und Parlament', *Politische Vierteljahresschrift Sonderheft* (special issue) 37: 275–98.

Kübler, Daniel and Brigitte Schwab (2007). 'New regionalism in five Swiss metropolitan areas: An assessment of inclusiveness, deliberation and democratic accountability', *European Journal of Political Research* 46(3): 473–502.

Lang, Amy (2007). 'But Is It for Real? The British Columbia Citizens' Assembly as a Model of State-Sponsored Citizen Empowerment', *Politics and Society* 35(1): 35–69.

Lavenex, Sandra and Frank Schimmelfennig (eds.) (2012). *Democracy Promotion in the EU's Neighbourhood: from Leverage to Governance?* London: Routledge.

Le Galès, Patrick (1995). 'Du gouvernement des villes à la gouvernance urbaine', *Revue française de science politique* 45(1): 57–95.

Leca, Jean (1996). 'La "gouvernance" de la France sous la Cinquième République: une perspective de sociologie comparative', in François d'Arcy and Luc Rouban (eds.) *De la Ve République à l'Europe* (pp. 329–65). Paris: Presses de Sciences Po.

Lehmbruch, Gerhard (1977). 'Liberal Corporatism and Party Government', *Comparative Political Studies* 10(1): 91–126.

Leibfried, Stephan and Michael Zürn (2005). *Transformations of the State?* Cambridge: Cambridge University Press.

Lever, Annabelle (2009). 'Democracy and Judicial Review: Are They Really Incompatible?', *Perspectives on Politics* 7(4): 805–22.

Levi-Faur, David (2006). 'Regulatory Capitalism: The Dynamics of Change beyond Telecoms and Electricity', *Governance* 19(3): 497–525.

Levi-Faur, David (2007). 'Regulatory Governance', in Paolo Graziano and Maarten P. Vink (eds.) *Europeanization. New Research Agendas* (pp. 102–14). Basingstoke: Palgrave Macmillan.

Litton, Frank and Muiris Maccartaigh (2007). 'Democratic governance and civil service accountability', *Administration* 55(1): 47–62.

Lloyd, Robert (2008). 'Promoting Global Accountability: The Experiences of the Global Accountability Project', *Global Governance* 14: 273–81.

Lord, Christopher (2004). *A Democratic Audit of the European Union.* Basingstoke: Palgrave Macmillan.

Loughlin, John (2007). 'Reconfiguring the State: Trends in Territorial Governance in European States', *Regional and Federal Studies* 14(4): 385–403.

Lupia, Arthur (2003). 'Delegation and its perils', in Kaare Strøm, Wolfgang C. Müller and Torbjörn Bergman (eds.) *Delegation and Accountability in Parliamentary Democracies* (pp. 33–54). Oxford: Oxford University Press.

Lynn, Laurence E. Jr. (2006). *Public Management: Old and New.* London: Routledge.

Macedo, Stephen (ed.) (2005). *Democracy at Risk: How Political Choices Undermine Citizen Participation and What We Can Do About It.* Washington DC: Brookings Institution Press.

Maggetti, Martino (2012). *Regulation in Practice. The de facto independence of regulatory agencies.* Colchester: ECPR Press.

Mair, Peter (2005). 'Democracy Beyond Parties'. Paper for presentation to the workshop 'Political Parties and Democracy', ECPR Joint Sessions, Granada, 14–19 April 2005.

Mair, Peter (2005a). 'Voting Alone', *European Political Science* 4(4): 421–29.

Mair, Peter (2008). 'The Challenge to Party Government', *West European Politics* 31(1): 211–34.

Mair, Peter (2009). 'Representative versus Responsible Government'. MPIFG Working Paper 09/8.

Mair, Peter and Petr Kopecky (2006). 'Political parties and patronage in contemporary democracies: An introduction'. Paper prepared for the workshop 'Political parties and Patronage', ECPR Joint Sessions, Nicosia, 25–30 April, 2006.

Majone, Giandomenico (1997). 'From the Positive to the Regulatory State: Causes and Consequences of Changes in the Mode of Governance.' *Journal of Public Policy* 17(2): 139–67.

Majone, Giandomenico (2001). 'Two Logics of Delegation: Agency and

Fiduciary Relations in EU Governance', *European Union Politics* 2: 103–22.

Majone, Giandomenico (2005). *Dilemmas of European Integration. The Ambiguities and Pitfalls of Integration by Stealth.* Oxford: Oxford University Press.

Malova, Darina and Tim Haughton (2002). 'Making Institutions in Central and Eastern Europe and the Impact of Europe', *West European Politics* 24(2): 101–20.

Mancini, Paolo (1999). 'New Frontiers in Political Professionalism.' *Political Communication* 16(3): 231–45.

Manin, Bernard (1994). 'Checks, balances and boundaries: the separation of powers in the constitutional debate of 1787', in Biancamaria Fontana (ed.) *The Invention of the Modern Republic* (pp. 27–62). Cambridge: Cambridge University Press.

Manin, Bernard (1997). *Principles of Representative Government.* Cambridge: Cambridge University Press.

Maravall, José Maria (2003). 'The Rule of Law as a Political Weapon', in José Maria Maravall and Adam Przeworski (eds.) *Democracy and the Rule of Law* (pp. 261–300). Cambridge: Cambridge University Press.

Marks, Gary and Carole Wilson (2000). 'The past in the present: a cleavage theory of party positions on European integration', *British Journal of Political Science* 30(3): 433–59.

Martens, Maria (2008). 'Administrative Integration through the Back Door? The Role and Influence of the European Commission in Transgovernmental Networks within the Environmental Policy Field', *Journal of European Integration* 30(5): 635–51.

Marty, Frédéric *et al.* (2006). *Les partenariats public-privé.* Paris: La Découverte.

Mattli, Walter and Tim Büthe (2003). 'Setting International Standards: Technological Rationality or Primacy of Power?', *World Politics* 57(1): 1–42.

Mayntz, Renate (1997). 'Politische Steuerung: Aufstieg, Niedergang und Transformation einer Theorie', in Renate Mayntz (ed.) *Soziale Dynamik und Politische Steuerung. Theoretische und Methodologische Überlegungen* (pp. 263–92). Frankfurt am Main: Campus.

Mayntz, Renate (2008). 'Von der Steuerungstheorie zu Global Governance', *Politische Vierteljahresschrift-Sonderheft* 41: 44–60.

Mazzoleni, Gianpietro and Winfried Schulz (1999). ' "Mediatization" of Politics: A Challenge for Democracy?', *Political Communication* 16(3): 247–61.

Menon, Anand (2003). 'Conclusion: Governing Europe', in Jack Hayward and Anan Menon (eds.) *Governing Europe* (pp. 411–32). Oxford: Oxford University Press.

Mény, Yves (2010). 'Democracy in troubled times', *European Political Science* 9(2): 259–68.

Mény, Yves and Yves Surel (2002). 'The Constitutive Ambiguity of Populism', in Yves Mény and Yves Surel (eds.) *Democracies and the Populist Challenge* (pp.1–21). Basingstoke: Palgrave Macmillan.

Merkel, Wolfgang (1999). 'Defekte Demokratien', in Wolfgang Merkel and Andreas Busch (eds.) *Demokratie in Ost und West* (pp. 361–81). Frankfurt am Main: Suhrkamp Verlag.

Meyer, Thomas (2002). *Media Democracy: How the Media Colonise Politics*. Cambridge: Polity Press.

Meynaud, Jean (1969). *Technocracy*. New York: The Free Press.

Michels, Roberto (1962). *Political Parties*. New York: The Free Press (1st edn. 1911).

Moravcsik, Andrew (1994). 'Why the European Community Strengthens the State: Domestic Politics and International Cooperation'. CES Working papers (52).

Moravcsik, Andrew (2002). 'In Defence of the 'Democratic Deficit': Reassessing Legitimacy in the European Union', *Journal of Common Market Studies* 40(4): 603–34.

Morlino, Leonardo (2008). 'Democracy and Change: How Research Tails Reality', *West European Politics* 31(1): 40–59.

Mudde, Cas (2004). 'The Populist Zeitgeist', *Government and Opposition* 39(3): 541–63.

Mudde, Cas (2007). *Populist Radical Right Parties in Europe*. Cambridge: Cambridge University Press.

Mulgan, Robert (2003). *Holding Power to Account. Accountability in Modern Democracies*. Basingstoke: Palgrave Macmillan.

Nanz, Patrizia (2006). 'Democratic Legitimacy and Constitutionalisation of Transnational Trade Governance: A View From Political Theory', in Christian Joerges and Ernst-Ulrich Petersmann (eds.) *Constitutionalism, Multilevel Trade Governance and Social Regulation* (pp. 59–82). Oxford: Hart Publishing.

Newton, Kenneth (1999). 'Politics and the News Media: Mobilization or Media Malaise?', *British Journal of Political Science* 29(4): 577–99.

Newton, Kenneth (2006). 'May the Weak Force be with You: The Power of the Mass Media in Modern Politics', *European Journal of Political Research* 45(2): 209–34.

Norris, Pippa (2011). *Democratic Deficit. Critical Citizens Revisited*. Cambridge: Cambridge University Press.

Norton, Philip (2004). 'Regulating the Regulatory State', *Parliamentary Affairs* 57(4): 785–99.

O'Donnell, Gulliermo (2007). *Dissonances: Democratic Critiques of Democracy*. Notre Dame, IN: University of Notre Dame Press.

OECD (2002). *Distributed Public Governance: Agencies, Authorities and Other Autonomous Bodies*. London: OECD.

Offe, Claus (1981). 'The Attribution of Public Status to Interest Groups', in

Susanne Berger (ed.) *Organized Interests in Western Europe* (pp. 123–58). Cambridge: Cambridge University Press.

Olsen, Johan P. (2005). 'Maybe It Is Time to Rediscover Bureaucracy', *Journal of Public Administration Research and Theory* 16(1): 1–24.

Olsen, Johan P. (2008). 'The Ups and Downs of Bureaucratic Organization', *Annual Review of Political Science* 11: 13–37.

Olson, Mancur (1965). *The Logic of Collective Action: Public Goods and the Theory of Groups*. Cambridge, MA: Harvard University Press.

Padioleau, Jean-Gustave (1982). *L'Etat au concret*. Paris: Presses universitaires de France.

Painter, Martin and B. Guy Peters (2010). *Tradition and Public Administration*. Basingstoke: Palgrave Macmillan.

Palier, Bruno (2003). 'Gouverner le changement des politiques de protection sociale', in Pierre Favre, Jack Hayward and Yves Schemeil (eds.) *Etre gouverné. Etudes en l'honneur de Jean Leca* (pp. 163–79). Paris: Presses de sciences Po.

Panebianco, Angelo (1988). *Political Parties: Organisation and Power*. Cambridge: Cambridge University Press.

Papadopoulos, Yannis (1995). *Complexité sociale et politiques publiques*. Paris: Montchrestien.

Papadopoulos, Yannis (2003). 'Cooperative Forms of Governance: Problems of Democratic Accountability in Complex Environments', *European Journal of Political Research* 42(4): 473–501.

Papadopoulos, Yannis (2007). 'Problems of Democratic Accountability in Network and Multi-Level Governance', *European Law Journal* 13(4): 469–86.

Papadopoulos, Yannis (2010). 'Accountability and Multi-Level Governance: More Accountability, Less Democracy?', *West European Politics* 33(5): 1030–49.

Papadopoulos, Yannis (2012). 'On the Embeddedness of Deliberative Systems: Why Elitist Innovations Matter More', in John Parkinson and Jane Mansbridge (eds.) *Deliberative Systems* (pp. 125–150). Cambridge: Cambridge University Press.

Papadopoulos, Yannis and Philippe Warin (eds.) (2007). 'Innovative, Participatory, and Deliberative Procedures in Policy-Making: Democratic and Effective?', special issue of the *European Journal of Political Research*, June 2007, 46(4).

Parkinson, John (2004). 'Why Deliberate? The Encounter between Deliberation and New Public Managers', *Public Administration* 82(2): 377–95.

Parkinson, John (2005). 'Rickety Bridges: Using the Media in Deliberative Democracy', *British Journal of Political Science* 37(1): 175–83.

Parkinson, John (2006). *Deliberating in the Real World*. Oxford: Oxford University Press.

Pateman, Carole (2012). 'Participatory Democracy Revisited', *Perspectives on Politics* 10(1): 7–19.

Pauly, Louis W. and Edgar Grande (2005). 'Reconstituting Political Authority: Sovereignty, Effectiveness, and Legitimacy in a Transnational Order', in Edgar Grande and Louis W. Pauly (eds.) *Complex Sovereignty: Reconstituting Political Authority in the Twenty-first Century* (pp. 3–21). Toronto: Toronto University Press.

Perrineau, Pascal (2007). 'La crise de la représentation politique', in Pascal Perrineau and Luc Rouban (eds.) *La Politique en France et en Europe* (pp. 15–34). Paris: Presses de Sciences Po.

Perry, James and Andreas Nölke (2006). 'The Political Economy of International Accounting Standards', *Review of International Political Economy* 13(4): 559–86.

Peters, B. Guy (2003). 'Dismantling and Rebuilding the Weberian State', in Jack Hayward and Anan Menon (eds.) *Governing Europe* (pp. 113–27). Oxford: Oxford University Press.

Peters, B. Guy (2007). 'Virtuous and Viscious Circles in Democratic Network Governance', in Eva Sörensen and Jacob Torfing (eds.) *Theories of Democratic Network Governance* (pp. 61–76). Basingstoke: Palgrave Macmillan.

Peters, B. Guy and Jon Pierre (2004). 'Conclusion: Political Control in a Managerialist World', in B. Guy Peters and Jon Pierre (eds.) *Politicization of the Civil Service in Comparative Perspective: The Quest for Control* (pp. 283–90). London: Routledge.

Peters, B. Guy *et al.* (2000). 'Staffing the Summit – the Administration of the Core Executive: Convergent Trends and National Specificities', in B. Guy Peters, R.A.W. Rhodes and Vincent Wright (eds.) *Administering the Summit: Administration of the Core Executive in Developed Countries* (pp. 3–23). Basingstoke: Palgrave Macmillan.

Pfetsch, Barbara (2004). 'From Political Culture to Political Communication Culture', in Frank Esser and Barbara Pfetsch (eds.) *Comparing Political Communication* (pp. 344–66). Cambridge: Cambridge University Press.

Pharr, Susan J. and Robert D. Putnam (eds.) (2000). *Disaffected Democracies: What's Troubling the Trilateral Countries?* Princeton, NJ: Princeton University Press.

Piattoni, Simona (2009). 'Multi-Level Governance: A Historical and Conceptual Analysis', *Journal of European Integration* 11(2): 163–80.

Pierre, Jon (2000). 'Introduction: Understanding Governance', in Jon Pierre (ed.). *Debating Governance* (pp. 1–10). Oxford: Oxford University Press.

Pierre, Jon (2009). 'Reinventing Governance, Reinventing Democracy?', *Policy and Politics*, 37 (4): 591–609.

Pierre, Jon and B. Guy Peters (2000). *Governance, Politics and the State*. Basingstoke: Palgrave Macmillan.

Pierre, Jon and B. Guy Peters (2005). *Governing Complex Societies: Trajectories And Scenarios*. Basingstoke: Palgrave Macmillan.

Pierson, Paul (1994). *Dismantling the Welfare State? Reagan, Thatcher and the Politics of Retrenchment.* Cambridge: Cambridge University Press.

Poguntke, Thomas and Paul Webb (2005). 'The Presidentialization of Politics in Democratic Societies: A Framework for Analysis', in Thomas Poguntke and Paul Webb (eds.) *The Presidentialization of Politics: A Comparative Study of Modern Democracies* (pp. 1–25). Oxford: Oxford University Press.

Poguntke, Thomas and Paul Webb (2005a). 'Presidentialization, Party Government and Democratic Theory'. Paper for presentation to the workshop 'Political Parties and Democracy', ECPR Joint Sessions, Granada, 14–19 April 2005.

Poguntke, Thomas *et al.* (2007). *The Europeanization of National Political Parties: Power and Organizational Adaptation.* London: Routledge.

Pollitt, Christopher (2003). 'Joined-up Government: a Survey', *Political Studies Review* 1(1): 34–49.

Pollitt, Christopher (2004). 'Theoretical Overview', in Christopher Pollitt and Colin Talbot (eds.) *Unbundled Government. A Critical Analysis of the Global Trend to Agencies, Quangos and Contractualisation* (pp. 319–41). London: Routledge.

Pollitt, Christopher (2007). 'Convergence or Divergence: What has been Happening in Europe', in Christopher Pollitt, Sandra van Thiel and Vincent Homburg (eds.) *New Public Management in Europe: Adaptation and Alternatives* (pp. 10–25). Basingstoke: Palgrave Macmillan.

Pollitt, Christopher and Geert Bouckaert (2004). *Public Management Reform: A Comparative Analysis.* Oxford: Oxford University Press. (2nd edn).

Pollitt Christopher and Colin Talbot (eds.) (2004). *Unbundled Government. A Critical Analysis of the Global Trend to Agencies, Quangos and Contractualisation.* London: Routledge.

Pollitt, Christopher *et al.* (2001). 'Agency Fever? Analysis of an International Policy Fashion', *Journal of Comparative Policy Analysis: Research and Practice* 3(3): 271–90.

Pollitt, Christopher *et al.* (2004). *Agencies. How Governments do Things Through Semi-Autonomous Organizations.* Basingstoke: Palgrave Macmillan.

Pollitt, Christopher *et al.* (2007). 'Introduction', in Pollitt, Christopher *et al.* (eds.) *New Public Management in Europe: Adaptation and Alternatives* (pp. 43–72). Basingstoke: Palgrave Macmillan.

Porter, Tony (2005). 'The Private Production of Public Goods: Private and Public Norms in Global Governance', in Edgar Grande and Louis W. Pauly (eds.) *Complex Sovereignty: Reconstituting Political Authority in the Twenty-first century* (pp. 217–37). Toronto: University of Toronto Press.

Prakash, Aseemand and Matthew Potoski (2010). 'The International Organization for Standardization as a Global Governor: A Club Theory Perspective', in Deborah D. Avant, Martha Finnemore and Susan K. Sell (eds.) *Who Governs the Globe?* (pp. 72–101). Cambridge: Cambridge University Press.

Przeworski, Adam (2010). *Democracy and the Limits of Self-Government.* Cambridge: Cambridge University Press.

Putnam, Robert D. (1988). 'Diplomacy and Domestic Politics. The Logic of Two-Level Games', *International Organization* 42(3): 427–60.

Putnam, Robert D. (2000). *Bowling Alone: The Collapse and Renewal of American Community.* New York: Simon and Schuster.

Putnam, Robert D. (ed.) (2002). *Democracies in Flux: The Evolution of Social Capital in Contemporary Society.* Oxford: Oxford University Press.

Quack, Sigrid (2010). 'Law, Expertise and Legitimacy in Transnational Governance: An Introduction', *Socio-Economic Review* 8(1): 3–16.

Ramachandran, Vijaya *et al.* (2009). 'Rethinking Fundamental Principles of Global Governance: How to Represent States and Populations in Multilateral Institutions', *Governance* 22(3): 341–51.

Raunio, Tapio (2002). 'Why European Integration Increases Leadership Autonomy Within Political Parties', *Party Politics* 8(4): 405–22.

Raunio, Tapio (2009). 'National Parliaments and European Integration: What We Know and Agenda for Future Research', *The Journal of Legislative Studies* 15(4): 317–34.

Raunio, Tapio and Simon Hix (2000). 'Backbenchers Learn to Fight Back: European Integration and Parliamentary Government', *West European Politics* 23(4): 142–68.

Reimann, Kim D. (2006). 'A View from the Top: International Politics, Norms and the Worldwide Growth of NGOs', *International Studies Quarterly* 50: 46–67.

Renn, Ortwin *et al.* (1995). *Fairness and Competence in Citizen Participation. Evaluating Models for Environmental Discourse.* Dordrecht: Kluwer.

Rethemeyer, R. Karl (2007). 'The Empires Strike Back: Is the Internet Corporatizing Rather than Democratizing Policy Processes?', *Public Administration Review* 67(2): 199–215.

Rhodes, R.A.W. (1997). *Understanding Governance.* Buckingham: Open University Press.

Rhodes, R.A.W. (2003). 'What is New about Governance and Why does it Matter?', in Jack Hayward and Anan Menon (eds.) *Governing Europe* (pp. 61–73). Oxford: Oxford University Press.

Risse, Thomas (2006). 'Transnational Governance and Legitimacy', in Arthur Benz and Yannis Papadopoulos (eds.) *Governance and Democracy. Comparing National, European, and International Experiences* (pp. 179–99). London: Routledge.

Roberts, Alasdair (2010). *The Logic of Discipline: Global Capitalism and the Architecture of Government.* Oxford: Oxford University Press.

Rokkan, Stein (1966). 'Norway: Numerical Democracy and Corporate Pluralism', in Robert A. Dahl (ed.) *Political Oppositions in Western Democracies* (pp. 70–115). New Haven: Yale University Press.

Ronit, Karsten (2007). 'Global Public Policy – the New Policy Arrangements of Business and Countervailing Groups', in Karsten Ronit (ed.) *Global Public Policy. Business and the Countervailing Powers of Civil Society* (pp. 1–42). London: Routledge.

Rosanvallon, Pierre (2006). *La contre-démocratie. La politique à l'âge de la défiance*. Paris: Editions du Seuil.

Rosanvallon, Pierre (2008). *La légitimité démocratique*. Paris: Editions du Seuil.

Rose, Richard and Ian McAllister (1986). *Voters Begin to Chose. From Closed-Class to Open Elections in Britain*. London: Sage.

Rosenau, James N. (2002). 'Governance in a New Global Order', in David Held and Anthony McGrew (eds.) *Governing Globalization* (pp. 70–86). Cambridge: Polity Press.

Rosenau, James N. (2004). 'Strong Demand, Huge Supply: Governance in an Emerging Epoch', in Ian Bache and Matthew Flinders (eds.) *Multi-level Governance* (pp. 31–48). Oxford: Oxford University Press.

Rousseau, Jean-Jacques (1973). 'The Social Contract', in *The Social Contract and Discourses*, trans. and ed. G.D.H. Cole, revised and augmented J.H. Brumfitt and J. Ch. Hall. London: Dent (1st edn. of *The Social Contract*: 1762).

Roussel, Violaine (2007). 'Les changements d'éthos des magistrats', in Jacques Commaille and Martine Kaluczynski (eds.) *La fonction politique de la justice* (pp. 27–46). Paris: La Découverte.

Rudder, Catherine E. (2008). 'Private Governance as Public Policy: A Paradigmatic Shift', *The Journal of Politics* 70(4): 899–913.

Sadurski, Wojciech (2002). 'Constitutional Justice, East and West: Introduction', in Wojciech Sadurski (ed.) *Constitutional Justice, East and West. Democratic Legitimacy and Constitutional Courts in Post-Communist Europe in a Comparative Perspective* (pp. 1–18). The Hague: Kluwer Law International.

Sahlin-Andersson, Kerstin (2001). 'National, International and Transnational Constructions of New Public Management', in Tom Christensen and Per Laegreid (eds.) *New Public Management. The Transformation of Ideas and Practice* (pp. 13–39). Aldershot: Ashgate.

Saint-Martin, Denis (2004). *Building the New Managerialist State: Consultants and the Politics of Public Sector Reform in Comparative Perspective*. Oxford: Oxford University Press.

Sassen, Saskia (2006). *Territory. Authority. Rights. From Medieval to Global Assemblages*. Princeton: Princeton University Press.

Savoie, Donald J. (2008). *Court Government and the Collapse of Accountability in Canada and the United Kingdom*. Toronto: University of Toronto Press.

Saward, Michael (2005). 'Authorisation and Authenticity: Does Democracy Really Need Political Parties?' Paper for presentation to the workshop

'Political Parties and Democracy', ECPR Joint Sessions, Granada, 14–19 April 2005.

Scarrow, Susan E. (2002). 'Parties without Members? Party Organization in a Changing Electoral Environment', in Russel J. Dalton and Martin P. Wattenberg (eds.) *Parties without Partisans. Political Change in Advanced Industrial Democracies* (pp. 79–101). Oxford: Oxford University Press.

Scarrow, Susan E. (2003). 'Making Elections More Direct? Reducing the Role of Parties in Elections', in Bruce E. Cain, Russell J. Dalton, and Susan E. Scarrow (eds.) *Democracy Transformed? Expanding Political Opportunities in Advanced Industrial Democracies* (pp. 44–58). Oxford: Oxford University Press.

Scarrow, Susan E. (2006). 'Party Subsidies and the Freezing of Party Competition: Do Cartel Mechanisms Work?', *West European Politics* 29(4): 619–39.

Scarrow, Susan E. *et al.* (2002). 'From Social Integration to Electoral Contestation. The Changing Distribution of Power within Political Parties', in Russel J. Dalton and Martin P. Wattenberg (eds.) *Parties without Partisans. Political Change in Advanced Industrial Democracies* (pp. 129–53). Oxford: Oxford University Press.

Scharpf, Fritz W. (1988). 'The Joint-Decision Trap. Lessons From German Federalism an European Integration', *Public Administration* 66(2): 239–78.

Scharpf, Fritz W. (1999). *Governing in Europe: Effective and Democratic?* Oxford: Oxford University Press.

Schattschneider, Elmer E. (1942). *Party Government*. New York: Holt, Rinehart and Winston.

Schattschneider, Elmer E. (1960). *The Semisovereign People*. Hinsdale, IL: The Dryden Press.

Schedler, Andreas (1999). 'Conceptualizing Accountability', in Andreas Schedler, Larry Diamond and Marc F. Plattner (eds.) *The Self-Restraining State* (pp. 13–28). Boulder, CO: Lynne Rienner.

Schlozman, Kay Lehman *et al.* (2010). 'Weapon of the Strong? Participatory Inequality and the Internet', *Perspectives on Politics* 8(2): 487–509.

Schmidt, Vivien (2006). *Democracy in Europe. The EU and National Polities.* Oxford: Oxford University Press.

Schmitter, Philippe C. (2008). 'The Changing Politics of Organised Interests', *West European Politics* 31(1): 195–210.

Schmitter, Philippe C. and Alexander H. Trechsel (coordinators) (2004). *The Future of Democracy in Europe. Trends, Analyses and Reforms.* Strasbourg: Council of Europe Publishing.

Schmitter, Philippe C. and Wolfgang Streeck (1999). 'The Organization of Business Interests. Studying the Associative Action of Business in Advanced Industrial Societies'. Discussion paper 99/1, Max-Planck-Institut für Gesellschaftsforschung, Köln.

Schneider, Volker (2000). 'Organisationsstaat und Verhandlungsdemokratie', in Raymund Werle and Uwe Schimank (eds.) *Gesellschaftliche Komplexität und Kollektive Handlungsfähigkeit* (pp. 243–69). Frankfurt am Main: Campus.

Scholte, Jan Aart (ed.) (2011). *Building Global Democracy? Civil Society and Accountable Global Governance.* Cambridge: Cambridge University Press.

Schrott, Andrea and Daniela Spranger (2007). 'Mediatization of political negotiations in modern democracies: institutional characteristics matter', *NCCR Challenges to Democracy in the 21st Century,* Working Paper No. 2.

Schulz, Winfried (2004). 'Reconstructing Mediatization as an Analytical Concept', *European Journal of Communication* 19(1): 87–101.

Schumpeter, Joseph (1994). *Capitalism, Socialism and Democracy.* London: Routledge (1st edn. 1942).

Scott, Colin (2003). 'Organizational Variety in Regulatory Governance: An Agenda for a Comparative Investigation of OECD Countries', *Public Organization Review* 3: 301–16.

Scott, Colin (2010). 'Regulatory Governance and the Challenge of Constitutionalism'. EUI Working Paper RSCAS 2010/07.

Sebaldt, Martin (2009). *Die Macht der Parlamente. Funktionen und Leistungsprofile nationaler Volksvertretungen in den alten Demokratien der Welt.* Wiesbaden: Verlag für Sozialwissenschaften.

Shapiro, Martin (1988). *Who Guards the Guardians? Judicial Control of Administration.* Athens, GA: University of Georgia Press.

Shapiro, Martin (2002). 'The Giving Reasons Requirement', in Martin Shapiro and Alec Stone Sweet (eds.) *On Law, Politics and Judicialization* (pp. 228–58). Oxford: Oxford University Press.

Shapiro, Martin (2002a). 'Some Conditions for the Success of Constitutional Courts: Lessons from the U.S. Experience', in Sadurski, Wojciech (ed.) *Constitutional Justice, East and West. Democratic Legitimacy and Constitutional Courts in Post-Communist Europe in a Comparative Perspective* (pp. 37–59). The Hague: Kluwer Law International.

Shapiro, Martin (2002b). 'The Success of Judicial Review and Democracy', in Martin Shapiro and Alec Stone Sweet (eds.) *On Law, Politics and Judicialization* (pp. 149–83). Oxford: Oxford University Press.

Shapiro, Martin and Alec Stone (1994). 'Special Issue: The New Constitutional Politics in Europe', *Comparative Political Studies* 26(4): 397–421.

Sieberer, Ulrich (2011). 'The Institutional Power of Western European Parliaments: A Multidimensional Analysis', *West European Politics* 34(4): 731–54.

Sintomer, Yves and Marion Gret (2005). *The Porto Alegre Experiment: Learning Lessons for a Better Democracy.* London: Zed Books.

Sintomer, Yves, Carsten Herzberg and Anja Röcke (2007). 'From Porto Alegre to Europe: Potentials and Limits of Participatory Budgeting', in Jochen Franzke, Linze Schaap, José Ruano and Marcel Boogers (eds.) *Tensions between Local Governance and Local Democracy* (pp. 113–27). The Hague: Reed Business.

Sintomer, Yves, Carsten Herzberg and Anja Röcke (2008). *Les Budgets participatifs en Europe. Des services publics au service du public.* Paris: La Découverte.

Skelcher, Chris (2005). 'Jurisdictional Integrity, Polycentrism, and the Design of Democratic Governance', *Governance* 18(1) : 89–110.

Skelcher, Chris (2005a). 'Public–Private Partnerships and Hybridity', in Ewan Ferlie, Lawrence E. Lynn Jr. and Christopher Pollitt (eds.) *The Oxford Handbook of Public Management* (pp. 347–70). Oxford: Oxford University Press.

Skelcher, Chris (2009). 'Fishing in Muddy Waters: Principals, Agents and Democratic Governance in Europe', *Journal of Public Administration Research and Theory* 20(1): 161–75.

Skelcher, Chris and Jacob Torfing (2010). 'Improving Democratic Governance through Institutional Design: Civic Participation and Democratic Ownership in Europe', *Regulation and Governance* 4(1): 71–91.

Skelcher, Chris *et al.* (2005). 'The Public Governance of Collaborative Spaces: Discourse, Design and Democracy', *Public Administration* 83(3): 573–596.

Skelcher, Chris *et al.* (2011). 'Explaining the Democratic Anchorage of Governance Networks. Evidence from Four European Countries', *Administrative Theory and Praxis*, 33 (1): 7–38.

Slaughter, Anne-Marie (2004). *A New World Order.* Princeton: Princeton University Press.

Smith, Graham (2005). *Beyond the Ballot: 57 Democratic Innovations from around the World.* London: Power Inquiry.

Smith, Graham (2009). *Democratic Innovations. Designing Institutions for Citizen Participation.* Cambridge: Cambridge University Press.

Smith, Jackie (2008). *Social Movements for Global Democracy.* Baltimore: Johns Hopkins University Press.

Smith, Mitchell P. (1997). 'The Commission Made Me Do It: The European Commission as a Strategic Asset in Domestic Politics', in Neill Nugent (ed.) *At the Heart of the Union: Studies of the European Commission* (pp. 167–86). New York: St. Martin's Press.

Song, Weiqing and Vincent Della Sala (2008). 'Eurosceptics and Europhiles in accord: The Creation of the European Ombudsman as an Institutional Isomorphism', *Policy and Politics* 36(4): 481–95.

Sosay, Gül (2006). 'Consequences of Legitimizing Independent Regulatory Agencies in Contemporary Democracies', in Dietmar Braun and Fabrizio Gilardi (eds.) *Delegation in Contemporary Democracies* (pp. 171–90). London: Routledge.

Sperling, Valerie (2009). *Altered States. The Globalization of Accountability.* Cambridge: Cambridge University Press.

Spörer-Wagner, Doreen and Frank Marcinkowski (2011). 'Politiker in der Oeffentichkeitsfalle? Zur Medialisierung politischer Verhandlungen in nationalen Kontexten', *Politische Vierteljahresschrift Sonderheft* (special issue) 44: 416–38.

Steffek, Jens (2008). 'Public Accountability and the Public Sphere of International Governance'. RECON Online Working Paper 2008/03.

Steffek, Jens and Kristina Hahn (eds.) (2010). *Evaluating Transnational NGOs: Legitimacy, Accountability, Representation.* Basingstoke: Palgrave Macmillan.

Steffek, Jens and Patrizia Nanz (2008). 'Emergent Patterns of Civil Society Participation in Global and European Governance', in Jens Steffek, Claudia Kissling and Patrizia Nanz (eds.). *Civil Society Participation in European and Global Governance* (pp. 1–29). Basingstoke: Palgrave Macmillan.

Stoker, Gerry (2006). *Why Politics Matters. Making Democracy Work.* Basingstoke: Palgrave Macmillan.

Stoker, Gerry (2010). 'Blockages on the Road to Relevance: Why has Political Science Failed to Deliver? *European Political Science* 9 (Supplement 1): S72–S84.

Stone Sweet, Alec (2000). *Governing with Judges. Constitutional Politics in Europe.* Oxford: Oxford University Press.

Stone Sweet, Alec (2002). 'Constitutional Politics in France and Germany', in Martin Shapiro and Alec Stone Sweet (eds.) *On Law, Politics and Judicialization* (pp. 184–208). Oxford: Oxford University Press.

Stone Sweet, Alec (2004). 'Islands of Transnational Governance', in Christopher K. Ansell and Giuseppe Di Palma (eds.) *Restructuring Territoriality. Europe and the United States Compared* (pp. 122–44). Cambridge: Cambridge University Press.

Stone Sweet, Alec (2010). 'The European Court of Justice and the judicialization of EU governance', *Living Reviews in European Governance* 5(2).

Streeck, Wolfgang and Kathleen Thelen (eds.) (2005). *Beyond Continuity: Institutional Change in Advanced Political Economies.* Oxford: Oxford University Press.

Street, John (2001). *Mass Media, Politics and Democracy.* Basingstoke: Palgrave Macmillan.

Strøm, Kaare, Wolfgang C. Müller and Torbjörn Bergman (eds.) (2003). *Delegation and Accountability in Parliamentary Democracies.* Oxford: Oxford University Press.

Sunstein, Cass (2001). *Republic.com.* Princeton: Princeton University Press.

Taggart, Paul and Aleks Szczerbiak (eds.) (2008). *Opposing Europe? The Comparative Party Politics of Euroscepticism: Volume 2: Comparative and Theoretical Perspectives.* Oxford: Oxford University Press.

Take, Ingo (2012). 'Legitimacy in Global Governance: International, Transnational and Private Institutions Compared', *Swiss Political Science Review* 18(2): 220–248.

Talbot, Colin (2004). 'The agency idea: sometimes old, sometimes new, sometimes borrowed, sometimes untrue', in Christopher Pollitt and Colin Talbot (eds.) *Unbundled Government. A Critical Analysis of the Global Trend to Agencies, Quangos and Contractualisation* (pp. 3–21). London: Routledge.

Tallberg, Jonas and Anders Uhling (2012). 'Civil society and global democracy. An assessment', in Daniele Archibugi, Mathias Koenig-Archibugi and Raffaele Marchetti (eds.). *Global Democracy. Normative and Empirical Perspectives* (pp. 210–32). Cambridge: Cambridge University Press.

Talpin, Julien (2008). 'Les effets politiques de l'inclusion des citoyens dans l'action publique. Résultats de l'étude de trois budgets participatifs', in Centre d'analyse stratégique. *La participation des citoyens et l'action publique* (pp. 112–26). Paris: La documentation française.

Tarrow, Sidney (2005). *The New Transnational Activism*. Cambridge: Cambridge University Press.

Thatcher, Mark (2002). 'Delegation to Independent Regulatory Agencies: Pressures, Functions and Contextual Mediation', *West European Politics* 25(1): 125–47.

Thatcher, Mark (2005). 'The Third Force? Independent Regulatory Agencies and Elected Politicians in Europe', *Governance* 18(3): 347–73.

Thatcher, Mark and Alec Stone Sweet (2002). 'Theory and Practice of Delegation to Non-Majoritarian Institutions', *West European Politics* 25(1): 1–22.

Thomann, Lars (2008). 'The ILO, Tripartism, and NGOs: Do Too Many Cooks Really Spoil the Broth?', in Jens Steffek, Claudia Kissling and Patrizia Nanz (eds.) *Civil Society Participation in European and Global Governance* (pp. 71–94). Basingstoke: Palgrave Macmillan.

Thompson, Dennis F. (2008). 'Deliberative Democratic Theory and Empirical Political Science', *Annual Review of Political Science* 11: 497–520.

Thorlakson, Lori (2003). 'Comparing Federal Institutions: Power and Representation in Six Federations', *West European Politics* 26(2): 1–22.

Tsakatika, Myrto (2007). 'A Parliamentary Dimension for EU Soft Governance', *Journal of European Integration* 29(5): 549–64.

Tyler, Tom R. (1998). 'Trust and Democratic Governance', in Valerie Braithwaite and Margaret Levi (eds.) *Trust and Governance* (pp. 269–94). New York: Russell Sage Foundation.

Urbinati, Nadia and Mark E. Warren (2008). 'The Concept of Representation in Contemporary Democratic Theory', *Annual Review of Political Science* 11: 387–412.

Van Biezen, Ingrid (2004). 'Political Parties as Public Utilities', *Party Politics* 10(6): 701–22.

Van Biezen, Ingrid and Richard S. Katz (2005). 'Democracy and Political Parties'. Paper for presentation to the workshop 'Political Parties and Democracy', ECPR Joint Sessions, Granada, 14–19 April 2005.

Van Biezen, Ingrid *et al.* (2012). 'Going, going, ... gone ? The decline of party membership in contemporary Europe', *European Journal of Political Research* 51(1): 24–56.

Van Slyke, David M. and Christine H. Roch (2004). 'What Do They Know, and Whom Do They Hold Accountable? Citizens in the Government–Nonprofit Contracting Relationship', *Journal of Public Administration Research and Theory* 14(2): 191–209.

Van Waarden, Frans and Youri Hildebrand (2009). 'From corporatism to lawyocracy? On liberalization and juridification', *Regulation and Governance* 3(3): 259–86.

Vatter, Adrian (ed.) (2011). *Die direkte Demokratie: Schutzmacht für religiöse Minderheiten oder Hort der Feindseligkeiten ?* Zurich: NZZ Libro.

Verhoest, Koen and Per Laegreid (2010). 'Organizing Public Sector Agencies: Challenges and Reflections', in Per Laegreid and Ken Verhoest (eds.) *Governance of Public Sector Organizations. Proliferation, Autonomy and Performance* (pp. 276–97). Basingstoke: Palgrave Macmillan.

Verhoest, Koen *et al.* (2010). *Autonomy and Control of State Agencies. Comparing States and Agencies.* Basingstoke: Palgrave Macmillan.

Verschuere, Bram (2009). 'The Role of Public Agencies in the Policy Making Process. Rhetoric versus Reality', *Public Policy and Administration* 24(1): 23–46.

Verweij, Marco and Timothy E. Josling (2003). 'Special Issue: Deliberately Democratizing Multilateral Organization (Introduction)', *Governance* 16(1): 1–21.

Vibert, Frank (2007). *The Rise of the Unelected.* Cambridge: Cambridge University Press.

Vogel, David (2008). 'Private Global Business Regulation', *Annual Review of Political Science* 11: 261–82.

Von Beyme, Klaus (2000). *Parliamentary Democracy. Democratization, Destabilization, Reconsolidation, 1789–1999.* Basingstoke: Palgrave Macmillan.

Waldron, Jeremy (2006). 'The Core of the Case Against Judicial Review', *The Yale Law Journal* 115: 1346–406.

Warren, Mark E. (2009). 'Governance-Driven Democratization', *Critical Policy Studies,* 3 (1): 3–13.

Warren, Mark E. and Hilary Pearse (eds.) (2008). *Designing Deliberative Democracy: The British Columbia Citizens' Assembly.* Cambridge: Cambridge University Press.

Wattenberg, Martin P. (2002). *Where Have All the Voters Gone?* Cambridge, MA: Harvard University Press.

Wattenberg, Martin P. (2002a). 'The Decline of Party Mobilization', in Russel J. Dalton and Martin P. Wattenberg (eds.) *Parties without Partisans. Political Change in Advanced Industrial Democracies* (pp. 64–76). Oxford: Oxford University Press.

Weale, Albert (2001). 'Science Advice, Democratic Responsiveness and Public Policy', *Science and Public Policy* 28(6): 413–21.

Webb, Paul (forthcoming), 'Who is willing to participate? Dissatisfied democrats, stealth democrats and populists in the UK', forthcoming in *European Journal of Political Research.*

Webb, Paul and Thomas Poguntke (2005). 'The Presidentialization of

Contemporary Democratic Politics: Evidence, Causes and Consequences', in Thomas Poguntke and Paul Webb (eds.) *The Presidentialization of Politics: A Comparative Study of Modern Democracies* (pp. 335–56). Oxford: Oxford University Press.

Webb, Paul et al. (2011). 'The Presidentialization of Party Leadership? Evaluating Party Leadership and Party Government in the Democratic World'. Paper presented to Annual Meeting of the American Political Science Association, Seattle, 1-4 September 2011.

Weber, Max (1994). *Political Writings*. (ed. by Peter Lassman and Ronald Spears). Cambridge: Cambridge University Press.

Wessel, Ramses A. (2007). 'Accountability and Multilevel Regulation'. Paper presented at Connex Wrapping Up Conference Research Group 2, Utrecht University, 11–12 October 2007.

Whytock, Christopher A. (2010). 'Private–Public Interaction in Global Governance: The Case of Transnational Commercial Arbitration', *Business and Politics* 12(3): Article 10.

Wilde, Pieter de *et al.* (2010). 'Contesting EU Legitimacy. The Prominence, Content and Justification of Euroscepticism during the 2009 EP Election Campaigns'. RECON Online Working Paper 2010/22.

Wilks, Stephen and Ian Bartle (2002). 'The Unanticipated Consequences of Creating Independent Competition Agencies', *West European Politics* 25(1): 148–72.

Wolf, Klaus-Dieter (2002). 'Contextualizing Normative Standards for Legitimate Governance beyond the State', in Bernard Gbikpi and Jürgen R. Grote (eds.) *Participatory Governance. Political and Societal Implications* (pp. 35–50). Opladen: Leske+Budrich.

Woods, Ngaire (2002). 'Global Governance and the Role of Institutions', in David Held and Anthony McGrew (eds.) *Governing Globalization* (pp. 25–45). Cambridge: Polity Press.

Woods, Ngaire (2006). *The Globalizers. The IMF, the World Bank, and their Borrowers*. Ithaca: Cornell University Press.

Woods, Ngaire (2007). 'Multilateralism and Building Stronger International Institutions', in Ebrahim Alnoor and Edward Weisband (eds.) *Global Accountabilities. Participation, Pluralism, and Public Ethics* (pp. 27–44). Cambridge: Cambridge University Press.

Yesilkagit, Kutsal and Sandra Van Thiel (2008). 'Political Influence and Bureaucratic Autonomy', *Public Organization Review* 8(2): 137–53.

Yesilkagit, Kutsal and Sandra Van Thiel (2012). 'Autonomous Agencies and Perceptions of Stakeholder Influence in Parliamentary Democracies', *Journal of Public Administration Research and Theory* 22(1): 101–119.

Zaller, John (2001). 'Monica Lewinsky and the Mainsprings of American Politics', in W. Lance Bennett and Robert M. Entman (eds.) *Mediated Politics. Communication uin the Future of Democracy* (pp. 252–78). Cambridge: Cambridge University Press.

Zangl, Bernhard (2005). 'Is there an Emerging International Rule of Law?', in Stephan Leibfried and M. Zürn (eds.) *Transformations of the State?* (pp. 73–91). Cambridge: Cambridge University Press.

Zolo, Danilo (1992). *Democracy and Complexity.* Cambridge: Polity Press.

Zürn, Michael (2003). 'Global Governance in der Legitimationskrise?', in Claus Offe (ed.) *Demokratisierung der Demokratie* (pp. 232–56). Frankfurt: Campus.

Zürn, Michael (2010). 'Global governance as multi-level governance', in Henrik Enderlein, Sonja Wälti and Michael Zürn (eds.) *Handbook on Multi-level Governance* (pp. 80–99). Cheltenham: Edward Elgar.

Zürn, Michael and Stephan Leibfried (2005). 'Reconfiguring the national constellation', in Stephan Leibfried and Michael Zürn (eds.) *Transformations of the State?* (pp. 1–36). Cambridge: Cambridge University Press.

Zweifel, Thomas D. (2006). *International Organizations and Democracy.* Boulder, CO: Lynne Rienner.

# Index

Page numbers in *italics* are references to figures.

Printed in China